CompTIA Security+ : Study Guide

+

CompTIA A+ Study Guide

+

CompTIA Network+ Study Guide

By SmartStudy Solutions

CompTIA Security+

CompTIA A+

CompTIA Network+

Introduction

In the ever-evolving landscape of information technology, one feature that stays the same is that security is paramount. The CompTIA Security+ certification is a crucial tool for those who aspire to safeguard digital spaces and fortify the integrity of data. This certification is viewed as a testament to a cybersecurity professional's ability to secure systems, protect networks, and uphold confidentiality. As the digital world continues to grow and evolve, the need for skilled security practitioners is greater than ever. Are you going to be the newest cybersecurity professional with a CompTIA Security+ certification? I hope so! The CompTIA Security+ certification is a vital endorsement of one's capabilities in the realm of cybersecurity; it is a cornerstone in the career paths of countless individuals worldwide.

Overview of SY0-601 Exam

The SY0-601 exam, an integral part of the CompTIA Security+ certification, has been meticulously crafted to ensure that those who attain this prestigious credential are well-prepared to tackle the multifaceted challenges of the cybersecurity domain. This latest iteration of the certification exam builds upon the foundation of its predecessors while adapting to the ever-shifting threat landscape. This exam tests your knowledge and proficiency in various security domains, from risk management and threat detection to cryptographic protocols and network security.

In the SY0-601 exam, you will encounter a diverse range of security topics, encompassing everything from access control measures and identity management to cloud security and incident response. This comprehensive examination serves as a true reflection of the multifaceted nature of modern cybersecurity, making it a robust measure of your preparedness to face real-world security challenges.

Tips for Effective Study

Preparation for the SY0-601 exam can be an exhilarating yet demanding journey. To excel in this pursuit, it is essential to develop a study strategy that aligns with the exam's rigor and breadth. In this study guide, I have distilled years of experience and expertise as a cybersecurity professional into a comprehensive resource designed to aid you in your quest to master the CompTIA Security+ certification. To help you navigate this often complex field of study, I provide valuable tips, strategies, and insights that will empower you to approach the SY0-601 exam with confidence.

My goal is to assist you in building a strong foundation of knowledge, honing your practical skills, and instilling the confidence necessary to excel in this assessment.

Whether you are an aspiring security professional or a seasoned IT veteran looking to enhance your credentials, this study guide will be your trusted companion on your path to CompTIA Security+ certification success.

As you delve into the pages that follow, you will find a wealth of information, hands-on exercises, and practice questions that mirror the complexity of the SY0-601 exam. By following the guidance and recommendations presented here, you can embark on your journey towards becoming a certified CompTIA Security+ professional!

So, let us begin this exciting and rewarding adventure together. Prepare to unlock the doors to a world where you are the guardian of digital fortresses and the protector of vital information! This study guide is your key to success in the SY0-601 exam and, ultimately, your gateway to a thriving career in the ever-evolving world of cybersecurity.

Theoretical Background

In the comprehensive journey towards mastering cybersecurity and preparing for the CompTIA Security+ SY0-601 certification, this chapter forms the bedrock upon which the edifice of knowledge and expertise is built. Here, I delve deep into the foundational principles and theories that underpin the world of information security. Aspiring security professionals will explore key concepts, fundamental models, and theoretical frameworks essential for understanding the ever-evolving landscape of cybersecurity. This chapter serves as an anchor to ground learners in the theoretical underpinnings required to navigate the complex and dynamic realm of security. Later chapters provide practical skills and insights that follow in this comprehensive study guide.

What Is a Use Case?

CompTIA frequently references the term "use case" across multiple objectives. A use case serves as a means to describe an objective that an organization aims to accomplish. It finds extensive application in systems analysis and software development, aiding in the identification and clarification of requirements essential for achieving the specified objective. Typically, a use case adopts a naming convention characterized by a verb-noun structure. For instance, let's consider a use case named "Place Order." Various departments within an organization may apply it differently, yet the use case maintains the same name throughout.

For software developers, the steps outlined within a use case serve as a blueprint for crafting software solutions that align with the defined objective. Meanwhile, marketing teams utilize the use case to gain insights into where they should direct their efforts to encourage customers to place orders. Similarly, billing and shipping departments leverage it to comprehend their roles and responsibilities after customers initiate orders.

Let us imagine a scenario where Lisa intends to place an order through an online e-commerce system. In this context, the "Place Order" use case encompasses several key elements:

Actors: Lisa represents one of the primary actors in this use case. Depending on her situation, she may either have an existing account as a registered user, complete with shipping and billing details within the database, or she might be a brand-new customer requiring data collection. Additionally, other actors come into play, including the billing system responsible for invoicing her order and the fulfillment system responsible for processing and dispatching the order.

Precondition: Prior to initiating the process, certain conditions must be met. In Lisa's case, the precondition necessitates her selection of an item for purchase before she can proceed to place the order.

Trigger: The trigger is the event that sets the use case in motion. In this instance, Lisa's action, such as clicking on the shopping cart to commence the purchase process, serves as the trigger.

Postcondition: These are the outcomes that materialize after the actor initiates the process. In this scenario, Lisa's order gets registered within the system upon her successful completion of the purchase. She receives an order acknowledgment. The Billing department might take additional steps to invoice her if billing was not completed during the purchase. Simultaneously, the Shipping department makes arrangements for product shipment.

Normal Flow: This component of a use case typically entails a sequential list of steps. In this example, you can expect to see a series of steps that begin with Lisa's selection of an item and conclude once she has successfully placed the order and exits the purchase system.

Alternate Flow: Recognizing that not all purchases are uniform, this section accounts for variations. For instance, Lisa might decide to use a different credit card or specify an alternative shipping address. She might even change her mind and abandon the process before completing the purchase, or opt to cancel the purchase post-process.

It is important to note that the elements outlined above are not an exhaustive representation of all potential components within a use case. Nevertheless, for the purposes of the CompTIA Security+ exam, it's not mandatory to be a project management expert with in-depth knowledge of all facets of use cases. Instead, the emphasis is on comprehending the fundamental concepts associated with a use case.

Encryption

The process of encryption involves the transformation of data into an unintelligible form, rendering it unreadable to unauthorized individuals. Authorized users can decipher the data, but encryption techniques significantly impede any attempts by unauthorized parties to access the content.

To illustrate, consider a scenario where there is a need to transmit Personally Identifiable Information (PII), such as medical records or credit card details via email. Preventing unauthorized access to this sensitive data is imperative, especially as it traverses the network. By encrypting the email prior to transmission, data confidentiality remains safeguarded during its journey.

Access Controls

Access controls encompass the trifecta of identification, authentication, and authorization, collectively ensuring that only individuals with proper permissions gain access to data. For instance, if you wish to grant data access to Maggie while restricting Homer from the same information, access controls become your ally. Here's an overview of key components within access controls:

Identification: Users establish their identity through unique usernames. In the example provided, Maggie and Homer possess distinct user accounts, each identifiable by a unique username. When Maggie employs her account, she asserts the identity associated with her account.

Authentication: Authentication validates a user's identity through mechanisms like passwords. Maggie knows her password, which should remain confidential to her alone. When she logs into her account using her username and password, she attests to the account's identity and proves her own identity through the password.

Authorization: With authorization, you can grant or restrict access to resources, often through permissions. For instance, you have the capability to provide Maggie's account with full access to specific files and folders. Likewise, you can ensure that Homer is devoid of any permissions related to data access.

Recall that data confidentiality ensures that information remains accessible solely to authorized users. The most effective strategy for preserving data confidentiality is encryption, a versatile safeguard applicable to various data types, such as PII, information residing in databases, and data stored on mobile devices. Access controls also play a pivotal role in upholding confidentiality by controlling access rights and permissions.

Ensuring Data Authenticity

Data integrity is the cornerstone of maintaining the trustworthiness of information. It serves to confirm that data remains unaltered, safeguarding against any unauthorized modifications, tampering, or corruption. In an ideal scenario, only those with the proper authorization can make alterations to data. However, there are situations where unauthorized or unintentional changes can occur. These alterations may be attributed to unauthorized users, malicious software (commonly known as malware), as well as system and human errors. When such changes take place, the data loses its integrity.

To uphold data integrity, hashing techniques come into play. In essence, a hash is essentially a numerical value generated by executing a hashing algorithm on a piece of data, such as a file or a message. This process results in an irreversible output of a fixed length. The key characteristic here is that if the original data remains unaltered, the resulting hash will always remain the same. By comparing hashes generated at two distinct points in time, it becomes possible to ascertain whether the original data has undergone any modifications. If the hashes match, the data remains unchanged. Conversely, if the hashes differ, this indicates that the data's integrity has been compromised.

Let us consider a practical example: Homer is sending a message to Marge, and both of them wish to ensure that the message retains its integrity. Homer's message reads, "The price is $19.99." He creates a hash for this message, for the sake of simplicity, let's call it 123. Subsequently, he transmits both the message and the hash to Marge.

Upon receiving the message and the hash, Marge, or software on her computer, can calculate the hash for the received message. She can then compare her calculated hash with the one sent by Homer. If the hash for the received message matches 123 (the same as the hash for the sent message), Marge can be confident that the message has not suffered any loss of data integrity. However, if the hash of the received message differs, say it's 456, Marge knows that the message she received is not the same as the one sent by Homer, signifying a loss of data integrity.

It is important to note that a variance in hashes doesn't reveal the specific cause of the message modification. It merely indicates that the message has indeed been altered. This realization, however, underscores the need to exercise caution and skepticism about the message's integrity.

Hashing techniques can also serve as a means to verify the integrity of files during downloads or transfers. Certain software programs have the capability to automatically validate hashes to determine if even a single bit of data has been altered during the download process. By comparing the source hash with the destination hash, the downloading program can detect any discrepancies. If the hashes do not align, this signals a loss of integrity, prompting the program to report the issue to the user.

To provide another instance, a website administrator can calculate and display the hash of a file on a website. Users who download this file can manually calculate its hash and then compare it with the hash provided on the website. In the event that a virus infects the file on the web server, the hash of the infected file would diverge from the hash of the original file, as well as from the hash posted on the website.

In summary, data integrity serves as the assurance that data remains unaltered, safeguarding against unauthorized or unintentional modifications. The utilization of hashing algorithms, such as SHA, offers a means to calculate hashes, which are numerical representations generated for data at different instances. The comparison of these hashes allows for the verification of data integrity.

Enhancing Data Accessibility

Availability is a pivotal factor in ensuring that data and services remain accessible when needed. The specific requirements for availability can vary significantly between different organizations. For some, it might mean ensuring data and services are accessible only during typical business hours (e.g., 8:00 a.m. to 5:00 p.m., Monday through Friday). In contrast, other organizations, especially those providing critical services, demand round-the-clock, year-round availability.

Organizations typically employ redundancy and fault-tolerant strategies to maintain high levels of availability for critical systems. Furthermore, keeping systems up-to-date with the latest patches is essential to prevent software-related issues from affecting their availability.

Redundancy and Fault Tolerance: Redundancy involves introducing duplicate components into critical systems, thereby enhancing fault tolerance. If a critical component experiences a fault or failure, the redundancy ensures that the service can continue without any interruption. In other words, systems with fault tolerance can withstand and continue to operate in the presence of a fault.

A common objective of employing fault tolerance and redundancy techniques is to eliminate any single point of failure (SPOF). An SPOF, when it fails, can lead to the failure of the entire system. For example, if a server relies on a single drive, that drive becomes an SPOF, and its failure could result in the server's downtime.

Here are some common examples of fault tolerance and redundancy techniques:

Disk Redundancies: Utilizing fault-tolerant disks like RAID-1 (mirroring), RAID-5 (striping with parity), and RAID-10 (striping with a mirror) enables a system to continue functioning even if a disk fails.

Server Redundancies: Failover clusters incorporate redundant servers to ensure that a service remains operational, even in the event of a server failure. In a failover cluster, the service transitions from the failed server to an operational one within the same cluster. Virtualization can also enhance server availability by minimizing unplanned downtime.

Network Redundancies: Load balancing leverages multiple servers to support a single high-volume website, distributing the traffic effectively. Network interface card (NIC) teaming offers both redundancy and increased bandwidth.

Power Redundancies: Uninterruptible power supplies (UPSs) and power generators can deliver power to critical systems, even in situations where commercial power fails.

Scalability and Elasticity: Scalability and elasticity are integral elements contributing to high availability. These concepts empower systems to adapt to fluctuations in workload by either increasing hardware resources (scaling up) or adding additional nodes or servers (scaling out). Systems can also scale down or scale in by removing excess resources or nodes. The crucial distinction is that static systems necessitate manual scaling up or out, whereas dynamic systems employ elasticity to adapt automatically.

Scalability implies a system's capability to manage increased workloads by manually augmenting resources. For instance, if a server has 16 GB of RAM, administrators can manually enhance its capacity by adding another 16 GB, resulting in a total of 32 GB. However, there's typically a scalability limit determined by the system's specifications. Once a system reaches its limit, such as supporting only 32 GB of RAM, further scaling is not possible.

Elasticity, on the other hand, pertains to a system's ability to dynamically adjust to varying workloads. It can add more memory, processors, or other resources in response to spikes in demand. When demand decreases, elasticity allows the system to shed excess resources automatically. This dynamic adaptability is akin to a rubber band; it stretches as needed but reverts to its original state when the demand subsides.

Cloud resources frequently feature elasticity capabilities, enabling them to promptly accommodate fluctuating demand. From the user's perspective, the elasticity of cloud resources often appears limitless.

Patching: To ensure that systems remain available, a vital practice is keeping them up-to-date with the latest patches. Software bugs can lead to a multitude of issues, including security vulnerabilities and sporadic system crashes. Software vendors regularly identify these bugs and develop code patches to resolve these issues. Organizations typically establish patch management procedures to ensure that their systems remain current with the latest patches.

In summary, availability assures that systems and data are accessible whenever required, and it often deals with the elimination of single points of failure. Enhanced availability is achieved through the implementation of fault tolerance and redundancies, such as RAID, failover clusters, backups, and power generators.

Understanding Resiliency

Contemporary trends lean towards bolstering the resiliency of systems rather than striving for the utmost availability. This approach ensures that systems remain reliable without incurring the substantial costs associated with achieving the highest possible availability, such as 99.999 percent uptime (five nines). Achieving such high availability typically involves the elimination of all conceivable single points of failure and the introduction of extensive redundancies, which can significantly elevate the total cost of ownership (TCO).

Resiliency methodologies focus on enabling systems to recover from faults or failures with minimal downtime. They frequently leverage techniques akin to those employed in high availability systems. For example, a system implementing resiliency may perform routine and rigorous backups, have backup power sources (e.g., uninterruptible power supplies or generators), employ network interface card (NIC) teaming, or incorporate redundant disk subsystems. If a power outage occurs or one of the NICs experiences issues, or if a disk drive fails, the system can swiftly recover.

Additionally, resiliency methodologies assume that components will attempt to re-run failed processes. In the event of an initial failure, the system retries the process. For instance, consider a web server experiencing unexpected slowdown or returning error messages. The cause of this slowdown or the errors may not be immediately apparent, but the system takes restorative actions. If a web browser requests the same page again, it succeeds. Some web browsers perform this recovery process automatically. As a practical illustration, if you momentarily lose Internet access and visit Google with the Chrome browser, it may initially fail to load the page. However, once your Internet access is restored, Chrome automatically recovers and displays the Google homepage.

This concept of retrying and recovering from failures is well-established in network protocols. When using Transmission Control Protocol (TCP), packets may occasionally fail to reach their intended destination. In such cases, TCP processes involve a simple request for the source to retransmit the missing packet.

Balancing Resource Availability and Security Constraints

Organizations frequently find themselves at the crossroads of resource availability and security constraints. Let us take data confidentiality, for instance, where encryption serves as a vital safeguard. The question naturally arises: why not encrypt all data? The reason lies in the resource consumption associated with encryption.

To illustrate, consider the preceding paragraph, which consists of roughly 260 characters. When encrypted, the same content expands to approximately 360 characters, marking a 40% increase in size—typical with many encryption methods. If a company opts for the blanket encryption of all its data, it must be prepared to allocate approximately 40% more disk space to accommodate the larger encrypted files. Furthermore, when processing this data, encryption and decryption operations consume additional memory and processing power, which can result in a slowdown in applications.

While security experts might argue that the cost of additional resources is a small price to pay for heightened security, business executives striving to maximize the company's value often hold a different perspective. Their responsibility is to minimize costs without compromising security, and this is achieved by finding the optimal balance between resource costs and security requirements.

Introducing Foundational Risk Concepts

One of the fundamental objectives in implementing IT security is to reduce risk, a notion that permeates throughout various chapters in this book. Hence, it's beneficial to introduce key risk concepts.

Risk, in essence, represents the likelihood or possibility of a threat exploiting a vulnerability, resulting in a potential loss. Threats encompass any circumstances or events with the potential to compromise the confidentiality, integrity, or availability of data. Vulnerabilities, on the other hand, signify weaknesses, which can manifest in hardware, software, configurations, or even in the actions of the system users.

When a threat, like an attacker, exploits a vulnerability, it can lead to a security incident. A security incident encompasses any adverse event or a series of events with the potential to negatively impact the confidentiality, integrity, or availability of an organization's IT systems and data. These incidents can span intentional attacks, malware infections, accidental data losses, and more.

Threats are diverse, emerging from both inside and outside the organization. Malicious insiders, such as disgruntled employees, can pose a threat from within, while external threats can come from attackers located anywhere globally with access to the Internet. Threats further categorize as natural, like hurricanes, tsunamis, or tornadoes, or human-made, including malware created by cybercriminals. Additionally, threats can be intentional, driven by malicious intent, or accidental, stemming from employee errors or system glitches.

The process of mitigating risk to reduce the likelihood of a threat exploiting a vulnerability is known as risk mitigation. This reduction of risk is primarily achieved by the implementation of controls, also referred to as countermeasures or safeguards. The actions detailed in this book encompass various types of controls. It's essential to recognize that while it may be impossible to prevent most threats—tornadoes cannot be halted, nor can criminals be deterred from creating malware—it is possible to reduce risk by either diminishing vulnerabilities or mitigating the impact of potential threats.

For instance, access controls, starting with authentication, ensure that only authorized personnel gain access to specific areas, systems, or data. These controls can limit the potential damage caused by disgruntled employees seeking to cause harm. In the event of a natural disaster, business continuity and disaster recovery plans play a pivotal role in mitigating the disaster's impact. Likewise, antivirus software proactively mitigates the impact of malware by intercepting it before any damage occurs.

In summary, risk signifies the likelihood of a threat exploiting a vulnerability, and risk mitigation involves implementing security controls to either reduce vulnerabilities or lessen the impact of potential threats.

Understanding Security Controls

A plethora of security controls are available to organizations to reduce risk. However, the good news is that you do not need to become an expert on all these controls to pass the CompTIA Security+ exam. What is important is to grasp the fundamental understanding of control categories and types.

CompTIA delineates security controls into the following categories in its objectives:

Managerial Controls: These controls are primarily administrative in nature and find their documentation in an organization's security policy. Their primary role is to manage risk.

Operational Controls: Operational controls focus on ensuring that day-to-day organizational operations align with the established security policy. They are the controls that people actively put into practice.

Technical Controls: Technical controls harness technology, including hardware, software, and firmware, to reduce vulnerabilities.

It is noteworthy to recall that the security controls may span multiple categories and are not limited to a single classification.

CompTIA also identifies several control types in its objectives:

- *Preventive Controls*: Preventive controls are geared towards thwarting incidents from happening in the first place.
- *Detective Controls*: Detective controls aim to identify and uncover incidents after they have transpired.
- *Corrective Controls*: Corrective controls are intended to reverse the impacts of an incident, restoring the system to its original state.
- *Deterrent Controls*: Deterrent controls are put in place to discourage individuals from engaging in malicious actions.
- *Compensating Controls*: Compensating controls come into play when the primary control is not viable.
- *Physical Controls*: These are the controls that are tangible and can be physically touched and manipulated.

National Institute of Standards and Technology (NIST) and SP 800 Documents

The National Institute of Standards and Technology (NIST), a part of the U.S. Department of Commerce, encompasses the Computer Security Division, hosting the Information Technology Laboratory (ITL). NIST issues Special Publications (SPs) in the 800 series, which are valuable references for the computer security community. These documents are frequently used by IT security professionals to design secure IT systems and networks.

Moreover, numerous security-related certifications, beyond the scope of the CompTIA Security+ certification, reference these SP 800 documents, either directly or indirectly.

For instance, SP 800-53 Revision 5, "Security and Privacy Controls for Information Systems and Organizations," offers a wealth of information on security controls. It consists of three chapters dedicated to security controls, followed by three appendices. Appendix C serves as a security control catalog, furnishing intricate insights into numerous individual security controls grouped into 20 distinct families.

Each of these families encompasses various subgroups. For instance, the Access Control family (AC) encompasses 25 different subgroups, ranging from AC-1 through AC-25. Many of these subgroups list individual controls and provide comprehensive guidance on their implementation. Take, for example, AC-2 (Account Management), which enumerates multiple controls (denoted as a. through l.) and offers detailed explanations for each control.

It is worth noting that in prior versions of SP 800-53, there was an attempt to classify every control as either managerial, operational, or technical. However, this classification became somewhat challenging, as many controls exhibited characteristics from multiple classifications. NIST has since removed these classifications.

Managerial Controls

Managerial controls serve primarily as administrative measures and are typically documented within an organization's written security policy. These controls employ planning and assessment techniques to consistently review the organization's capacity to minimize and manage risks. Chapter 8, "Using Risk Management Tools," delves into vulnerability assessments and penetration tests, both of which fall under this category.

For instance, two common managerial controls are:

- *Risk Assessments*: These assist organizations in quantifying and qualifying risks, enabling them to concentrate on significant risks. For example, quantitative risk assessments employ cost and asset values to quantify risks in monetary terms, while qualitative risk assessments classify risks based on probability and impact.
- *Vulnerability Assessments*: These assessments aim to identify existing vulnerabilities. When necessary, additional controls are introduced to mitigate the risks associated with these vulnerabilities.

Operational Controls

Operational controls play a crucial role in ensuring that an organization's day-to-day operations align with its overarching security plan. These controls are primarily executed by individuals rather than automated systems. The operational controls encompass several families, including:

- *Awareness and Training*: Training is of paramount importance in risk reduction. It helps users maintain password security, adhere to clean desk policies, recognize threats such as phishing and malware, and more.
- *Configuration Management*: Configuration management often leverages baselines to ensure systems commence in a secure, hardened state. Change management procedures are instrumental in averting unintended configuration errors.

- *Media Protection*: This category involves safeguarding physical media such as USB flash drives, external and internal drives, and backup tapes.
- *Physical and Environmental Protection*: It includes both physical security elements like cameras and door locks, and environmental controls such as heating and ventilation systems.

Technical Controls

Technical controls harness technology, including hardware, software, and firmware, to diminish vulnerabilities. These controls are typically installed and configured by administrators, offering automated protection. Throughout this book, you'll encounter numerous examples of technical controls. Some of these examples are:

- *Encryption*: Encryption is a robust technical control used to preserve data confidentiality, both during transmission over a network and storage on devices like servers, desktop computers, and mobile devices.
- *Antivirus Software*: Once installed, antivirus software serves as a defense against malware infections. Chapter 6, "Comparing Threats, Vulnerabilities, and Common Attacks," provides a more detailed exploration of malware and antivirus software.
- *Intrusion Detection Systems (IDSs) and Intrusion Prevention Systems (IPSs)*: IDSs and IPSs are designed to monitor networks or hosts for intrusions, delivering ongoing protection against diverse threats. Chapter 4, "Securing Your Network," delves into various types of IDSs and IPSs.
- *Firewalls*: Network firewalls restrict incoming and outgoing network traffic. Chapter 3, "Exploring Network Technologies and Tools," offers a deeper examination of firewalls.
- *Least Privilege*: The principle of least privilege stipulates that individuals or processes should be granted only the privileges necessary for their designated tasks or functions, and no more. Privileges comprise both rights and permissions.

Control Types

Control types serve specific functions concerning security incidents. Some common classifications encompass preventive, detective, corrective, deterrent, compensating, and physical controls. As you explore these, you'll notice some overlap between control categories and control types. For example, training appears both in the operational category and among preventive controls.

Preventive Controls: The primary aim of preventive controls is to forestall security incidents from occurring. Preventive controls might also be referred to as preventative controls, with the two terms being synonymous. Some examples include:

Hardening: Hardening involves enhancing the security of a system or application beyond its default configuration. This approach employs a defense-in-depth strategy that combines layered security measures. It encompasses actions like disabling unnecessary ports and services, implementing secure protocols, maintaining system patches, deploying strong passwords alongside robust password policies, and deactivating default and superfluous accounts.

Training: Ensuring that users are informed about security vulnerabilities and threats plays a pivotal role in preventing incidents. Educated users are less susceptible to social engineering tactics, making it challenging for malicious actors to trick them.

Security Guards: Security guards act as a deterrent, preventing many security breaches. Their role may involve verifying user identities before allowing access to secure areas, effectively deterring social engineers from attempting unauthorized access.

Change Management: Change management serves to avert unintended outages by ensuring that changes do not lead to configuration errors. It straddles both operational and preventive controls, aiming to prevent incidents by submitting changes through a formal change management process.

Account Disablement Policy: An account disablement policy guarantees the deactivation of user accounts when employees leave the organization, preventing ex-employees and others from exploiting these accounts.

Intrusion Prevention System (IPS): IPSs can block malicious traffic before it infiltrates a network, preventing potential security incidents.

Detective Controls: While preventive controls seek to forestall security incidents, some incidents will invariably occur. Detective controls come into play to identify when vulnerabilities have been exploited, resulting in a security incident. It's important to note that detective controls uncover incidents after they have transpired. Some examples of detective controls include:

Log Monitoring: Numerous logs document activity on systems and networks. For instance, firewall logs record details of all traffic blocked by the firewall. By vigilantly monitoring these logs, it becomes possible to detect security incidents. Some automated log monitoring methods can instantly flag potential incidents.

Security Information and Event Management (SIEM) Systems: SIEM systems can not only monitor logs to detect individual incidents but also identify trends and issue real-time alerts. Analyzing past alerts can help pinpoint patterns, such as a surge in attacks on a specific system.

Security Audit: Security audits examine an organization's security posture. For instance, an account audit can assess whether personnel and technical policies correctly adhere to account policies.

Video Surveillance: Closed-circuit television (CCTV) systems record activities and can detect past incidents. Moreover, video surveillance serves as a deterrent control.

Motion Detection: Many alarm systems feature motion detection capabilities, raising alarms in response to potential intruders.

Intrusion Detection System (IDS): IDSs are designed to identify malicious network traffic once it has entered the network. They often trigger alarms to notify IT personnel of potential attacks.

Corrective and Recovery Controls

Corrective and recovery controls aim to mitigate the consequences of an incident or issue after it has occurred. Here are some examples of corrective and recovery controls:

- *Data Backups and System Recovery*: Data backups ensure that personnel can retrieve data if it is lost or compromised. Similarly, system recovery procedures enable administrators to restore a system following a failure. Chapter 9 provides a more in-depth exploration of backups and disaster recovery plans.
- *Incident Handling Processes*: Incident handling processes establish the steps to take in response to security incidents. This typically commences with the formulation of an incident response policy and an incident response plan.

Physical Controls

Physical controls encompass any controls that are tangible or can be physically touched. They include various items such as bollards, access control vestibules (sometimes referred to as mantraps), lighting, signs, fences, sensors, and more. It is important to understand that physical controls can also be categorized as other control types. For instance, locks are not only physical controls but also preventive and deterrent controls. A locked door, for example, prevents unauthorized personnel from entering a secure area and deters individuals from attempting entry, knowing that the door is locked.

Deterrent Controls

Deterrent controls strive to discourage potential threats. Some deterrent controls aim to dissuade potential attackers from launching attacks, while others aim to discourage employees from violating security policies. Many deterrent controls can also be described as preventive controls. For example, consider an organization that employs a security guard to control access to a restricted building area. The mere presence of the guard deters most individuals from attempting unauthorized access, thus preventing security incidents related to unauthorized entry.

The following list identifies some physical security controls used to deter threats:

- *Cable Locks:* Securing laptops to furniture with cable locks deters thieves from stealing laptops, as the laptops cannot be easily removed. Any attempt to remove the lock would likely destroy it. However, a thief could potentially cut the cable using a large cable cutter, which would appear suspicious.
- *Physical Locks:* Physical locks, such as locked doors securing a wiring closet or a server room, deter unauthorized access. Many server bay cabinets include locking cabinet doors.

Compensating Controls

Compensating controls are alternative measures used in place of a primary control. For example, an organization may require employees to use smart cards for authentication on a system. However, new employees might experience delays in receiving their smart cards. To maintain a high level of security while allowing new employees to access the network, the organization might choose to implement a Time-based One-Time Password (TOTP) as a compensating control. This compensating control still offers robust authentication.

Response Controls

Response controls, often referred to as incident response controls, are designed to prepare for security incidents and respond to them when they occur. These controls typically involve the creation of security policies, including incident response policies, and personnel training on how to respond to incidents. Chapter 11 provides more comprehensive coverage of incident response controls.

Combining Control Categories and Types

It is essential to recognize that control categories (managerial, operational, and technical) and control types (such as preventive, detective, corrective, etc.) are not mutually exclusive. In other words, most controls can be described using multiple categories and types. For example, encryption is both a preventive and technical control. It helps prevent data confidentiality breaches and is implemented using technology. Understanding these control categories should enable you to select the correct answers on the exam, even when CompTIA combines them in a question.

Similarly, a fire suppression system is both a physical and technical control. It qualifies as a physical security control because it can be physically touched, but it also falls under the technical control category because it employs technology to detect, suppress, or extinguish fires.

Using Command-Line Tools

The CompTIA Security+ objectives include several command-line tools. Some questions will present these tools directly in the question, while others will require you to choose the best tool from the answers. Familiarity with these tools can simplify your approach to such questions. Appendix A, "Command-Line Basics," provides a foundational understanding of working with command-line tools in both Windows and Linux environments. For those not accustomed to working with command-line tools, this appendix can be especially helpful.

Network Reconnaissance and Discovery

Network discovery is the process by which devices on a network identify other devices within the same network. Network reconnaissance, on the other hand, aims to gather additional information about the network and its devices. Many command-line tools are utilized by administrators (and sometimes malicious actors) for network reconnaissance and discovery, often for legitimate troubleshooting purposes. However, these tools can also be used by attackers to gain insight into a network and its hosts as part of their efforts to exploit vulnerabilities and extend their control within an attack.

The CompTIA Security+ objectives list several command-line tools that are essential for assessing organizational security. These tools are often specific to Windows systems and run via the Windows Command Prompt, while others are specific to Linux systems and are used within the Linux terminal or shell. During the exam, you can expect to encounter command-line commands both within the questions and in multiple-choice answers. Familiarizing yourself with these tools, their use cases, and command syntax is crucial for success. Practice and hands-on experience can further enhance your proficiency in working with these tools.

Ping

Ping is a fundamental command used to assess the connectivity of remote systems. It can also be employed to verify a system's ability to resolve hostnames to IP addresses, test network interface cards (NICs), and assess security within an organization.

The ping command evaluates connectivity by sending Internet Control Message Protocol (ICMP) echo request packets. Remote systems respond to these packets with ICMP echo reply packets. If you receive echo replies, it indicates that the remote system is operational. For instance, the following command can be used to test your computer's connection with another computer on your network, provided the other computer's IP address is 192.168.1.1: ping 192.168.1.1

On Windows systems, the ping command sends four ICMP echo requests. Systems receiving these requests respond with ICMP echo replies. On Linux-based systems, ping continues until you manually stop it using the Ctrl + C keyboard shortcut. To mimic this continuous behavior on Windows, you can use the -t switch, like so: ping -t 192.168.1.1

Conversely, to mimic the behavior of Windows ping on a Linux system, you can use the -c switch (for count), as demonstrated in the following example: ping -c 4 192.168.1.1

This command can test connectivity with an IP address on a local network, but it can also be used to assess connectivity with any system. For example, if you have the IP address of a system hosting a website on the internet, you can use ping to check its accessibility.

Using Ping for Name Resolution Checks

The name resolution process involves converting a hostname (such as google.com) into an IP address. This typically entails a computer querying a Domain Name System (DNS) server with the hostname, and the DNS server responding with an IP address.

Some malware attempts to disrupt the name resolution process for specific hosts. For example, on Windows systems, malware may modify the name resolution process to prevent systems from connecting to the Windows Update server and obtaining updates.

You can use the ping command to verify if the name resolution process is functioning correctly by pinging the hostname of a remote system. For instance, the following command resolves the hostname (google..com) to its corresponding IP address: ping google.com

Executing this command would result in a response indicating that the hostname (google.com) has been resolved to the IP address (8.8.8.8). The subsequent responses from the server confirm its operational status, ensuring that it is up and running.

Caution Regarding Firewalls

When you receive responses from a system, it confirms the operational status and reachability of the other system. However, if the ping command fails, it does not necessarily imply that the remote system is non-operational or unreachable. Even if the remote system functions correctly, the ping command may return a 'Reply Timed Out' error.

Numerous denial-of-service (DoS) attacks employ ICMP to disrupt services on internet-based systems. One such attack is the 'ping flood' attack, which endeavors to disrupt systems by bombarding them with repeated ping requests. In response to this threat, administrators often configure firewalls to either block ICMP traffic or disallow ICMP echo requests. This proactive measure prevents such attacks from succeeding. In essence, while a remote system may be fully operational, ping may fail due to the firewall blocking ICMP traffic.

Employing Ping for Organizational Security Evaluation

Ping can also serve as a tool for assessing organizational security. For example, if you have configured firewalls and routers to block ping traffic, you can employ the ping command to verify that these network components effectively block the traffic. In brief, IPSs can identify and automatically thwart attacks. For example, in the case of a distributed denial-of-service (DDoS) attack, which inundates a server with thousands of ping requests, an IPS can detect the attack and automatically block ICMP ping traffic, thereby neutralizing the threat.

You can utilize the ping command to confirm that the IPS functions as expected. To do so, you can simulate an attack by sending continuous pings from a couple of computers. If the IPS is functioning correctly, it will thwart these attacks, causing the ping requests to stop receiving responses.

Remember This: Administrators utilize the ping command to verify the connectivity of remote systems, validate the functioning of name resolution, and evaluate the security posture of systems and networks. This evaluation involves confirming that routers, firewalls, and IPSs block ICMP traffic as configured.

hping

The hping command shares similarities with the ping command, but it offers the flexibility to send pings using TCP, UDP, and ICMP. This tool is valuable for assessing whether a firewall blocks ICMP traffic, though it is exclusively available on Linux-like systems. Notably, hping boasts additional capabilities, such as scanning systems for open ports, a topic that will be explored further in Chapter 8.

Ipconfig and ifconfig

The ipconfig command, an abbreviation for 'Internet Protocol configuration,' reveals Transmission Control Protocol/Internet Protocol (TCP/IP) configuration details on Windows systems. This includes information such as the computer's IP address, subnet mask, default gateway, MAC address, and Domain Name System (DNS) server address. Furthermore, the command furnishes configuration details for all network interface cards (NICs) on a system, encompassing both wired and wireless NICs. Technicians frequently initiate ipconfig as an initial step in diagnosing network issues.

On Linux-based systems, ifconfig (abbreviated from 'interface configuration') serves a similar purpose as ipconfig. Ifconfig, however, offers more extensive capabilities compared to ipconfig. It allows for NIC configuration and property listing.

Here are some common command usages:

- *ipconfig*: When executed alone, this command provides essential information about the NIC, including the IP address, subnet mask, and default gateway.
- *ipconfig /all and ifconfig -a*: These commands offer comprehensive listings of TCP/IP configuration data for each NIC. This data encompasses details such as the Media Access Control (MAC) address, assigned DNS server addresses, and the address of a Dynamic Host Configuration Protocol (DHCP) server, if the system operates as a DHCP client. On Linux systems, the equivalent command is ifconfig -a.
- *ipconfig /displaydns*: This command displays the contents of the DNS cache, revealing results of system queries for hostname-to-IP address resolution. Additionally, it exposes hostname-to-IP address mappings included in the hosts file.
- *ipconfig /flushdns*: When executed, this command purges the contents of the DNS cache. It is employed to clear incorrect information from the cache, ensuring that the system queries DNS for up-to-date data.

Linux systems feature commands unique to their environment. It is important to note that some of these commands may require administrative permissions on certain Linux distributions. You can often gain these permissions by preceding the command with 'sudo.' For instance, instead of running 'ifconfig eth0,' you would execute 'sudo ifconfig eth0.'

Some of the Linux-specific commands are as follows:

- *ifconfig eth0*: This command reveals the configuration details of the first Ethernet interface (NIC) on a Linux system. In cases where a system has multiple NICs, designations like eth1, eth2, and so on are used. For the first wireless interface, 'wlan0' can be employed.
- *ifconfig eth0 promisc*: The execution of this command activates promiscuous mode on the initial Ethernet interface, allowing the NIC to process all incoming traffic. Ordinarily, a NIC operates in non-promiscuous mode, disregarding packets not explicitly destined for it. To deactivate promiscuous mode, the command 'ifconfig eth0 -promisc' can be utilized.
- *ifconfig eth0 allmulti*: This command enables multicast mode on the NIC, permitting the NIC to process all multicast traffic it receives. Typically, a NIC only processes multicast traffic associated with multicast groups it has joined. Deactivating multicast mode can be achieved with 'ifconfig eth0 -allmulti.'

Promiscuous mode is employed when you want a system to process all incoming packets that reach the NIC. A prime example is the use of a protocol analyzer application, where the desire is to capture and analyze all traffic. Activating promiscuous mode facilitates this process by allowing the NIC to see all packets in the protocol analyzer application.

Many Linux distributions have deprecated the use of the 'ifconfig' command. While deprecated, it implies that using the command is discouraged but still tolerated. 'ifconfig' is part of the 'net-tools' package, and it is important to note that Linux Debian developers no longer maintain this package. Nonetheless, 'ifconfig' and other tools within the 'net-tools' package are still prevalent on most Linux systems, including Kali Linux.

Instead of 'ifconfig,' Linux developers recommend the use of the 'ip' command. While the 'ip' command can display information and configure network interfaces, it employs distinct commands and provides different capabilities. For instance, it lacks a command for enabling promiscuous mode on a NIC. Here are some 'ip' commands:

- *ip link show*: This command lists the interfaces along with relevant details.
- *ip link set eth0 up*: This command activates a network interface.
- *ip -s link*: ByNetstat, short for network statistics, is a command that provides insights into TCP/IP protocols and active network connections on a system. It is a valuable tool for identifying active connections, which can be useful for detecting

potential security threats. Netstat offers various commands, some of which include:

- *netstat*: Displays a list of all open TCP connections.
- *netstat -a*: Shows all TCP and UDP ports the system is listening on, along with open connections. It also displays the corresponding IP addresses and port numbers, which can help identify the associated protocols.
- *netstat -r*: Displays the routing table.
- *netstat -e*: Provides details on network statistics, such as the number of bytes sent and received.
- *netstat -s*: Offers statistics on packets sent or received for specific protocols like IP, ICMP, TCP, and UDP.
- *netstat -n*: Shows addresses and port numbers in numerical order, which can be helpful when looking for specific IP addresses or ports.
- *netstat -p protocol*: Displays statistics for a particular protocol, such as TCP or UDP. For instance, you can use netstat -p tcp to view only TCP statistics.

These commands allow you to gather information about network connections and system routing. Combining different options can provide more specific data, enabling you to investigate network activity or troubleshoot network-related issues.

Tracert and traceroute are commands used to list the routers (hops) between two systems. They identify the IP addresses and sometimes the hostnames of each hop, along with round-trip times (RTTs). Tracert is used on Windows-based systems, while traceroute is used on Linux-based systems. These commands help network administrators identify problematic routers and track the path taken by network traffic. It's a valuable tool for diagnosing network connectivity issues and identifying modified network paths.

Pathping combines the functionalities of ping and tracert. It identifies all hops on the path and sends pings to each hop, calculating statistics based on the responses. This command is often used to locate potential issues in the network path between two systems, making it useful for identifying intermittent problems or segment issues between hops.

The arp command is used to view and manipulate the ARP (Address Resolution Protocol) cache. ARP resolves IP addresses to MAC addresses and stores the results in the ARP cache. It can be used to check the MAC address of other systems on the local network, identify potential ARP cache poisoning attacks, and verify the accuracy of ARP entries.

Linux and LAMP stack are becoming increasingly prevalent in network environments. The LAMP stack consists of Linux, Apache, MySQL, and PHP (or Perl or Python). The book introduces several Linux command-line tools commonly used for file manipulation and log management, including:

- cat command: Displays the contents of files.
- grep command: Searches for specific strings or patterns within files.
- head and tail commands: Display the beginning or end of files, respectively.
- logger command: Adds log entries to the syslog.
- journalctl command: Queries system logs stored in the journal.
- chmod command: Modifies file and folder permissions on Linux systems.

These Linux commands are crucial for managing files, troubleshooting issues, and maintaining system security. running this command, statistics on network interfaces are displayed.

On Windows systems, 'ipconfig' is used to view network interfaces, while Linux systems utilize 'ifconfig.' Additionally, 'ifconfig' allows the manipulation of network interface settings. In many scenarios, the 'ip' command is recommended in lieu of 'ifconfig,' especially for viewing and configuring NIC settings.

Comprehending Log Entries

The CompTIA Security+ exam requires candidates to analyze log entries and interpret their meaning. For system administrators who regularly work with logs, this becomes second nature. However, for those who don't deal with logs daily, log entries can sometimes appear as a foreign language.

Log entries play a crucial role in helping administrators and security investigators understand what occurred, when it occurred, where it happened, and who or what was involved. By examining entries from various logs, personnel can establish an audit trail that identifies all the events leading up to a security incident. Subsequent sections will cover various concepts related to logs that you should grasp before the test day.

Windows Logs

Operating systems maintain basic logs that record events. For instance, Windows systems possess several common logs that keep track of activities on a Windows computer system. You can view these logs using the Windows Event Viewer. The primary Windows logs include:

- *Security log*: The Security log serves as a security, audit, and access log. It records auditable events, such as successes and failures. A success signifies the successful completion of an audited event, like a user successfully logging on or deleting a file. On the other hand, failure indicates that a user attempted an action but failed, such as an unsuccessful login or an attempt to delete a file resulting in a permission error. While Windows enables some auditing by default, administrators can add additional auditing.

- *System log*: The System log records events related to the functioning of the operating system, such as system startup, shutdown, information about services, driver loading or failures, and other important system component events.
- *Application log*: The Application log records events sent to it by applications or programs running on the system, including warnings, errors, and routine messages.

If a system is under attack, reviewing the operating system logs can provide insights into the nature of the attack. Depending on the type of attack, any of the operating system logs may prove useful.

Network Logs

Network logs keep a record of network traffic. These logs exist on various devices like routers, firewalls, web servers, and network intrusion detection/prevention systems. Administrators can often configure these devices to log specific information, such as all the traffic they pass or block. These logs prove valuable when troubleshooting connectivity issues and identifying potential intrusions or attacks, providing information about the source and destination of packets, including IP addresses, MAC addresses, and ports.

Web servers usually log requests made to the server for web pages, following the Common Log format standardized by the World Wide Web Consortium (W3C). A typical log entry includes details like:

- *Host*: The IP address or hostname of the client making the request.
- *User-identifier*: The name of the user requesting the page, if known.
- *Authuser*: The logon name of the user requesting the page, if the user logged on.
- *Date*: The date and time of the request.
- *Request*: The actual request line sent by the client.
- *Status*: The HTTP status code returned to the client.
- *Bytes*: The byte length of the reply.

Centralized Logging Methods

Routine checking of logs on all network devices can be quite challenging. A common solution is to employ a centralized system for collecting log entries. Two popular methods for achieving this are through a Security Information and Event Management (SIEM) system and the syslog protocol.

SIEM Systems

A Security Information and Event Management (SIEM) system offers a centralized solution for collecting, analyzing, and managing data from multiple sources. It combines the functions of Security Event Management (SEM) and Security Information Management (SIM) solutions. SEM provides real-time monitoring, analysis, and notification of security events, while SIM offers long-term data storage and tools for data analysis, including trend analysis and compliance reporting.

SIEM systems prove highly valuable for large enterprises with substantial data and activity volumes, as they enable automated monitoring and reporting. Vendors offer SIEMs as applications that can be installed on centralized systems or as dedicated hardware appliances. Common capabilities of SIEMs include:

- *Log collectors*: Collect log data from various devices and store them in a searchable database.
- *Data inputs*: Accept log entries from a variety of sources, including firewalls, routers, network intrusion detection and prevention systems, as well as other systems like web servers, proxy servers, and database servers.
- *Log aggregation*: Combine data from different systems into a common format to make analysis and searching more straightforward.
- *Correlation engine*: Analyze log data from various systems to identify patterns indicative of potential security events and raise alerts.
- *Reports*: Provide built-in reports across different categories, including network traffic event monitoring, device events, threat events, logon/logoff events, and compliance with specific regulations.
- *Packet capture*: Capture network traffic for in-depth analysis, often integrated into SIEM systems.
- *User behavior analysis*: Monitor user activity, such as launched applications and network behavior, to identify abnormal patterns that may suggest malicious intent.
- *Sentiment analysis*: Employ artificial intelligence to analyze large data sets for user behavior anomalies.
- *Security monitoring*: Continuously monitor systems for predefined alerts, both built-in and user-defined.
- *Automated triggers*: Set triggers to perform actions in response to repeated events, such as modifying firewall rules to block malicious activity.

- *Time synchronization*: Ensure that all servers sending data to the SIEM have synchronized time, critical for incident investigation and for organizations with multiple locations in different time zones.
- *Event deduplication*: Remove duplicate log entries, improving efficiency and data consistency.
- *Logs/WORM*: Prevent the modification of log entries, ensuring data integrity.
- *SIEM location*: Place SIEM within the private network for data protection. In large organizations, consider off-loading some processing tasks to separate servers, allowing the primary SIEM appliance to focus on alerts and triggers.

SIEM dashboards provide administrators with real-time views of significant activities, which can be customized. These dashboards may be displayed on large screens in network operations centers or on a single computer in smaller networks. Key components of a SIEM dashboard include sensors (collecting logs), alerts, sensitivity settings, correlation capabilities, and trend analysis.

Syslog Protocol

The syslog protocol defines a standard log entry format and specifies how to transport log entries. You can deploy a centralized syslog server to collect syslog entries from various devices in the network, similar to a SIEM server collecting log entries.

Syslog, developed in the 1980s, initially lacked a single defining publication, but it was later documented by the IEEE in informational RFCs (RFC 3164 in 2001 and RFC 5424 in 2009). Systems sending syslog messages are originators, while collectors (syslog servers) receive messages from external devices or services and applications on the same system.

It is important to note that the syslog protocol defines the formatting and transmission of log messages but not how the syslog server handles these entries. On Linux systems, syslog messages are managed by the syslogd daemon, which collects and processes logs based on the /etc/syslog.conf file. Many syslog messages are routed to the /var/syslog file.

Alternatively, additional applications can collect and process syslog entries, offering functions similar to SIEM systems. Historically, syslog messages were sent via UDP using port 514, but modern implementations can use TCP port 6514 with Transport Layer Security (TLS) for reliability and encryption.

Syslog-ng and Rsyslog

On Linux-like systems, syslogd can be replaced with two open-source software utilities, syslog-ng and rsyslog, which extend its capabilities. Both offer rich filtering, content-based filtering, and support for TCP and TLS.

Syslog-ng extends syslogd, enabling log collection from various sources, routing capabilities, and extensions using tools and modules in other languages.

Rsyslog, an improvement over syslog-ng, allows direct insertion of log entries into database engines and supports TCP and TLS.

NXLog

NXLog is another log management tool that supports log formats for Windows, including event log entries. It can be installed on both Windows and Linux-like systems, serving as a log collector. It integrates with most SIEM systems and is available in two versions: Community Edition (free, with features comparable to some SIEM solutions) and Enterprise Edition (includes additional capabilities like real-time event correlation and remote administration).

Linux Logs

The CompTIA Security+ exam includes several Linux-based commands, as discussed earlier in this chapter. It is valuable to be aware of common Linux logs located in the /var/log directory. These logs can be viewed using the System Log Viewer on Linux systems or through the terminal using commands like cat. Common Linux logs include:

- /var/log/syslog: Stores system activity, including startup events (not to be confused with the syslog protocol).
- /var/log/messages: Contains a wide variety of general system messages, covering topics like startup, mail, kernel, and authentication.
- /var/log/boot.log: Records entries created during system boot.
- /var/log/auth.log: Contains information about successful and unsuccessful logins.
- /var/log/faillog: Logs failed login attempts, accessible using the faillog command.
- /var/log/kern.log: Contains kernel-related information logged by the system kernel, which is at the core of the Linux operating system.
- /var/log/httpd/: If the system serves as an Apache web server, this directory houses access and error logs that follow the Common Log format.

Understanding these log entries and knowing how to access them is essential for Linux administrators.

Threats, Attacks, and Vulnerabilities

Threats, attacks, and vulnerabilities comprise a significant portion of the attention directed by cybersecurity professionals to their work. These three elements form the foundation upon which the security profession is built. This chapter will delve into the multifaceted world of threats, exploring various malware types and their characteristics, as well as attack types, and the importance of threat intelligence and vulnerability management.

1. Malware Types and Characteristics
Viruses, Worms, and Trojans
Viruses are the familiar adversaries that attach themselves to legitimate programs or files, enabling them to spread, replicate, and inflict damage as they go. These infectious agents can cause havoc within your systems, corrupting or deleting data, and disrupting day-to-day operations. Understanding viruses, their propagation methods, and their distinct characteristics is pivotal for effective defense.

Worms, like viruses, are malicious entities that replicate themselves; however, they possess the capability to spread independently across networks without the need for a host file. Worms can rapidly propagate, making them a formidable threat to network security.

Trojans derive their name from the mythological Trojan Horse, and these deceitfully infiltrate systems under the guise of legitimate software. Concealing a malicious payload, they can steal data, provide unauthorized access, or conduct other malicious actions, making them a potent weapon in the attacker's arsenal.

Ransomware and Spyware
Ransomware is a nefarious breed of malware that encrypts your valuable data and demands a ransom for its safe release. This insidious software can bring businesses and individuals to their knees; the prevalence and effectiveness of ransomware highlighting the critical need for robust defenses and backup strategies.

Spyware, as the name suggests, covertly infiltrates systems, silently collecting sensitive information and transmitting it to malicious actors. Detecting and eradicating these stealthy spies is essential to protect your privacy and data.

Rootkits and Logic Bombs
Rootkits delve into the very core of an operating system, granting attackers elevated privileges and enabling them to manipulate the system undetected. Their ability to remain

concealed makes them a formidable threat. Rootkits require a deep understanding of their characteristics and detection methods.

Logic bombs are time-activated malware designed to execute a destructive action when specific conditions are met. These are often triggered by a predetermined event or date. Recognizing the presence of logic bombs and defusing them is crucial to preventing catastrophic system failures.

Understanding these malware types and their characteristics is the first step in building a robust defense against the ever-present menace of cyberattacks.

2. Attack Types
Social Engineering Attacks
Social engineering attacks exploit human psychology to manipulate individuals into divulging confidential information or taking certain actions. These attacks often rely on deception and trust. Attackers may use tactics such as phishing, pretexting, baiting, or tailgating to trick their targets into revealing sensitive data or granting unauthorized access.

Network Attacks
Network attacks target vulnerabilities in network infrastructure to disrupt services or gain unauthorized access. These attacks encompass a wide range of techniques, including packet sniffing, denial of service (DoS), and distributed denial of service (DDoS) attacks. Understanding network attacks is critical for safeguarding the integrity of data transmission and network infrastructure.

Wireless Attacks
Wireless attacks target vulnerabilities in wireless networks, exploiting weaknesses in encryption or authentication methods. Techniques such as eavesdropping, session hijacking, and deauthentication attacks pose serious threats to wireless security. Protecting your wireless networks is essential to prevent unauthorized access and data compromise.

3. Threat Intelligence and Vulnerability Management
Sources of Threat Intelligence
Threat intelligence is the lifeblood of proactive cybersecurity. This process provides insights into emerging threats, attacker tactics, and vulnerabilities that may be exploited. In this section, I will explore various sources of threat intelligence, including open-source feeds, commercial threat intelligence services, and information sharing and analysis centers (ISACs).

Vulnerability Scanning and Penetration Testing

Vulnerability management is the process of identifying, prioritizing, and mitigating security vulnerabilities in an organization's systems and applications. Vulnerability scanning tools help automate the discovery of weaknesses, while penetration testing simulates real-world attacks to assess an organization's security posture. In this section, I delve into the methods and best practices for conducting vulnerability scanning and penetration testing.

These methods and best practices for conducting vulnerability scanning and penetration testing are vital components of a proactive and comprehensive security strategy. They also play a crucial role in identifying, assessing, and mitigating vulnerabilities within an organization's systems and networks. Let us delve deeper into these essential practices:

Vulnerability Scanning:

Automated Scanning Tools: Utilizing specialized software tools, vulnerability scanning automates the process of identifying potential weaknesses in your systems and applications. These tools assess various aspects, including open ports, outdated software, misconfigurations, and known vulnerabilities. Commonly used scanning tools include Nessus, OpenVAS, and Qualys.

Regular Scans: To maintain a strong security posture, it is essential to conduct regular vulnerability scans. This practice ensures that newly discovered vulnerabilities are promptly identified and addressed, reducing the window of opportunity for potential attackers.

Risk Prioritization: Not all vulnerabilities are equal in terms of risk. Effective scanning involves a process of risk prioritization, allowing organizations to focus on addressing the most critical vulnerabilities first. This is often achieved by assigning a risk score or severity rating to each identified vulnerability.

Compliance Assessment: Vulnerability scanning tools can also aid in assessing compliance with industry standards and regulations. This ensures that organizations meet specific security requirements, which is particularly important in regulated industries such as healthcare and finance.

Penetration Testing:

Simulated Attacks: Penetration testing, also known as ethical hacking, involves conducting simulated attacks on your systems and networks. These controlled tests aim to identify vulnerabilities and weaknesses in a real-world scenario, providing a better understanding of the potential impact of an actual breach.

White Box and Black Box Testing: Penetration testing can take on different forms, including white box and black box testing. White box testing involves testing with full knowledge of the system's architecture, while black box testing simulates the perspective of an external attacker with no internal information. Both methods offer valuable insights.

Engagement Scoping: Prior to penetration testing, a scoping phase is crucial. This defines the objectives, scope, and rules of engagement for the test. It also helps ensure that testing activities are conducted within predefined boundaries to avoid unintended disruption.

Detailed Reporting: Penetration testing results in a detailed report that outlines the vulnerabilities discovered, their potential impact, and recommendations for remediation. This report is a valuable resource for making informed decisions and implementing security improvements.

Recurring Tests: Just like vulnerability scanning, penetration testing should be a recurring practice. Regular testing helps organizations stay ahead of evolving threats and vulnerabilities and continuously improve their security posture.

As you prepare for the CompTIA Security+ SY0-601 exam, understanding threats, attacks, and vulnerabilities is fundamental. To help you assess your knowledge and readiness, here are three practice questions:

Practice Question 1: Which type of malware conceals its presence and can potentially grant unauthorized access to a system?

A) Ransomware
B) Worm
C) Spyware
D) Rootkit

Answer: D) Rootkit

Explanation: A rootkit is a type of malware that is designed to hide its presence on a system and provide unauthorized access. It often replaces or modifies system files to maintain stealth.

Practice Question 2: What type of attack involves an attacker intercepting communication between two parties and relaying messages between them without their knowledge?

A) Phishing
B) Man-in-the-Middle (MitM)
C) DoS (Denial of Service)
D) SQL Injection

Answer: B) Man-in-the-Middle (MitM)

Explanation: A Man-in-the-Middle (MitM) attack occurs when an attacker intercepts and possibly alters communication between two parties, typically without their knowledge. It can lead to eavesdropping, data tampering, or identity theft.

Practice Question 3: A security incident response process typically follows a sequence of phases. Which phase focuses on restoring systems to normal operations and verifying their integrity?

A) Identification
B) Containment
C) Recovery
D) Eradication

Answer: C) Recovery

Explanation: The Recovery phase in an incident response process focuses on restoring systems to normal operations after a security incident. It also involves verifying the integrity of systems and data to ensure that they are secure.

As you continue your journey into the world of cybersecurity, the knowledge and insights presented in this chapter will serve as a sturdy foundation for understanding the threats and attacks that challenge our digital world. Equipped with this understanding, you can take proactive steps to defend against these adversaries and secure your digital assets. Stay vigilant—the realm of cybersecurity is ever-changing, and knowledge is your greatest weapon!

Architecture and Design

In the world of cybersecurity, the foundation of security is rooted in the architecture and design of the systems and networks that underpin our digital interactions. In this chapter, I delve into the critical aspects of architecture and design, focusing on how a well-structured foundation can mitigate potential threats and vulnerabilities.

1. Secure Network Design
Network Segmentation
Network segmentation is a fundamental concept in the pursuit of a robust security infrastructure. This strategy involves dividing a network into smaller, isolated segments to minimize the potential impact of a security breach. By compartmentalizing sensitive data and systems, organizations can restrict lateral movement for attackers and limit the scope of security incidents.

Secure Network Topologies
The design of *network topologies* plays a crucial role in safeguarding data and ensuring efficient communication. By understanding and implementing secure network topologies, you can reduce the attack surface and enhance the overall security posture of your network.

Common secure network topologies are the architectural blueprints that organizations use to design their network infrastructures, and they play a pivotal role in enhancing security. In this section, I explore some of these secure network topologies and their practical implications:

Perimeter Network Topology (DMZ): The DMZ (Demilitarized Zone) is an isolated network segment situated between the internal and external networks. It houses services that need to be publicly accessible but must be separated from the internal network. By placing web servers, email gateways, or public-facing services in the DMZ, organizations can reduce the attack surface and protect their sensitive internal resources.

Segmentation with VLANs: Using Virtual Local Area Networks (VLANs), organizations can divide their networks into smaller, isolated segments. This segmentation reduces the lateral movement for potential attackers. For instance, separating departments into VLANs limits the scope of a security breach to the compromised segment, enhancing overall network security.

Ring Topology: Ring topologies connect devices in a circular or ring-like configuration. The practical implication of this design is redundancy and fault tolerance. Even if one segment of the ring is compromised, communication can continue through the other part. This topology is often used in industrial networks and critical infrastructure to ensure continuous operation.

Star Topology: In a star topology, all devices are connected to a central hub or switch. This design simplifies management and monitoring of the network, making it easier to detect and respond to security incidents. It also provides isolation between network segments, enhancing security and control.

Mesh Topology: Mesh networks have every device connected to every other device, creating redundancy and multiple paths for data to travel. While this topology can be complex and expensive, it provides fault tolerance and resiliency. In the context of security, if one path is compromised, data can still find alternative routes, reducing the risk of network downtime.

Hybrid Topologies: Hybrid topologies combine elements of different network topologies to meet specific organizational needs. For example, a combination of star and ring topologies can offer a balance between centralized management and fault tolerance. Hybrid topologies allow organizations to adapt to their unique security and operational requirements.

Flat Network Topology: In a flat network, all devices are on a single network segment, often with minimal security measures. While this design can simplify network management, it poses security risks. Practical implications involve implementing robust security measures like network segmentation, firewalls, and intrusion detection to mitigate the vulnerabilities associated with flat networks.

Understanding these network topologies and their practical implications is fundamental to designing a secure network that not only facilitates efficient communication but also defends against potential security threats. By carefully selecting and implementing the right topology based on an organization's specific needs and risk tolerance, security professionals can establish a strong foundation for protecting digital assets and ensuring data integrity.

2. Secure Systems Design
Trusted OS and Hardening Techniques
A trusted *operating system* (OS) is the cornerstone of secure systems. This section explores the concept of a trusted OS, emphasizing the importance of OS selection and configuration. Additionally, we delve into hardening techniques, which involve securing

the OS by removing unnecessary features, applying patches, and configuring settings to minimize vulnerabilities.

Secure Boot and BIOS/UEFI Settings

The security of a system begins even before the OS loads. *Secure Boot* and the *BIOS/UEFI settings* are integral components of the boot process. In this section, I explore the significance of Secure Boot and provides guidance on configuring BIOS/UEFI settings to protect against firmware-level attacks and unauthorized access.

Secure Boot and the configuration of BIOS/UEFI settings are crucial aspects of system security, as they are the first line of defense against firmware-level attacks and unauthorized access. Let us explore the significance of Secure Boot and provide guidance on configuring BIOS/UEFI settings to enhance security.

The Significance of Secure Boot:

Protection Against Malicious Bootkits: Secure Boot is a security feature that ensures the integrity of the bootloader and kernel during the boot process. It prevents the execution of unsigned or altered bootloaders and bootkits, which are commonly used by attackers to compromise the system's firmware. By enforcing the use of signed, trusted bootloaders, Secure Boot safeguards the system against these types of threats.

Early Threat Detection: Firmware-level attacks often go undetected by traditional security tools and antivirus software. Secure Boot's role in early threat detection is critical; it ensures that any unauthorized modifications to the bootloader are detected during the boot process, triggering alerts and preventive actions.

Mitigation of Unauthorized Changes: Secure Boot mitigates the risk of unauthorized changes to the bootloader, which could be caused by attackers or misconfigurations. By only allowing the system to boot using authorized, signed code, it ensures the system's firmware remains in a known, secure state.

Configuring BIOS/UEFI Settings:

Enabling Secure Boot: The first step is to enable Secure Boot in the BIOS/UEFI settings. It is essential to verify that the system's firmware supports Secure Boot and that it is enabled. Depending on the system, this setting may be found in the security or boot sections of the BIOS/UEFI interface.

Managing Secure Boot Keys: Secure Boot relies on cryptographic keys to verify the integrity of bootloaders and components. The BIOS/UEFI settings allow users to manage these keys. Best practices include ensuring that only trusted keys are used, and regularly updating keys when necessary.

Boot Order and Boot Device Control: In BIOS/UEFI settings, configure the boot order to prioritize the boot from the trusted source, such as the internal hard drive or SSD, where the authorized bootloader resides. This prevents attackers from booting from external devices to compromise the system.

Setting BIOS/UEFI Passwords: Set strong, unique passwords for the BIOS/UEFI settings to prevent unauthorized access and changes. BIOS/UEFI passwords add an additional layer of security, especially if physical access to the system is possible.

Regular Firmware Updates: Keep the system's firmware up to date by regularly checking for and applying manufacturer-provided updates. Firmware updates often include security patches that address known vulnerabilities.

System Recovery and Backup: Plan for system recovery by creating backup copies of the system's firmware settings and keys. This ensures that in the event of a firmware-related issue, you can restore the system to a known good state.

Configuring BIOS/UEFI settings to enable Secure Boot and protect against firmware-level attacks is a fundamental aspect of system security. By following these best practices, organizations and individuals can reduce the risk of unauthorized access, malicious firmware modifications, and boot-level attacks, thus enhancing the overall security posture of their systems. Firmware-level security is a critical consideration in the ever-evolving landscape of cybersecurity, and these measures provide a strong foundation for protecting the integrity of system firmware.

3. Cloud and Virtualization
Cloud Service Models
Cloud computing has become an integral part of modern IT infrastructure. Understanding the various cloud service models (Infrastructure as a Service, Platform as a Service, and Software as a Service) is crucial for selecting the right model to meet your organization's needs while maintaining security.

Cloud Deployment Models
Different organizations have different cloud deployment preferences, ranging from public and private to hybrid and multicloud. Exploring these cloud deployment models helps in making informed decisions to align your cloud strategy with security objectives.

Virtualization Security Best Practices

Virtualization technology has revolutionized data center management and resource allocation. However, it also introduces new security challenges. This section provides an overview of virtualization security best practices, covering topics like hypervisor security, virtual machine isolation, and secure configuration of virtualization environments.

Chapter 3 covered secure network and systems design, which is essential knowledge for the SY0-601 exam. To assess your understanding, here are three practice questions:

Practice Question 1: Which of the following secure network design practices helps limit the lateral movement of attackers within a network?

A) Encryption
B) DMZ
C) Network Segmentation
D) Intrusion Detection System

Answer: C) Network Segmentation

Explanation: Network segmentation is a secure network design practice that divides a network into smaller segments, limiting the ability of attackers to move laterally between segments. It enhances security by isolating different parts of the network.

Practice Question 2: What is the primary function of a Trusted OS in secure system design?

A) Enforce encryption for all data in transit
B) Ensure all employees have access to critical data
C) Provide a secure and controlled environment for running applications
D) Automatically update all system software

Answer: C) Provide a secure and controlled environment for running applications

Explanation: A Trusted OS (Operating System) is designed to provide a secure and controlled environment for running applications, protecting them from unauthorized access or tampering.

Practice Question 3: In the context of cloud computing, which cloud service model provides users with the highest level of control and responsibility for managing infrastructure and applications?

A) Software as a Service (SaaS)

B) Platform as a Service (PaaS)
C) Infrastructure as a Service (IaaS)
D) Function as a Service (FaaS)

Answer: C) Infrastructure as a Service (IaaS)

Explanation: Infrastructure as a Service (IaaS) provides users with the highest level of control and responsibility for managing infrastructure, including virtual machines, storage, and networking. Users are responsible for managing and securing the underlying infrastructure.

By mastering the principles and best practices outlined in this chapter, you will be better equipped to design and architect systems and networks that not only function effectively but also resist the constant onslaught of potential threats and vulnerabilities. The security landscape is ever-changing, and a solid architecture and design approach serve as the bedrock upon which robust security solutions are built.

Implementation

In an age where digital communication is omnipresent, securing protocols and services, network infrastructure devices, and addressing the unique challenges posed by mobile and IoT (Internet of Things) devices is paramount. In this chapter, I explore these crucial facets of cybersecurity and provide valuable insights into safeguarding your digital environment.

1. Secure Protocols and Services

Secure Protocols and Services are essential components of a robust cybersecurity strategy. They aim aim to protect data, communications, and digital assets from potential threats and vulnerabilities. In this section, I will delve into the significance and practical implications of some key secure protocols and services:

DNSSEC (Domain Name System Security Extensions): DNSSEC is a critical protocol designed to address the inherent vulnerabilities in the Domain Name System (DNS). By adding digital signatures to DNS data, it ensures data integrity and authenticity, preventing DNS cache poisoning attacks. This secures the critical process of domain name resolution, a foundational aspect of internet communication.

Practical Implications:

- *Data Integrity*: DNSSEC guarantees that DNS responses have not been tampered with during transit, reducing the risk of domain name manipulation by malicious actors.
- *Authentication*: By cryptographically verifying the source and integrity of DNS data, it helps ensure that users are directed to legitimate websites and not malicious counterparts.
- *Mitigation of Cache Poisoning*: DNSSEC counters cache poisoning attacks, protecting users from being redirected to malicious websites via compromised DNS data.

SSH (Secure Shell): SSH is a secure, encrypted protocol used for remote access and secure file transfers. It addresses the security concerns associated with traditional remote access methods, such as Telnet or FTP, by providing strong encryption and authentication.

Practical Implications:

- *Secure Remote Access*: SSH ensures that remote access to servers and network devices is encrypted and protected from eavesdropping or interception.
- *Authentication*: Strong authentication methods like public-key authentication add an extra layer of security, making it challenging for unauthorized users to gain access.
- *Secure File Transfer*: SSH's secure file transfer capabilities provide a safe means to transmit files between systems, safeguarding data in transit.

S/MIME (Secure/Multipurpose Internet Mail Extensions): S/MIME is an email security protocol that enhances the security of email communications. It achieves this by providing end-to-end encryption, digital signatures, and data integrity validation for email messages.

Practical Implications:

- *Confidentiality*: S/MIME ensures that email messages remain confidential, as they are encrypted and only decipherable by the intended recipient.
- *Message Integrity*: Digital signatures verify that email messages haven't been altered in transit, offering assurance that the content is authentic.
- *Authentication*: The use of certificates and digital signatures enhances email authentication, reducing the risk of email spoofing and phishing attacks.

Secure Protocols and Services play a crucial role in maintaining the confidentiality, integrity, and authenticity of data and communications. By implementing these protocols, organizations and individuals can mitigate the risk of data breaches, unauthorized access, and other security threats in an interconnected digital environment. Understanding their significance and practical implications is key to building a robust and secure cybersecurity framework.

2. Network Infrastructure Devices

Network Infrastructure Devices are the critical components that form the backbone of any organization's IT infrastructure. These devices play a pivotal role in ensuring the secure and efficient functioning of networks. In this section, I explore the significance and practical implications of key network infrastructure devices:

Firewalls: Firewalls are a fundamental component of network security. They act as a barrier between an organization's internal network and the external, often untrusted, network (usually the internet). Firewalls filter and control incoming and outgoing network traffic, enforcing security policies and protecting against unauthorized access and threats.

Practical Implications:

- *Access Control*: Firewalls establish rules to permit or deny traffic based on defined criteria, ensuring that only authorized communication is allowed.
- *Threat Mitigation*: They provide protection against common threats like malware, denial of service attacks, and unauthorized access attempts.
- *Logging and Monitoring*: Firewalls generate logs and alerts, allowing security teams to monitor network traffic and detect potential security incidents in real-time.

IDS/IPS (Intrusion Detection and Prevention Systems): IDS and IPS are security systems designed to monitor network traffic and detect suspicious activities or known attack patterns. While IDS identifies potential threats, IPS takes it a step further by actively blocking and preventing those threats from compromising the network.

Practical Implications:

- *Threat Detection:* IDS alerts security teams to unusual or suspicious network activities, enabling them to investigate and respond to potential threats.
- *Threat Prevention*: IPS takes the detection process a step further by automatically blocking or mitigating threats, reducing the risk of successful attacks.
- *Real-time Monitoring*: These systems provide real-time visibility into network traffic, assisting security professionals in identifying emerging threats and vulnerabilities.

VPNs (Virtual Private Networks): VPNs establish secure, encrypted connections over untrusted networks, enabling remote users to access corporate resources while ensuring the confidentiality and integrity of data in transit. They are crucial for safeguarding sensitive information when transmitted over public networks like the internet.

Practical Implications:

- *Remote Access:* VPNs allow remote employees, partners, and authorized users to securely access corporate resources and data from anywhere with an internet connection.
- *Data Encryption:* VPNs employ encryption to protect data during transmission, making it difficult for eavesdroppers to intercept or tamper with the data.
- *Secure Communication*: They facilitate secure communication between geographically distributed offices, protecting sensitive internal communications and data.

Network Infrastructure Devices are the foundation upon which a secure and efficient network is built. Their proper configuration and management are essential to safeguard data, ensure network integrity, and protect against unauthorized access and a wide range of cyber threats. By understanding their significance and practical implications, organizations can create a robust security posture that defends against the evolving threat landscape.

3. Security for Mobile and IoT

Security for Mobile and IoT is a crucial aspect of contemporary cybersecurity. Mobile and Internet of Things (IoT) devices have proliferated in both personal and business environments, offering convenience and efficiency but also introducing significant security challenges. This section explores the significance and practical implications of securing these diverse and dynamic devices:

Mobile Device Management (MDM): MDM solutions are designed to manage and secure mobile devices, including smartphones, tablets, and laptops. They have become essential in the context of remote work and bring your own device (BYOD) policies. MDM ensures that organizations can enforce security policies, track device locations, and protect sensitive data on mobile devices.

Practical Implications:

- *Remote Device Management*: MDM allows organizations to remotely configure, monitor, and manage mobile devices, reducing the risk of data breaches.
- *Data Protection*: MDM enables the implementation of data encryption, remote data wiping, and access control measures to safeguard data on lost or stolen devices.
- *Compliance and Policy Enforcement*: It helps enforce security policies and ensure that mobile devices adhere to organizational compliance standards.

IoT Security Considerations: The IoT consists of a vast array of connected devices, ranging from smart thermostats and wearable fitness trackers to industrial sensors and connected vehicles. These devices often have limited computing power and security features, making them vulnerable to attacks and exploitation. IoT security focuses on protecting these devices and the data they collect and transmit.

Practical Implications:

- *Authentication and Authorization*: Implementing strong authentication and authorization mechanisms is essential to ensure that only authorized users or devices can access IoT systems.

- *Data Encryption*: Encrypting data at rest and in transit helps protect the confidentiality and integrity of information collected and transmitted by IoT devices.
- *Firmware Updates*: Regularly updating IoT device firmware is crucial to patch known vulnerabilities and enhance security. However, this process must be carefully managed to prevent device disruptions.
- *Monitoring and Anomaly Detection*: Employing monitoring solutions that can detect unusual behavior or security incidents in the IoT network is essential for early threat detection.
- *Access Control*: Implementing access control measures to restrict access to IoT devices and systems can prevent unauthorized manipulation of critical infrastructure or data.

Mobile and IoT security are complex challenges due to the sheer variety and numbers of devices in use. Ensuring the security of these devices involves a combination of policy, technology, and user education. By recognizing the significance and practical implications of securing mobile and IoT environments, organizations can navigate this evolving landscape while minimizing security risks and protecting sensitive data.

Chapter 4 focused on implementation. Below are three practice questions to help you prepare for the SY0-601 exam:

Practice Question 1: Secure Protocols and Services

Which secure protocol is commonly used to secure email communication by providing authentication and encryption for email messages?

A) DNSSEC
B) SSH
C) S/MIME
D) SNMP

Answer: C) S/MIME

Explanation: Secure/Multipurpose Internet Mail Extensions (S/MIME) is a widely used protocol for securing email communication. It provides authentication, message integrity, and encryption for email messages.

Practice Question 2: Network Infrastructure Devices

Which network infrastructure device is designed to inspect network traffic, detect suspicious activity, and respond to potential threats by blocking or allowing traffic based on predefined rules?

A) Firewall
B) IDS/IPS
C) VPN
D) DNSSEC

Answer: B) IDS/IPS (Intrusion Detection System/Intrusion Prevention System)

Explanation: IDS/IPS devices are designed to inspect network traffic, detect suspicious activity, and respond to potential threats. Intrusion Detection Systems (IDS) identify and alert on security incidents, while Intrusion Prevention Systems (IPS) can take active measures to block or allow traffic based on predefined rules.

Practice Question 3: Security for Mobile and IoT

In the context of Mobile Device Management (MDM), what is the primary purpose of remote wipe functionality?

A) To update device firmware
B) To unlock a locked device
C) To locate a lost device
D) To erase data on a lost or stolen device

Answer: D) To erase data on a lost or stolen device

Explanation: Remote wipe functionality in Mobile Device Management (MDM) allows administrators to remotely erase data on a lost or stolen device. This helps protect sensitive information and maintain data security in case the device is compromised.

In this chapter, I provided a comprehensive guide to understanding and implementing secure protocols, network infrastructure devices, and security practices for mobile and IoT devices. By mastering these critical aspects of cybersecurity, you can establish a resilient security framework to protect digital assets, data, and communications in an ever-evolving and interconnected world.

55

Operations and Incident Response

In the dynamic field of cybersecurity, Operations and Incident Response are paramount to maintaining a resilient security posture. This chapter delves into the essential procedures and techniques that underpin effective incident response, as well as the importance of disaster recovery and business continuity planning.

1. Incident Response Procedures

Identification, Containment, Eradication, Recovery (ICER): The ICER framework represents the cornerstone of incident response. It provides a structured approach to handling security incidents, ensuring that they are effectively managed and mitigated.

Incident Response Procedures are a critical component of a robust cybersecurity strategy. These procedures provide organizations with a structured approach to handling security incidents, ensuring that they are detected, contained, eradicated, and that operations are smoothly recovered. Let us explore the significance and practical implications of each phase of the Incident Response Procedures.

Identification: Prompt and accurate identification of a security incident is crucial to minimize its impact and prevent further damage. Identifying incidents can be challenging, as cyber threats constantly evolve, and attackers become more sophisticated.

Practical Implications:

- *Anomaly Detection*: Implementing anomaly detection systems can help identify unusual network traffic patterns or user behavior, potentially indicating a security incident.
- *Intrusion Detection Systems (IDS)*: IDS are valuable tools for recognizing known attack patterns or signatures, triggering alerts when suspicious activities are detected.
- *Continuous Monitoring*: Organizations should maintain continuous monitoring of their networks, systems, and applications to detect security incidents as they happen.

Containment: Containment is the immediate response to an identified incident. It aims to prevent the threat from spreading further and causing additional damage. Effective containment can mitigate the extent of a breach.

Practical Implications:

- Isolation: Isolating affected systems or network segments can prevent attackers from moving laterally within the environment.
- Blocking Attack Vectors: Identifying and blocking the attack vectors used by the attacker, such as closing specific ports or services.
- User Access Control: Temporarily revoking user access to compromised accounts to prevent unauthorized actions.

Eradication: Eradication involves eliminating the root cause of the security incident. This phase aims to ensure that the incident does not reoccur by removing vulnerabilities, malware, or other threats.

Practical Implications:

- *Vulnerability Patching*: Identifying and patching known vulnerabilities that the attacker exploited is a critical step in the eradication phase.
- *Malware Removal*: If malware is detected, it should be thoroughly removed from affected systems to prevent further infection.
- *Configuration Changes*: Making necessary changes to system configurations or security policies to prevent similar incidents in the future.

Recovery: The recovery phase focuses on restoring systems and services to normal operations. It is essential for minimizing downtime and returning to business as usual.

Practical Implications:

- *Data Restoration*: Ensuring that lost or compromised data is restored from backups or unaffected sources.
- *System Validation*: Verifying the integrity of systems to ensure that they are secure and that there are no residual threats.
- *Post-Incident Review*: Conducting a post-incident review to analyze the incident response process and identify areas for improvement.

A well-structured incident response plan is an indispensable part of a cybersecurity strategy. It not only helps organizations mitigate the impact of security incidents but also ensures that they are well-prepared to respond effectively. By implementing these procedures, organizations can recover from incidents more swiftly and minimize the damage caused by security breaches.

2. Forensic Techniques

Disk and memory forensics are crucial for understanding how an incident occurred, identifying the extent of the breach, and collecting evidence for potential legal or disciplinary action.

Forensic Techniques are essential in the field of cybersecurity for investigating security incidents, understanding their nature, and collecting evidence for potential legal or disciplinary actions. Two critical areas within forensic techniques are disk forensics and memory forensics.

Disk Forensics: Disk forensics involves the examination of data stored on disk drives, which is essential for understanding how a security incident occurred, identifying the extent of the breach, and collecting evidence for further investigation.

Practical Implications:

- *Data Recovery*: In the aftermath of a security incident, data recovery tools and techniques are used to retrieve deleted or damaged files. This process can yield crucial evidence related to the incident.
- *File Analysis*: Forensic analysts examine files to identify signs of tampering or unauthorized access. They can analyze file metadata, access times, and file signatures to trace the actions of an intruder.
- *Timeline Reconstruction*: Disk forensics allows investigators to reconstruct a timeline of events leading up to and following the security incident. This timeline helps to establish the sequence of activities.

Memory Forensics: Memory forensics focuses on analyzing a computer's volatile memory (RAM). This technique is invaluable for detecting active threats and uncovering the runtime behavior of malicious processes.

Practical Implications:

- *Malware Detection*: Memory forensics is effective for identifying and analyzing malware that resides in memory, as well as identifying unusual processes or system behavior.
- *Root Cause Analysis*: Investigating memory can help identify the root cause of a security incident, such as the specific malware strain or the exploitation of a vulnerability.
- *Live Memory Analysis*: Real-time analysis of memory can provide insights into active threats and ongoing attacks. This is especially valuable for detecting advanced persistent threats.

Chain of Custody and Evidence Handling: Preserving the integrity and admissibility of digital evidence in legal proceedings is crucial. The chain of custody and evidence handling procedures ensure that evidence collected is protected, accurately documented, and uncontaminated throughout the investigation.

Practical Implications:

- *Chain of Custody Documentation*: Every step in the handling, transfer, and storage of evidence must be meticulously documented. This establishes a clear record of who had possession of the evidence at all times.
- *Secure Evidence Storage*: Physical and digital evidence must be stored securely to prevent tampering or contamination. Secure storage facilities and systems are critical.
- *Access Control*: Access to evidence should be strictly controlled, with only authorized personnel permitted to handle it.
- *Maintaining Evidence Integrity*: Measures are taken to ensure that evidence is not altered or corrupted during the investigation. This includes protecting evidence from physical and digital tampering.

Forensic techniques and the proper chain of custody and evidence handling procedures are essential for conducting thorough and reliable investigations. They are vital in understanding the scope of security incidents, determining the causes, and collecting evidence that can be used for legal proceedings or internal disciplinary actions. By adhering to best practices in forensic analysis and evidence handling, organizations can effectively respond to incidents and improve their overall security posture.

3. Disaster Recovery and Business Continuity Planning

Disaster recovery and business continuity planning are vital to ensure that organizations can continue operations and recover from disruptive incidents.

Disaster Recovery (DR) and Business Continuity Planning (BCP) are integral components of a comprehensive cybersecurity strategy. These plans help organizations ensure the resilience of their operations in the face of disruptions, whether caused by natural disasters, cyberattacks, or system failures.

Disaster Recovery (DR): Disaster recovery planning focuses on preparing for and recovering from catastrophic events that could lead to significant data loss, system failures, or extended downtime. A well-structured DR plan helps organizations restore critical IT systems and data promptly, minimizing disruptions and data loss.

Practical Implications:

- *Identifying Critical Systems*: Organizations must identify their critical IT systems and data to prioritize recovery efforts. These systems could include customer databases, financial records, and essential applications.
- *Recovery Time Objectives (RTOs)*: Determining RTOs for each critical system is essential. RTO is the maximum acceptable downtime for a system. It guides the speed of recovery efforts.
- *Backup and Restore Procedures*: Implementing robust backup strategies, both onsite and offsite, is crucial. Organizations must regularly test their backup and restore procedures to ensure data integrity and a quick recovery.
- *Failover Mechanisms*: For high-availability systems, setting up failover mechanisms, such as redundant servers or cloud-based solutions, is an effective way to minimize downtime.
- *Training and Testing*: Conducting regular training sessions and drills for IT staff ensures they can execute recovery procedures effectively.

Business Continuity Planning (BCP): Business continuity planning goes beyond IT systems to address the broader aspects of an organization's operations. BCP ensures that businesses can continue to provide essential services and products even during disruptions, sustaining their reputation and minimizing financial losses.

Practical Implications:

- *Identifying Critical Functions*: Similar to DR, organizations must identify essential business functions, which extend beyond IT systems to encompass areas like customer service, finance, and communications.
- *Alternate Work Locations*: Establishing alternate work locations or remote work capabilities ensures that employees can continue working in case the primary workplace is inaccessible.
- *Communication Plans*: Creating communication plans ensures that stakeholders are informed of disruptions, and employees know how to contact one another and management.
- *Personnel Readiness*: Ensuring that employees are trained and ready to execute their roles during a disruption is vital for maintaining operations.
- *BCP and DR Synergy*: BCP and DR plans should be complementary, with DR covering the technical aspects of recovery, and BCP addressing broader business functions. When used together, these plans provide a holistic approach to ensuring business resilience.

Both DR and BCP plans should be tested and updated regularly to remain effective and relevant in a constantly changing business and threat landscape. These plans not only protect against natural disasters and cyberattacks but also help organizations recover from hardware failures, data corruption, and other unforeseen issues. By understanding their significance and practical implications, organizations can navigate disruptions with minimal impact and ensure business continuity.

Chapter 4 focused on operations and incident response. Here are three practice questions to help you prepare for the SY0-601 exam:

Practice Question 1: In an incident response process, which phase is responsible for identifying potential security incidents and ensuring they are reported?

A) Containment
B) Eradication
C) Identification
D) Recovery

Answer: C) Identification

Explanation: The Identification phase in an incident response process focuses on identifying potential security incidents, verifying their validity, and ensuring that they are reported for further action.

Practice Question 2: What forensic technique involves analyzing a computer's volatile memory (RAM) to identify active threats and uncover the runtime behavior of malicious processes?

A) Disk Forensics
B) Network Forensics
C) Memory Forensics
D) Database Forensics

Answer: C) Memory Forensics

Explanation: Memory forensics involves analyzing a computer's volatile memory (RAM) to identify active threats, such as malware, and uncover the runtime behavior of malicious processes. It is valuable for detecting and analyzing in-memory attacks.

Practice Question 3: In the context of incident response, what is the primary goal of the "Containment" phase?

A) Identify the root cause of the incident
B) Restore affected systems to normal operations
C) Prevent further damage and stop the incident from spreading
D) Verify the integrity of systems and data

Answer: C) Prevent further damage and stop the incident from spreading

Explanation: The primary goal of the "Containment" phase in incident response is to prevent further damage by isolating and stopping the incident from spreading within the environment. This phase aims to limit the impact of the incident.

By mastering the procedures and techniques of incident response, as well as disaster recovery and business continuity planning, organizations can enhance their resilience in the face of unforeseen events and cyber threats. The ability to respond effectively to incidents and ensure business continuity is a hallmark of a robust cybersecurity strategy.

Governance, Risk, and Compliance

In the realm of cybersecurity, Governance, Risk, and Compliance (GRC) are critical components of a comprehensive strategy. This chapter explores the various aspects of GRC, from establishing policies and procedures to managing risks and ensuring compliance with relevant laws and regulations.

1. Policies, Plans, and Procedures

Policies, Plans, and Procedures serve as the cornerstone of an effective Governance, Risk, and Compliance (GRC) framework. They provide the necessary structure, rules, and guidelines to govern an organization's approach to cybersecurity. Here, we delve into the significance and practical implications of this crucial aspect of cybersecurity.

Significance

- *Defining a Clear Direction*: Policies set the organization's security posture, conveying what is acceptable and unacceptable in terms of security practices. They provide a clear direction, outlining the organization's commitment to protecting its assets and data.
- *Consistency and Standardization*: Policies and procedures establish a common set of rules and practices that apply consistently across the organization. This uniformity simplifies management and enforcement.
- *Risk Mitigation*: By outlining security measures and best practices, these documents are instrumental in identifying and mitigating potential security risks. They provide a roadmap for addressing vulnerabilities and threats.
- *Legal and Regulatory Compliance*: Many regulations and laws require organizations to have specific security policies and procedures in place. Compliance with these regulations is essential to avoid legal repercussions.

Practical Implications

- *Policy Development and Maintenance*: Developing a comprehensive set of cybersecurity policies is the first step. These policies cover various aspects of security, such as data protection, access control, acceptable use of technology, and incident response. Regularly review and update these policies to keep pace with evolving threats and technologies.
- *Planning and Documentation*: Disaster recovery plans, incident response plans, and other documentation are essential for ensuring the organization can respond

effectively to security incidents and disruptions. Well-documented procedures are vital for guiding employees during a crisis.

- *User Training and Awareness*: Policies are only effective if employees and stakeholders are aware of them and understand their implications. Conduct regular training and awareness programs to ensure that everyone in the organization comprehends and adheres to established policies and procedures.
- *Access Control*: Implement access control procedures to govern who has access to what resources within the organization. Proper access control safeguards sensitive data and prevents unauthorized access.
- *Incident Response Framework*: Establish a clear incident response framework, including policies and procedures for reporting incidents, containment, eradication, and recovery. This ensures that security incidents are managed efficiently, minimizing damage and downtime.
- *Data Protection*: Develop data protection policies that specify how sensitive data should be handled, stored, and transmitted. Encryption, data classification, and data retention policies are essential elements of data protection.
- *Acceptable Use Policies*: Clearly define acceptable use policies for the organization's IT resources. These policies set guidelines for the proper use of company technology and help prevent misuse or abuse.
- *Review and Revision*: Regularly review and revise policies and procedures. As the threat landscape evolves, policies should adapt to address new risks and challenges.
- *Policy Enforcement*: Establish procedures for monitoring and enforcing compliance with policies. This may involve conducting audits, assessing employee compliance, and applying sanctions for policy violations.
- *Legal and Regulatory Adherence*: Ensure that all policies and procedures align with relevant laws and regulations. Stay informed about changes in legislation that may affect your organization and make necessary adjustments.

Policies, plans, and procedures are indispensable components of a holistic cybersecurity strategy. They provide a structured framework for addressing security challenges, maintaining compliance, and ensuring that everyone within the organization is aligned with security objectives and best practices.

2. Risk Management

Risk Management is a crucial component of an organization's Governance, Risk, and Compliance (GRC) framework. It involves assessing potential threats and vulnerabilities, quantifying the potential impact, and taking steps to mitigate and manage those risks effectively. Here, we explore the significance and practical implications of risk management in the context of cybersecurity.

Significance

- *Proactive Approach*: Risk management takes a proactive approach to identifying and addressing potential threats and vulnerabilities before they materialize into security incidents. It is a fundamental element of a preventative cybersecurity strategy.
- *Resource Allocation*: Risk management helps organizations allocate resources effectively. By understanding which risks pose the greatest threat, organizations can prioritize security measures and investments where they will have the most significant impact.
- *Regulatory Compliance*: Many regulatory frameworks, such as GDPR, HIPAA, and PCI-DSS, require organizations to conduct risk assessments and implement appropriate security measures. Compliance with these regulations is vital to avoid legal consequences.
- *Business Continuity*: Effective risk management minimizes the chances of significant disruptions to an organization's operations, ensuring business continuity and protecting its reputation.

Practical Implications

- *Risk Assessments*: Conduct regular risk assessments to identify and evaluate potential security risks. This process involves analyzing the likelihood of an event occurring and its potential impact on the organization. Common risk assessment methodologies include qualitative, quantitative, and semi-quantitative assessments.
- *Asset Identification*: Clearly identify and classify organizational assets. This includes tangible assets like hardware and data, as well as intangible assets such as intellectual property.
- *Vulnerability Identification*: Identify and catalog potential vulnerabilities in systems, software, and processes. This should include known vulnerabilities, configuration weaknesses, and new vulnerabilities that may emerge.
- *Risk Quantification*: Assign values to the likelihood and potential impact of identified risks. This step helps organizations prioritize risks based on their potential consequences.
- *Risk Mitigation Strategies*: Develop strategies to mitigate identified risks. These strategies may involve implementing security controls, improving security awareness, or transferring risk through insurance or third-party partnerships.
- *Ongoing Monitoring*: Continuously monitor the threat landscape and adapt risk management strategies as new threats emerge. Regular updates to risk assessments and risk mitigation plans are essential to keep pace with the evolving threat landscape.

- *Incident Response Plan*: Part of risk management involves having a robust incident response plan in place. This plan outlines the steps to take when a security incident occurs, ensuring that risks are managed effectively during and after an incident.
- *Business Impact Analysis*: Assess the potential financial and operational impact of identified risks. This information helps organizations prioritize risk mitigation efforts and allocate resources strategically.
- *Documentation and Reporting*: Maintain comprehensive documentation of risk assessments, mitigation strategies, and progress reports. This documentation is vital for audits and compliance purposes.
- *Regular Review and Updates*: Regularly review and update the organization's risk management program. As the threat landscape evolves, so too should risk management strategies to address new risks and challenges.
- *Executive and Stakeholder Involvement*: Ensure that key stakeholders, including executive leadership, are involved in the risk management process. Their input and support are critical for effective risk management.

Risk management is an integral part of an organization's commitment to cybersecurity. By identifying, quantifying, and proactively addressing potential threats and vulnerabilities, organizations can safeguard their assets, protect their operations, and maintain compliance with regulatory requirements. Effective risk management is a dynamic and ongoing process, essential for navigating the ever-evolving landscape of cybersecurity threats.

3. Compliance with Laws and Regulations

Compliance with Laws and Regulations is a critical component of an organization's Governance, Risk, and Compliance (GRC) framework. It ensures that organizations adhere to the appropriate standards and guidelines, protecting sensitive data, maintaining legal standing, and upholding the trust of customers and stakeholders. Here, we explore the significance and practical implications of compliance with specific laws and regulations in the realm of cybersecurity.

Significance

- *Legal Obligation*: Compliance with relevant laws and regulations is not just good practice; it's a legal and ethical obligation. Non-compliance can lead to severe legal consequences, financial penalties, and reputational damage.
- *Data Protection*: Many regulations and laws are designed to safeguard sensitive data, such as personal information, healthcare records, or payment card data. Compliance is essential to protect this information.

- *Reputation and Trust*: Maintaining compliance enhances an organization's reputation and builds trust with customers and stakeholders. Compliance demonstrates a commitment to security and data privacy.
- *Global Operations*: As organizations operate globally, they must navigate a complex web of international, national, and industry-specific regulations. Compliance ensures a consistent approach to security across different regions and sectors.

Practical Implications

GDPR (General Data Protection Regulation)

- *Data Protection Measures*: Implement data protection measures to safeguard the personal data of European Union citizens. This includes encryption, access controls, and data breach notification procedures.
- *Consent Mechanisms*: Ensure that data processing activities are conducted based on informed consent mechanisms. Individuals must have a clear understanding of how their data will be used.
- *Data Subject Rights*: Develop procedures to accommodate data subject rights, such as the right to access, rectify, or delete personal data upon request.
- *Data Protection Impact Assessments*: Conduct data protection impact assessments (DPIAs) for high-risk data processing activities.

HIPAA (Health Insurance Portability and Accountability Act)

- PHI Safeguarding: Comply with HIPAA regulations to protect the privacy and security of protected health information (PHI).
- Privacy Policies: Develop and maintain privacy policies and procedures that govern the use, disclosure, and access to PHI.
- Incident Response: Implement an incident response plan specific to HIPAA to address breaches involving PHI.
- Breach Notification: Adhere to HIPAA's breach notification requirements, which mandate timely notification of data breaches to affected individuals and regulatory authorities.

PCI-DSS (Payment Card Industry Data Security Standard)

- *Security Controls*: Implement security controls and best practices to protect payment card data during storage, transmission, and processing.
- *Regular Security Assessments*: Conduct regular security assessments, including penetration testing and vulnerability scanning, to ensure compliance.

- *Secure Access Control*: Enforce access controls to limit access to payment card data to authorized personnel only.
- *Data Encryption*: Utilize encryption to protect payment card data, both in transit and at rest.
- *Audits and Reporting*: Prepare for and participate in audits and assessments to verify compliance with relevant laws and regulations. Compliance reports must be generated and submitted to regulatory authorities as required.
- *Legal Consultation*: Maintain a relationship with legal counsel or compliance experts who can provide guidance and interpretation of complex regulatory requirements.
- *Ongoing Education*: Continuously educate employees and stakeholders about the importance of compliance and the specifics of relevant laws and regulations.
- *Data Inventory and Classification*: Create an inventory of data and classify it according to the type and level of sensitivity to apply appropriate controls and protections.
- *Regular Review and Updates*: Regularly review and update compliance procedures to address changes in the regulatory environment and the organization's operations.

Chapter 5 focused on operations and incident response. Below are some practice questions to help you prepare for the SY0-601 exam:

Practice Question 1: Secure Protocols and Services

Which secure protocol is commonly used to secure email communication by providing authentication and encryption for email messages?

A) DNSSEC
B) SSH
C) S/MIME
D) SNMP

Answer: C) S/MIME

Explanation: Secure/Multipurpose Internet Mail Extensions (S/MIME) is a widely used protocol for securing email communication. It provides authentication, message integrity, and encryption for email messages.

Practice Question 2: Network Infrastructure Devices

Which network infrastructure device is designed to inspect network traffic, detect suspicious activity, and respond to potential threats by blocking or allowing traffic based on predefined rules?

A) Firewall
B) IDS/IPS
C) VPN
D) DNSSEC

Answer: B) IDS/IPS (Intrusion Detection System/Intrusion Prevention System)

Explanation: IDS/IPS devices are designed to inspect network traffic, detect suspicious activity, and respond to potential threats. Intrusion Detection Systems (IDS) identify and alert on security incidents, while Intrusion Prevention Systems (IPS) can take active measures to block or allow traffic based on predefined rules.

Practice Question 3: Security for Mobile and IoT

In the context of Mobile Device Management (MDM), what is the primary purpose of remote wipe functionality?

A) To update device firmware
B) To unlock a locked device
C) To locate a lost device
D) To erase data on a lost or stolen device

Answer: D) To erase data on a lost or stolen device

Explanation: Remote wipe functionality in Mobile Device Management (MDM) allows administrators to remotely erase data on a lost or stolen device. This helps protect sensitive information and maintain data security in case the device is compromised.

Compliance with laws and regulations in the realm of cybersecurity is not only a legal requirement but also a strategic investment in protecting an organization's data, reputation, and operations. By adhering to the specific requirements of GDPR, HIPAA, PCI-DSS, and other relevant regulations, organizations can demonstrate their commitment to security and data privacy while avoiding legal repercussions and financial penalties.

Practice Exams

Exam 1

1. Which of the following describes a denial-of-service (DoS) attack?
   A) A malicious actor gains unauthorized access to a system.
   B) A vulnerability is exploited to execute arbitrary code.
   C) Legitimate users are prevented from accessing a resource.
   D) Sensitive data is intercepted and disclosed.

2. Which of the following is an example of two-factor authentication?
   A) Entering a username and password.
   B) Scanning a fingerprint and entering a PIN.
   C) Using a strong password.
   D) Encrypting data in transit.

3. Which type of cryptographic algorithm uses the same key for both encryption and decryption?
   A) Asymmetric encryption
   B) Symmetric encryption
   C) Hashing algorithm
   D) Digital signature algorithm

4. Which of the following is a security control that can help prevent SQL injection attacks?
   A) Input validation and parameterized queries
   B) Intrusion Prevention System (IPS)
   C) Firewall
   D) Network segmentation

5. Which of the following is an example of a social engineering attack?
   A) Exploiting a software vulnerability to gain unauthorized access.
   B) Intercepting network traffic to obtain sensitive information.
   C) Tricking someone into revealing their password.
   D) Using brute-force techniques to crack a password.

6. Which of the following is a characteristic of a strong password?
   A) Using common words or phrases.
   B) Including personal information, such as birthdates.

C) Using a combination of uppercase and lowercase letters, numbers, and special characters.

D) Using the same password for multiple accounts.

7. Which of the following protocols is commonly used for secure web browsing?
   A) HTTP
   B) FTP
   C) HTTPS
   D) SMTP

8. What is the purpose of a virtual private network (VPN)?
   A) To protect against malware infections.
   B) To secure data in transit over a public network.
   C) To restrict access to authorized users.
   D) To prevent unauthorized physical access to a network.

9. Which of the following best describes the concept of defense in depth?
   A) Implementing multiple layers of security controls to protect against various threats.
   B) Granting users only the permissions necessary to perform their job functions.
   C) Regularly updating software and systems to ensure they are running the latest versions.
   D) Encrypting sensitive data to protect it from unauthorized access.

10. What is the purpose of a security incident response plan?
    A) To prevent security incidents from occurring.
    B) To restore normal operations after a security incident.
    C) To identify vulnerabilities in a system or network.
    D) To perform routine security assessments and audits.

11. Which of the following is an example of a public key infrastructure (PKI) component?
    A) Certificate Authority (CA)
    B) Intrusion Detection System (IDS)
    C) Virtual Private Network (VPN)
    D) Firewall

12. What is the purpose of a security control known as "access control lists" (ACL)?
    A) To prevent unauthorized physical access to a facility.
    B) To regulate and control network traffic based on predefined rules.
    C) To encrypt sensitive data during transit.
    D) To detect and respond to security incidents.

13. Which of the following is a characteristic of an asymmetric encryption algorithm?
    A) It uses the same key for both encryption and decryption.
    B) It is faster and more efficient than symmetric encryption.
    C) It requires the distribution of public keys.
    D) It is primarily used for hashing data.

14. Which of the following is a common security measure to protect against malware infections?
    A) Intrusion Prevention System (IPS)
    B) Proxy server
    C) Network Address Translation (NAT)
    D) Demilitarized Zone (DMZ)

15. What is the purpose of a security assessment?
    A) To identify and exploit vulnerabilities in a system.
    B) To ensure compliance with industry regulations and standards.
    C) To recover from a security incident.
    D) To encrypt sensitive data.

16. Which of the following is an example of a physical security control?
    A) Antivirus software
    B) Biometric authentication
    C) Intrusion Detection System (IDS)
    D) Encryption algorithm

17. What is the purpose of a data loss prevention (DLP) solution?
    A) To encrypt sensitive data in transit.
    B) To detect and prevent unauthorized access to data.
    C) To track and log user activity on a network.
    D) To recover data after a system failure.

18. Which of the following is a best practice for securing wireless networks?
    A) Disabling encryption to improve network performance.
    B) Using default administrator credentials.
    C) Enforcing strong passwords for Wi-Fi connections.
    D) Broadcasting the SSID (Service Set Identifier).

19. What is the primary purpose of a security information and event management (SIEM) system?
    A) To identify and block malicious network traffic.

B) To analyze and correlate security event logs from various sources.

C) To encrypt sensitive data at rest.

D) To enforce access control policies on a network.

20. Which of the following is a characteristic of a distributed denial-of-service (DDoS) attack?

A) It involves gaining unauthorized access to a system.

B) It targets a specific individual or organization.

C) It uses multiple compromised systems to flood a target with traffic.

D) It focuses on exploiting vulnerabilities in software or systems.

21. Which of the following is an example of a network-based security control?

A) Intrusion Detection System (IDS)

B) Anti-malware software

C) Full disk encryption

D) Patch management system

22. What is the purpose of a security policy in an organization?

A) To enforce physical access controls

B) To define the acceptable use of IT resources

C) To encrypt sensitive data at rest

D) To monitor network traffic for anomalies

23. Which of the following is a common wireless security protocol?

A) WPA2 (Wi-Fi Protected Access II)

B) SSL (Secure Sockets Layer)

C) AES (Advanced Encryption Standard)

D) PGP (Pretty Good Privacy)

24. What is the primary purpose of penetration testing?

A) To identify and exploit vulnerabilities in a system

B) To recover data after a system failure

C) To enforce access control policies on a network

D) To encrypt sensitive data during transit

25. Which of the following is an example of a security control that provides confidentiality?

A) Firewall

B) Intrusion Prevention System (IPS)

C) VPN (Virtual Private Network)

D) Security Information and Event Management (SIEM) system

26. What is the purpose of a hardware security module (HSM)?
    A) To secure physical access to a facility
    B) To enforce password complexity requirements
    C) To provide secure storage and processing of cryptographic keys
    D) To monitor and respond to security incidents

27. Which of the following is a characteristic of a brute-force attack?
    A) It involves exploiting vulnerabilities in software or systems
    B) It uses social engineering techniques to deceive users
    C) It relies on trial-and-error to guess passwords or encryption keys
    D) It targets a specific individual or organization

28. What is the purpose of an incident response plan?
    A) To prevent unauthorized access to a system
    B) To guide actions and responses during a security incident
    C) To analyze and correlate security event logs from various sources
    D) To ensure compliance with industry regulations and standards

29. Which of the following is a best practice for securing mobile devices?
    A) Disabling automatic software updates
    B) Connecting to public Wi-Fi networks without encryption
    C) Enabling biometric authentication
    D) Sharing sensitive data over unencrypted channels

30. What is the purpose of data classification in information security?
    A) To monitor and control user access to data
    B) To identify and prevent social engineering attacks
    C) To categorize data based on its sensitivity and value
    D) To encrypt data at rest and in transit

31. What is the purpose of a security incident response plan?
    A) To detect and prevent unauthorized access attempts
    B) To guide actions and responses during security incidents
    C) To enforce data retention and disposal policies
    D) To encrypt sensitive data during transit

32. Which of the following is an example of a security control that provides integrity?
    A) Intrusion Detection System (IDS)
    B) Data loss prevention (DLP) system
    C) Public Key Infrastructure (PKI)

D) Secure Sockets Layer (SSL) certificate

33. What is the primary goal of a ransomware attack?
    A) To steal sensitive information and sell it on the dark web
    B) To gain unauthorized access to a network for future exploitation
    C) To encrypt data and demand a ransom for its release
    D) To overload a network or system with malicious traffic

34. What is the purpose of a security control known as "blacklisting"?
    A) To simulate real-world attacks and identify vulnerabilities
    B) To monitor and correlate security event logs from various sources
    C) To prevent access or communication with known malicious entities
    D) To enforce password complexity requirements

35. What is the purpose of network segmentation in information security?
    A) To provide redundancy and fault tolerance in a network infrastructure
    B) To enforce access control policies and permissions
    C) To monitor and analyze network traffic for anomalies
    D) To divide a network into smaller, isolated segments for improved security

36. Which of the following is an example of a security control that provides non-repudiation?
    A) Intrusion Prevention System (IPS)
    B) Secure File Transfer Protocol (SFTP)
    C) Public Key Infrastructure (PKI)
    D) Two-factor authentication (2FA)

37. What is the purpose of a security information and event management (SIEM) system?
    A) To encrypt sensitive data at rest and in transit
    B) To generate one-time passwords for authentication
    C) To monitor and correlate security event logs from various sources
    D) To simulate real-world attacks and identify vulnerabilities

38. Which of the following is an example of a physical security control?
    A) Firewall
    B) Intrusion Detection System (IDS)
    C) Biometric door lock
    D) Virtual Private Network (VPN)

39. What is the purpose of a data loss prevention (DLP) system?

A) To enforce password complexity requirements

B) To identify and prevent unauthorized access attempts

C) To monitor and protect sensitive data from unauthorized disclosure or exfiltration

D) To perform vulnerability scans on network systems

40. Which of the following is an example of a security control that provides availability?

A) Firewall

B) Data encryption

C) Uninterruptible Power Supply (UPS)

D) Intrusion Prevention System (IPS)

41. What is the purpose of a security control known as "secure coding practices"?

A) To encrypt sensitive data during transit

B) To regulate and restrict user access to resources

C) To develop software with fewer vulnerabilities and security flaws

D) To monitor and analyze network traffic for anomalies

42. What is the primary purpose of a security control known as "file integrity monitoring"?

A) To enforce password complexity requirements

B) To monitor and analyze network traffic for anomalies

C) To detect unauthorized changes to files and systems

D) To prevent distributed denial-of-service (DDoS) attacks

43. Which of the following is an example of a security control that provides non-repudiation?

A) Data loss prevention (DLP) system

B) Public Key Infrastructure (PKI)

C) Secure Sockets Layer (SSL) certificate

D) Intrusion prevention system (IPS)

44. What is the purpose of a security control known as "two-factor authentication" (2FA)?

A) To simulate real-world attacks and identify vulnerabilities

B) To enforce access control policies and permissions

C) To authenticate users based on two or more factors

D) To encrypt sensitive data at rest and in transit

45. Which of the following is a characteristic of a hash function?

A) Uses a pair of different keys for encryption and decryption

B) Provides a higher level of encryption security compared to symmetric algorithms

C) Requires a secure key exchange between the communicating parties

D) Generates a fixed-size output unique to the input data

46. What is the purpose of a security control known as "network segmentation"?
    A) To enforce password complexity requirements
    B) To monitor and analyze network traffic for anomalies
    C) To divide a network into smaller, isolated segments for improved security
    D) To prevent unauthorized access attempts to a network

47. What is the primary purpose of a security control known as "security incident response"?
    A) To encrypt data during transit between two endpoints
    B) To block unauthorized access attempts to a network
    C) To guide actions and responses during security incidents
    D) To detect, prevent, and remove malicious software from systems

48. Which of the following is an example of a security control that provides availability?
    A) Data backup and recovery
    B) Intrusion detection system (IDS)
    C) Public Key Infrastructure (PKI)
    D) Secure Shell (SSH) encryption

49. What is the purpose of a security control known as "vulnerability scanning"?
    A) To enforce access control policies and permissions
    B) To monitor and analyze network traffic for anomalies
    C) To identify and assess weaknesses in systems and applications
    D) To encrypt sensitive data during transit

50. What is the purpose of a security control known as "physical access controls"?
    A) To encrypt data at rest and in transit
    B) To regulate and restrict user access to resources
    C) To monitor and analyze network traffic for anomalies
    D) To prevent unauthorized physical access to facilities or assets

51. Which of the following is an example of a physical security control?
    A) Firewall
    B) Intrusion Detection System (IDS)

C) Biometric access control

D) VPN

52. Which type of malware is designed to encrypt a user's files and demand a ransom for their decryption?

A) Spyware

B) Worm

C) Trojan

D) Ransomware

53. In the context of public key infrastructure (PKI), what is the purpose of a certificate authority (CA)?

A) To encrypt data

B) To issue digital certificates

C) To authenticate users

D) To monitor network traffic

54. Which of the following authentication methods relies on something the user knows?

A) Fingerprint recognition

B) Smart card

C) PIN (Personal Identification Number)

D) Retina scan

55. What type of attack involves sending unsolicited emails or messages to deceive recipients into disclosing sensitive information?

A) Man-in-the-middle attack

B) Phishing attack

C) Brute-force attack

D) SQL injection

56. A security policy that specifies the maximum number of failed login attempts before locking out an account is an example of which security principle?

A) Least privilege

B) Account lockout

C) Strong password

D) Data classification

57. Which of the following access control models assigns permissions based on job roles or functions within an organization?

A) Discretionary Access Control (DAC)

B) Mandatory Access Control (MAC)
C) Role-Based Access Control (RBAC)
D) Rule-Based Access Control (RBAC)

58. Which protocol provides secure communication over a network, ensuring confidentiality and integrity of data in transit?
A) FTP (File Transfer Protocol)
B) HTTPS (Hypertext Transfer Protocol Secure)
C) DNS (Domain Name System)
D) POP3 (Post Office Protocol version 3)

59. What security concept is the practice of segmenting a network to limit the spread of malicious software or unauthorized access?
A) Network address translation (NAT)
B) Virtual Private Network (VPN)
C) Defense in Depth (DiD)
D) Network segmentation

60. In the context of security risk management, what is the process of identifying and assessing potential threats and vulnerabilities?
A) Incident response
B) Risk assessment
C) Business continuity planning
D) Security awareness training

61. Which of the following is an example of a network security control designed to prevent unauthorized access by filtering traffic based on source and destination IP addresses and ports?
A) Antivirus software
B) Intrusion Detection System (IDS)
C) Firewall
D) Biometric authentication

62. What type of attack is characterized by an attacker intercepting and altering communication between two parties without their knowledge?
A) Brute-force attack
B) Phishing attack
C) Man-in-the-middle attack
D) Denial of Service (DoS) attack

63. In the context of information security, what does the CIA triad stand for?

A) Centralized, Isolated, Anonymous
B) Confidentiality, Integrity, Availability
C) Continuous Integration and Automation
D) Certified Information Auditor

64. Which encryption protocol is commonly used to secure email communication?
A) SSL (Secure Sockets Layer)
B) TLS (Transport Layer Security)
C) SSH (Secure Shell)
D) IPsec (Internet Protocol Security)

65. What is the primary purpose of a Security Information and Event Management (SIEM) system?
A) Data encryption
B) Intrusion prevention
C) Security incident detection and response
D) Network monitoring

66. Which security principle involves ensuring that users are granted only the minimum level of access needed to perform their job functions?
A) Least privilege
B) Defense in Depth
C) Strong password policy
D) Security awareness training

67. What type of malware disguises itself as legitimate software but carries out malicious activities without the user's knowledge or consent?
A) Ransomware
B) Spyware
C) Adware
D) Worm

68. Which of the following protocols is commonly used to secure remote access to a corporate network?
A) FTP (File Transfer Protocol)
B) SSH (Secure Shell)
C) SNMP (Simple Network Management Protocol)
D) HTTP (Hypertext Transfer Protocol)

69. What is the process of verifying the identity of a user, device, or application before granting access to a system or network?

A) Authorization
B) Authentication
C) Encryption
D) Intrusion Detection

70. What technology provides an additional layer of security by generating a time-sensitive one-time code for authentication, often used in two-factor authentication (2FA)?
A) Biometric authentication
B) Public Key Infrastructure (PKI)
C) Two-factor authentication (2FA)
D) Time-based One-Time Password (TOTP)

71. What is the primary purpose of a penetration test in the context of cybersecurity?
A) To exploit vulnerabilities and gain unauthorized access
B) To test the effectiveness of security controls and identify weaknesses
C) To monitor network traffic for suspicious activities
D) To encrypt data during transmission

72. Which of the following is a common authentication factor in two-factor authentication (2FA)?
A) Username and password
B) Fingerprint scan
C) Security token
D) Email address

73. What does the term "zero-day vulnerability" refer to in the field of cybersecurity?
A) A vulnerability that has been patched with a software update
B) A vulnerability that has been known for zero days
C) A previously undisclosed vulnerability for which there is no available patch
D) A vulnerability that only affects zero-day attacks

74. Which security concept involves ensuring that data is not altered during transmission and that the recipient can verify its origin?
A) Confidentiality
B) Integrity
C) Availability
D) Authentication

75. Which of the following is an example of a security control that enforces access based on user identity and role within an organization?

A) Firewall
B) Intrusion Detection System (IDS)
C) Role-Based Access Control (RBAC)
D) Antivirus software

Answers

1. C) Legitimate users are prevented from accessing a resource: A denial-of-service (DoS) attack is designed to disrupt or deny access to a system, network, or service for legitimate users by overwhelming the target with a flood of malicious traffic or resource consumption.

2. B) Scanning a fingerprint and entering a PIN: Two-factor authentication (2FA) involves using two different factors to verify a user's identity. In this example, the fingerprint scan represents the biometric factor, while the PIN serves as the knowledge factor.

3. B) Symmetric encryption: Symmetric encryption algorithms use the same key for both the encryption and decryption processes. This means that the same key is used to both scramble and unscramble the data.

4. A) Input validation and parameterized queries: Input validation ensures that user-supplied data conforms to expected formats or patterns, while parameterized queries separate the query from the user-supplied input, preventing SQL injection attacks by treating the input as data rather than executable code.

5. C) Tricking someone into revealing their password: Social engineering attacks exploit human psychology to manipulate individuals into divulging sensitive information, such as passwords or other confidential data, through deception or manipulation.

6. C) Using a combination of uppercase and lowercase letters, numbers, and special characters: A strong password is complex and includes a combination of uppercase and lowercase letters, numbers, and special characters. This complexity makes passwords more resistant to brute-force attacks or dictionary-based password cracking attempts.

7. C) HTTPS: HTTPS (Hypertext Transfer Protocol Secure) is a secure version of HTTP that uses encryption to protect the confidentiality and integrity of data transmitted between a web browser and a web server.

8. B) To secure data in transit over a public network: A VPN creates a secure and encrypted connection over a public network, such as the internet. Its purpose is to ensure the confidentiality and integrity of data transmitted between two endpoints by encapsulating the data in a secure tunnel.

9. A) Implementing multiple layers of security controls to protect against various threats:: Defense in depth is a security strategy that involves implementing multiple layers of security controls, such as firewalls, intrusion detection systems, access controls, and encryption, to provide overlapping protection and mitigate the impact of a single security control failure.

10. B) To restore normal operations after a security incident: A security incident response plan outlines the steps and procedures to be followed in the event of a security incident. Its purpose is to minimize the impact of an incident, contain the

damage, investigate the cause, and restore normal operations as quickly as possible.

11. A) Certificate Authority (CA): A Certificate Authority (CA) is a component of a Public Key Infrastructure (PKI) that issues and manages digital certificates. It verifies the identity of entities and signs their certificates, enabling secure communication through encryption and authentication.

12. B) To regulate and control network traffic based on predefined rules: Access Control Lists (ACLs) are security controls used to regulate and control network traffic. They are typically configured on network devices, such as routers or firewalls, and enforce rules that allow or deny access to network resources based on source/destination IP addresses, port numbers, or other criteria.

13. C) It requires the distribution of public keys: Asymmetric encryption algorithms, also known as public-key encryption, use a pair of mathematically related keys: a public key for encryption and a private key for decryption. Public keys are distributed freely, while private keys are kept secret. The distribution of public keys enables secure communication without the need to share a common secret key.

14. A) Intrusion Prevention System (IPS): An Intrusion Prevention System (IPS) is a security measure designed to detect and block malicious activities, including malware infections. It monitors network traffic, analyzes patterns, and can take proactive measures to prevent attacks or unauthorized access attempts.

15. B) To ensure compliance with industry regulations and standards: Security assessments are conducted to evaluate the security posture of an organization or system. One of the primary purposes is to ensure compliance with industry regulations and standards, such as HIPAA or PCI DSS, and identify any security vulnerabilities or weaknesses that may exist.

16. B) Biometric authentication: Biometric authentication involves using physical or behavioral characteristics, such as fingerprints or facial recognition, to verify the identity of an individual. It is a physical security control that enhances access control by relying on unique and difficult-to-replicate attributes.

17. B) To detect and prevent unauthorized access to data: A Data Loss Prevention (DLP) solution is designed to identify and prevent unauthorized access, transmission, or disclosure of sensitive data. It uses various techniques, such as data classification, content inspection, and policy enforcement, to ensure the protection of sensitive information.

18. C) Enforcing strong passwords for Wi-Fi connections: One best practice for securing wireless networks is to enforce strong passwords for Wi-Fi connections. Strong passwords should be complex, unique, and resistant to dictionary or brute-force attacks, reducing the risk of unauthorized access to the wireless network.

19. B) To analyze and correlate security event logs from various sources: A Security Information and Event Management (SIEM) system collects and analyzes security event logs from various sources, such as firewalls, intrusion detection systems, and

servers. It correlates the data to identify patterns, detect security incidents, and provide centralized visibility and reporting for effective security management.

20. C) It uses multiple compromised systems to flood a target with traffic: A distributed denial-of-service (DDoS) attack involves using multiple compromised systems, often forming a botnet, to flood a target with a massive volume of traffic. This overwhelms the target's resources, such as bandwidth or processing power, causing service disruption or unavailability.

21. A) Intrusion Detection System (IDS): An Intrusion Detection System (IDS) is an example of a network-based security control. It monitors network traffic and systems for suspicious activities or known attack patterns, alerting administrators when potential intrusions are detected.

22. B) To define the acceptable use of IT resources: The purpose of a security policy in an organization is to define the acceptable use of IT resources. It outlines guidelines and rules that employees must follow to ensure the security and proper usage of organizational assets and systems.

23. A) WPA2 (Wi-Fi Protected Access II): WPA2 (Wi-Fi Protected Access II) is a widely used wireless security protocol. It provides stronger encryption and security features compared to its predecessor, WPA, and is commonly used to secure Wi-Fi networks.

24. A) To identify and exploit vulnerabilities in a system: The primary purpose of penetration testing is to identify and exploit vulnerabilities in a system or network. It involves simulating real-world attacks to assess the security posture and identify potential weaknesses that could be exploited by malicious actors.

25. C) VPN (Virtual Private Network): Virtual Private Network (VPN) is an example of a security control that provides confidentiality. It creates a secure, encrypted tunnel over a public network, such as the internet, allowing remote users to access private network resources securely.

26. C) To provide secure storage and processing of cryptographic keys: A hardware security module (HSM) is a physical device designed to provide secure storage and processing of cryptographic keys. It offers high-level protection for sensitive cryptographic operations, such as key generation, encryption, and decryption.

27. C) It relies on trial-and-error to guess passwords or encryption keys: A brute-force attack is a method where an attacker systematically tries all possible combinations of passwords or encryption keys until the correct one is found. It relies on trial-and-error rather than exploiting vulnerabilities or using deception techniques.

28. B) To guide actions and responses during a security incident: An incident response plan is designed to guide actions and responses during a security incident. It outlines the steps to be taken, roles and responsibilities of the incident response team, communication protocols, and recovery procedures to mitigate the impact of security incidents.

29. C) Enabling biometric authentication: Enabling biometric authentication is a best practice for securing mobile devices. Biometrics, such as fingerprints or facial recognition, provide an additional layer of security by using unique biological characteristics for user authentication.

30. C) To categorize data based on its sensitivity and value: The purpose of data classification in information security is to categorize data based on its sensitivity and value. It helps organizations apply appropriate security controls, such as access controls and encryption, based on the classification level to ensure the confidentiality, integrity, and availability of data.

31. B) To guide actions and responses during security incidents: A security incident response plan outlines the steps and procedures to be followed when a security incident occurs. It provides guidance on how to detect, respond to, mitigate, and recover from security incidents effectively.

32. C) Public Key Infrastructure (PKI): PKI is a security control that provides integrity by using digital certificates and cryptographic keys. It ensures that data remains intact and unaltered during storage, transmission, and processing.

33. C) To encrypt data and demand a ransom for its release: The primary goal of a ransomware attack is to encrypt important data on a victim's system or network and demand a ransom payment from the victim in exchange for the decryption key.

34. C) To prevent access or communication with known malicious entities: Blacklisting is a security control that blocks or denies access to known malicious entities such as IP addresses, domain names, or specific software applications, preventing communication or interaction with them.

35. D) To divide a network into smaller, isolated segments for improved security: Network segmentation involves dividing a network into smaller subnetworks or segments to enhance security. It helps in containing potential threats, limiting lateral movement, and reducing the impact of a security breach.

36. C) Public Key Infrastructure (PKI): PKI is a security control that provides non-repudiation by using digital signatures. It ensures that the sender of a message cannot deny sending it and that the message has not been altered in transit.

37. C) To monitor and correlate security event logs from various sources: A security information and event management (SIEM) system collects and analyzes security event logs generated by various sources within an organization's network. It helps to identify potential security incidents and detect patterns or anomalies by correlating information from different sources.

38. C) Biometric door lock: A biometric door lock is a physical security control that uses unique physical characteristics, such as fingerprints or retina scans, to grant access to a secure area. It helps to prevent unauthorized physical access.

39. C) To monitor and protect sensitive data from unauthorized disclosure or exfiltration: A data loss prevention (DLP) system is designed to monitor, detect,

and prevent the unauthorized disclosure or exfiltration of sensitive data. It helps in enforcing data security policies and preventing data breaches.

40. C) Uninterruptible Power Supply (UPS): A UPS is a security control that provides availability by supplying backup power to critical systems or devices during power outages or electrical disruptions. It helps to prevent downtime and ensure uninterrupted operation.

41. C) To develop software with fewer vulnerabilities and security flaws: Secure coding practices help developers write code that is resistant to common security threats, reducing the likelihood of vulnerabilities and security flaws in software development.

42. C) To detect unauthorized changes to files and systems: File integrity monitoring (FIM) tools are designed to monitor and detect any unauthorized modifications or tampering with files and systems, ensuring the integrity and security of data.

43. B) Public Key Infrastructure (PKI): PKI provides non-repudiation by using digital signatures and certificates to verify the authenticity and integrity of messages, ensuring that the sender cannot deny sending the message.

44. C) To authenticate users based on two or more factors: Two-factor authentication (2FA) requires users to provide multiple pieces of evidence to establish their identity, enhancing security by adding an extra layer of authentication beyond just a password.

45. D) Generates a fixed-size output unique to the input data: A hash function is a mathematical function that generates a fixed-size output, known as a hash value or digest, which is unique to the input data. This property allows for data integrity verification and identification.

46. C) To divide a network into smaller, isolated segments for improved security: Network segmentation involves dividing a network into smaller segments, isolating different parts to enhance security by limiting the impact of security breaches and controlling access between segments.

47. C) To guide actions and responses during security incidents: Security incident response involves having predefined processes and procedures to detect, respond to, and mitigate security incidents effectively, providing a structured approach to handle security events.

48. A) Data backup and recovery: Data backup and recovery measures ensure the availability of data by creating copies and storing them separately, allowing for data restoration in the event of data loss or system failures.

49. C) To identify and assess weaknesses in systems and applications: Vulnerability scanning is the process of scanning networks, systems, and applications to identify vulnerabilities or misconfigurations, enabling organizations to proactively address and mitigate potential security weaknesses.

50. B) To regulate and restrict user access to resources: Physical access controls help regulate and restrict user access to facilities or assets, ensuring that only authorized individuals can gain entry, enhancing physical security.

51. C) Biometric access control: Biometric access control, such as fingerprint or retina scans, is an example of a physical security control because it relies on a physical characteristic for authentication. Firewalls and VPNs are network security controls, while Intrusion Detection Systems (IDS) are designed to monitor and detect network threats.

52. D) Ransomware: Ransomware is a type of malware that encrypts a user's files and demands a ransom for their decryption. Spyware, worms, and Trojans are different types of malware with distinct characteristics.

53. B) To issue digital certificates: A Certificate Authority (CA) is responsible for issuing digital certificates in a Public Key Infrastructure (PKI). These certificates are used for various security purposes, such as secure communications and authentication. The other options do not accurately describe the role of a CA.

54. C) PIN (Personal Identification Number): Something the user knows is typically a PIN (Personal Identification Number). Biometric methods, such as fingerprint recognition and retina scans, rely on something the user is. Smart cards are examples of something the user has.

55. B) Phishing attack: Phishing attacks involve sending unsolicited emails or messages to deceive recipients into disclosing sensitive information, such as login credentials or financial details. Man-in-the-middle, brute-force, and SQL injection attacks are different types of cyberattacks with distinct characteristics.

56. B) Account lockout: A security policy that specifies the maximum number of failed login attempts before locking out an account is an example of an account lockout policy. It helps protect against brute-force attacks. Least privilege, strong password, and data classification are related but different security principles.

57. C) Role-Based Access Control (RBAC): Role-Based Access Control (RBAC) assigns permissions based on job roles or functions within an organization. Discretionary Access Control (DAC) allows users to determine access permissions, while Mandatory Access Control (MAC) is based on security labels. Rule-Based Access Control (RBAC) uses rules to determine access.

58. B) HTTPS (Hypertext Transfer Protocol Secure): HTTPS provides secure communication over a network, ensuring the confidentiality and integrity of data in transit. It is widely used for secure web browsing. FTP, DNS, and POP3 are different network protocols with specific purposes

59. D) Network segmentation: Network segmentation is the practice of dividing a network into smaller segments to limit the spread of malicious software or unauthorized access. It enhances security by isolating potential threats. Network address translation (NAT) and Virtual Private Network (VPN) serve different

purposes in network security. Defense in Depth (DiD) is a comprehensive security strategy.

60. B) Risk assessment: Risk assessment is the process of identifying and assessing potential threats and vulnerabilities to an organization's assets. It helps organizations understand their security risks and make informed decisions. Incident response, business continuity planning, and security awareness training are related but distinct concepts in security management.

61. C) Firewall: Firewalls are network security controls that filter traffic based on source and destination IP addresses and ports. They are designed to prevent unauthorized access and protect network resources.

62. C) Man-in-the-middle attack: In a man-in-the-middle attack, an attacker intercepts and alters communication between two parties without their knowledge. This type of attack allows the attacker to eavesdrop on sensitive information or manipulate the data being transmitted.

63. B) Confidentiality, Integrity, Availability: The CIA triad stands for Confidentiality, Integrity, and Availability. It is a fundamental concept in information security, where Confidentiality ensures data privacy, Integrity ensures data accuracy and trustworthiness, and Availability ensures data is accessible when needed.

64. B) TLS (Transport Layer Security): TLS is commonly used to secure email communication by encrypting data transmitted between the email client and the email server. It helps ensure the confidentiality and integrity of email content.

65. C) Security incident detection and response: A Security Information and Event Management (SIEM) system is primarily used for security incident detection and response. It collects and analyzes security event data to identify and respond to security incidents in real time.

66. A) Least privilege: The principle of least privilege (POLP) involves granting users only the minimum level of access needed to perform their job functions. This minimizes the potential for unauthorized access and reduces the impact of security breaches.

67. B) Spyware: Spyware disguises itself as legitimate software but carries out malicious activities without the user's knowledge or consent. It often collects information about the user or their activities.

68. B) SSH (Secure Shell): SSH is commonly used to secure remote access to a corporate network. It provides encrypted and secure communication for remote administration and data transfer.

69. B) Authentication: Authentication is the process of verifying the identity of a user, device, or application before granting access to a system or network. It ensures that only authorized entities can access resources.

70. D) Time-based One-Time Password (TOTP): Time-based One-Time Password (TOTP) technology generates time-sensitive one-time codes for authentication. It is commonly used in two-factor authentication (2FA) to enhance security by

requiring users to enter a code that changes at regular intervals, typically every 30 seconds.

71. B) To test the effectiveness of security controls and identify weaknesses: The primary purpose of a penetration test (pen test) is to test the effectiveness of security controls and identify weaknesses in an organization's security posture. Pen testers simulate real-world attacks to find vulnerabilities before malicious attackers do, allowing organizations to strengthen their defenses.

72. A) Username and password: Two-factor authentication (2FA) commonly involves the use of two authentication factors, one of which is usually something the user knows (e.g., username and password). The second factor may be something the user has (e.g., a security token) or something the user is (e.g., a fingerprint scan).

73. C) A previously undisclosed vulnerability for which there is no available patch: A zero-day vulnerability is a security flaw that is not publicly known and for which there is no available patch or fix. These vulnerabilities are attractive to attackers because they can be exploited before the software vendor or organization can respond.

74. B) Integrity: Ensuring data integrity involves protecting data from unauthorized alteration during transmission and verifying its origin. Data should remain unchanged and reliable throughout its transmission or storage. Encryption and digital signatures are commonly used to maintain data integrity.

75. C) Role-Based Access Control (RBAC): Role-Based Access Control (RBAC) enforces access based on user identity and role within an organization. It assigns permissions to roles rather than individual users, simplifying access management and reducing the risk of granting excessive privileges. Firewalls, IDS, and antivirus software are security controls with different functions.

Test 2

1. Which of the following is a security control used to prevent unauthorized access to a network by inspecting and filtering packets at the network layer?
   a) Intrusion Detection System (IDS)
   b) Firewall
   c) Antivirus software
   d) Proxy server

2. Which of the following is a security control used to verify the identity of individuals accessing a network by requiring them to provide multiple forms of authentication?
   a) Single Sign-On (SSO)
   b) Multifactor Authentication (MFA)

c) Access Control List (ACL)
d) Intrusion Prevention System (IPS)

3. Which of the following is a type of attack that involves intercepting and altering communication between two parties without their knowledge?
a) Spoofing
b) Phishing
c) Man-in-the-Middle (MitM)
d) Smurf

4. Which of the following is a security control that restricts access to certain resources based on the time of day or week?
a) Role-Based Access Control (RBAC)
b) Mandatory Access Control (MAC)
c) Discretionary Access Control (DAC)
d) Time-of-Day Restrictions

5. Which of the following is a secure method for transmitting data over an untrusted network by creating a secure "tunnel"?
a) SSH (Secure Shell)
b) FTPS (FTP Secure)
c) Telnet
d) HTTP

6. Which of the following is a security control used to prevent unauthorized access to a network by monitoring and analyzing network traffic patterns?
a) Intrusion Detection System (IDS)
b) Firewall
c) Antivirus software
d) Network Behavior Analysis (NBA)

7. Which of the following is a security concept that ensures that data is protected from unauthorized disclosure or access?
a) Confidentiality
b) Availability
c) Integrity
d) Non-repudiation

8. Which of the following is a secure method for authenticating and authorizing users by requiring them to provide something they have, such as a smart card?
a) RADIUS (Remote Authentication Dial-In User Service)

b) LDAP (Lightweight Directory Access Protocol)

c) TACACS+ (Terminal Access Controller Access Control System Plus)

d) Smart Card Authentication

9. Which of the following is a security control used to prevent unauthorized access to a network by analyzing and filtering packets at the application layer?
a) Intrusion Detection System (IDS)
b) Firewall
c) Antivirus software
d) Web Application Firewall (WAF)

10. Which of the following is a security principle that states that a user should only have access to the information and resources necessary to perform their job functions?
a) Principle of least privilege
b) Defense in depth
c) Separation of duties
d) Need to know

11. Which of the following is a type of malware that encrypts a victim's files and demands a ransom to decrypt them?
a) Trojan horse
b) Rootkit
c) Ransomware
d) Logic bomb

12. Which of the following is a security control that uses biometric characteristics, such as fingerprints or iris scans, to verify an individual's identity?
a) Token-based authentication
b) Biometric authentication
c) Password authentication
d) Certificate-based authentication

13. Which of the following is a security principle that ensures that individuals cannot deny their actions or transactions?
a) Confidentiality
b) Availability
c) Integrity
d) Non-repudiation

14. Which of the following is a security control used to prevent unauthorized access to a network by identifying and blocking known malicious IP addresses?
a) Intrusion Detection System (IDS)
b) Firewall
c) Antivirus software
d) IP blacklist

15. Which of the following is a cryptographic protocol used to provide secure communication over an untrusted network?
a) HTTPS (Hypertext Transfer Protocol Secure)
b) FTP (File Transfer Protocol)
c) SMTP (Simple Mail Transfer Protocol)
d) POP3 (Post Office Protocol Version 3)

16. Which of the following is a security control used to detect and prevent unauthorized access attempts by repeatedly entering different passwords?
a) Account lockout
b) Account expiration
c) Password complexity
d) Account disablement

17. Which of the following is a social engineering attack that involves an attacker pretending to be a trusted individual or entity in order to deceive victims?
a) Phishing
b) Spoofing
c) Smurfing
d) Brute-force

18. Which of the following is a security control that assigns specific privileges and permissions to users based on their roles within an organization?
a) Role-Based Access Control (RBAC)
b) Discretionary Access Control (DAC)
c) Mandatory Access Control (MAC)
d) Access Control List (ACL)

19. Which of the following is a security control that monitors and records events occurring within a system or network for later analysis?
a) Intrusion Detection System (IDS)
b) Security Information and Event Management (SIEM)
c) Intrusion Prevention System (IPS)
d) Antivirus software

20. Which of the following is a security principle that ensures that data is accurate and has not been modified or tampered with?
a) Confidentiality
b) Availability
c) Integrity
d) Non-repudiation

21. Which of the following is a type of attack that involves overwhelming a target system or network with a flood of requests to disrupt its normal operation?
a) Denial of Service (DoS)
b) Distributed Denial of Service (DDoS)
c) Phishing
d) Man-in-the-Middle (MitM)

22. Which of the following is a security control that encrypts data transmitted over a wireless network to prevent unauthorized interception?
a) WPA2 (Wi-Fi Protected Access 2)
b) MAC filtering
c) SSID hiding
d) NAT (Network Address Translation)

23. Which of the following is a security concept that ensures that resources and services are accessible and usable when needed?
a) Confidentiality
b) Availability
c) Integrity
d) Non-repudiation

24. Which of the following is a security control used to detect and prevent malicious software from infecting a system or network?
a) Intrusion Detection System (IDS)
b) Firewall
c) Antivirus software
d) Network Behavior Analysis (NBA)

25. Which of the following is a cryptographic algorithm used to securely hash passwords or data?
a) AES (Advanced Encryption Standard)
b) RSA (Rivest-Shamir-Adleman)
c) SHA (Secure Hash Algorithm)

d) 3DES (Triple Data Encryption Standard)

26. Which of the following is a security control used to monitor and filter network traffic based on predefined rules?
a) Intrusion Detection System (IDS)
b) Firewall
c) Antivirus software
d) Proxy server

27. Which of the following is a security principle that involves implementing multiple layers of security controls to protect against various threats?
a) Principle of least privilege
b) Defense in depth
c) Separation of duties
d) Need to know

28. Which of the following is a type of attack that involves sending unsolicited messages or requests to a large number of recipients?
a) Phishing
b) Spamming
c) Spoofing
d) Smurfing

29. Which of the following is a security control that validates the integrity and authenticity of digital documents or communications?
a) VPN (Virtual Private Network)
b) PKI (Public Key Infrastructure)
c) EFS (Encrypting File System)
d) IPSec (Internet Protocol Security)

30. Which of the following is a security control used to prevent unauthorized access to a network by blocking certain types of network traffic?
a) Intrusion Detection System (IDS)
b) Firewall
c) Antivirus software
d) VPN (Virtual Private Network)

31. Which of the following is a cryptographic protocol used to secure email communication by encrypting the message content?
a) HTTPS (Hypertext Transfer Protocol Secure)
b) SSL/TLS (Secure Sockets Layer/Transport Layer Security)

c) PGP (Pretty Good Privacy)
d) IPsec (Internet Protocol Security)

32. Which of the following is a security control that limits the number of login attempts a user can make within a certain time period?
a) Account lockout
b) Account expiration
c) Password complexity
d) Account disablement

33. Which of the following is a type of attack that involves sending deceptive emails or messages to trick recipients into revealing sensitive information?
a) Phishing
b) Spoofing
c) Smurfing
d) Brute-force

34. Which of the following is a security control used to verify the integrity and authenticity of digital certificates?
a) Certificate Authority (CA)
b) Registration Authority (RA)
c) Certificate Revocation List (CRL)
d) Certificate Signing Request (CSR)

35. Which of the following is a security control that monitors and analyzes network traffic in real time to detect and block suspicious or malicious activities?
a) Intrusion Detection System (IDS)
b) Firewall
c) Antivirus software
d) Network Behavior Analysis (NBA)

36. Which of the following is a security principle that states that a user should only have access to the information necessary to perform their job functions?
a) Principle of least privilege
b) Defense in depth
c) Separation of duties
d) Need to know

37. Which of the following is a type of malware that disguises itself as legitimate software to deceive users into installing it?
a) Trojan horse

b) Rootkit

c) Ransomware

d) Logic bomb

38. Which of the following is a security control that verifies the identity of individuals accessing a network by requiring them to provide something they know, such as a password?

a) RADIUS (Remote Authentication Dial-In User Service)

b) LDAP (Lightweight Directory Access Protocol)

c) TACACS+ (Terminal Access Controller Access Control System Plus)

d) Password authentication

39. Which of the following is a security control used to prevent unauthorized access to a network by inspecting and filtering packets at the application layer?

a) Intrusion Detection System (IDS)

b) Firewall

c) Antivirus software

d) Web Application Firewall (WAF)

40. Which of the following is a cryptographic algorithm used to securely encrypt data and ensure its confidentiality?

a) AES (Advanced Encryption Standard)

b) RSA (Rivest-Shamir-Adleman)

c) SHA (Secure Hash Algorithm)

d) 3DES (Triple Data Encryption Standard)

41. Which of the following is a security control that restricts access to certain resources based on the time of day or week?

a) Role-Based Access Control (RBAC)

b) Mandatory Access Control (MAC)

c) Discretionary Access Control (DAC)

d) Time-of-Day Restrictions

42. Which of the following is a secure method for transmitting data over an untrusted network by creating a secure "tunnel"?

a) SSH (Secure Shell)

b) FTPS (FTP Secure)

c) Telnet

d) HTTP

43. Which of the following is a security control used to prevent unauthorized access to a network by monitoring and analyzing network traffic patterns?
a) Intrusion Detection System (IDS)
b) Firewall
c) Antivirus software
d) Network Behavior Analysis (NBA)

44. Which of the following is a security concept that ensures that data is protected from unauthorized disclosure or access?
a) Confidentiality
b) Availability
c) Integrity
d) Non-repudiation

45. Which of the following is a secure method for authenticating and authorizing users by requiring them to provide something they have, such as a smart card?
a) RADIUS (Remote Authentication Dial-In User Service)
b) LDAP (Lightweight Directory Access Protocol)
c) TACACS+ (Terminal Access Controller Access Control System Plus)
d) Smart Card Authentication

46. Which of the following is a security control used to prevent unauthorized access to a network by analyzing and filtering packets at the network layer?
a) Intrusion Detection System (IDS)
b) Firewall
c) Antivirus software
d) Proxy server

47. Which of the following is a security principle that states that a user should only have access to the information and resources necessary to perform their job functions?
a) Principle of least privilege
b) Defense in depth
c) Separation of duties
d) Need to know

48. Which of the following is a type of malware that encrypts a victim's files and demands a ransom to decrypt them?
a) Trojan horse
b) Rootkit
c) Ransomware

d) Logic bomb

49. Which of the following is a security control that uses biometric characteristics, such as fingerprints or iris scans, to verify an individual's identity?
a) Token-based authentication
b) Biometric authentication
c) Password authentication
d) Certificate-based authentication

50. Which of the following is a security principle that ensures that individuals cannot deny their actions or transactions?
a) Confidentiality
b) Availability
c) Integrity
d) Non-repudiation

51. Which of the following is a security control used to prevent unauthorized access to a network by identifying and blocking known malicious IP addresses?
a) Intrusion Detection System (IDS)
b) Firewall
c) Antivirus software
d) IP blacklist

52. Which of the following is a security control that monitors and analyzes system activities and events to detect and respond to potential security incidents?
a) Security Information and Event Management (SIEM)
b) Intrusion Detection System (IDS)
c) Firewall
d) Antivirus software

53. Which of the following is a security principle that ensures that data remains complete, accurate, and unmodified?
a) Confidentiality
b) Availability
c) Integrity
d) Non-repudiation

54. Which of the following is a technique used to verify the integrity and authenticity of a message by generating a fixed-size hash value?
a) Encryption
b) Key exchange

c) Digital signature

d) Hashing

55. Which of the following is a security control that enforces restrictions on data transfers between different security domains or networks?
a) Data Loss Prevention (DLP)
b) Intrusion Detection System (IDS)
c) Firewall
d) Data Diode

56. Which of the following is a security concept that ensures that data and services are available and accessible to authorized users when needed?
a) Confidentiality
b) Availability
c) Integrity
d) Non-repudiation

57. Which of the following is a security control used to prevent unauthorized access to a network by examining and filtering packets based on their source and destination IP addresses?
a) Intrusion Detection System (IDS)
b) Firewall
c) Antivirus software
d) Network Address Translation (NAT)

58. Which of the following is a security principle that advocates for implementing multiple layers of security controls to protect systems and data?
a) Principle of least privilege
b) Defense in depth
c) Separation of duties
d) Need to know

59. Which of the following is a technique used to protect sensitive information by converting it into an unreadable format?
a) Encryption
b) Key exchange
c) Digital signature
d) Hashing

60. Which of the following is a security control used to prevent unauthorized access to a network by authenticating and authorizing users based on their digital certificates?
a) RADIUS (Remote Authentication Dial-In User Service)
b) LDAP (Lightweight Directory Access Protocol)
c) TACACS+ (Terminal Access Controller Access Control System Plus)
d) Certificate-based authentication

61. Which of the following is a security concept that ensures that actions and transactions cannot be denied by the parties involved?
a) Confidentiality
b) Availability
c) Integrity
d) Non-repudiation

62. Which of the following is a security control used to prevent unauthorized access to a network by examining and filtering packets at the transport layer?
a) Intrusion Detection System (IDS)
b) Firewall
c) Antivirus software
d) Intrusion Prevention System (IPS)

63. Which of the following is a security principle that advocates for dividing responsibilities among multiple individuals to prevent fraud and misuse of privileges?
a) Principle of least privilege
b) Defense in depth
c) Separation of duties
d) Need to know

64. Which of the following is a type of malware that remains hidden on a system and provides unauthorized access to an attacker?
a) Trojan horse
b) Rootkit
c) Ransomware
d) Logic bomb

65. Which of the following is a security control used to prevent unauthorized access to a network by authenticating and authorizing users based on their unique physical characteristics?
a) Token-based authentication

b) Biometric authentication

c) Password authentication

d) Certificate-based authentication

66. Which of the following is a security concept that ensures that data cannot be altered without detection?

a) Confidentiality

b) Availability

c) Integrity

d) Non-repudiation

67. Which of the following is a security control used to prevent unauthorized access to a network by examining and filtering packets based on their protocol and port numbers?

a) Intrusion Detection System (IDS)

b) Firewall

c) Antivirus software

d) Network Load Balancer

68. Which of the following is a security control used to detect and block known malicious software from infecting a system?

a) Intrusion Detection System (IDS)

b) Firewall

c) Antivirus software

d) Security Information and Event Management (SIEM)

69. Which of the following is a security principle that requires individuals to have a legitimate need to access specific information or resources?

a) Principle of least privilege

b) Defense in depth

c) Separation of duties

d) Need to know

70. Which of the following is a security control used to protect against social engineering attacks by verifying the identity of individuals before disclosing sensitive information?

a) Two-factor authentication

b) Single sign-on

c) Identity verification system

d) Security awareness training

71. Which of the following is a security concept that ensures that data is consistently available and accessible by authorized users?
a) Resilience
b) Redundancy
c) Availability
d) Reliability

72. Which of the following is a security control used to prevent unauthorized access to a network by monitoring and controlling incoming and outgoing network traffic based on predetermined security policies?
a) Network Access Control (NAC)
b) Intrusion Prevention System (IPS)
c) Data Loss Prevention (DLP)
d) Security Information and Event Management (SIEM) system

73. Which of the following best describes a distributed denial-of-service (DDoS) attack?

A) Unauthorized access to a network device or system
B) A malicious program that replicates itself across multiple systems
C) Flooding a network or website with excessive traffic to disrupt its availability
D) Intercepting and altering data packets in transit

74. Which of the following authentication factors is considered the strongest?

A) Something the user knows
B) Something the user has
C) Something the user is
D) Something the user does

75. Which of the following encryption algorithms is commonly used for securing wireless networks?

A) AES (Advanced Encryption Standard)
B) RSA (Rivest-Shamir-Adleman)
C) DES (Data Encryption Standard)
D) MD5 (Message Digest Algorithm 5)

Answers

1. b) Firewall: A firewall is a security control used to prevent unauthorized access to a network by inspecting and filtering packets at the network layer. It examines network traffic and applies rules to allow or deny access based on predetermined criteria.

2. b) Multifactor Authentication (MFA): Multifactor Authentication is a security control used to verify the identity of individuals accessing a network by requiring them to provide multiple forms of authentication. This can include something they know (e.g., password), something they have (e.g., security token), or something they are (e.g., biometric data).

3. c) Man-in-the-Middle (MitM): A Man-in-the-Middle (MitM) attack involves intercepting and altering communication between two parties without their knowledge. The attacker secretly relays and possibly modifies the communication, allowing them to eavesdrop or manipulate the information exchanged.

4. d) Time-of-Day Restrictions: Time-of-Day Restrictions is a security control that restricts access to certain resources based on the time of day or week. It allows organizations to define time-based policies, determining when users can or cannot access specific resources.

5. a) SSH (Secure Shell): SSH is a secure method for transmitting data over an untrusted network by creating a secure "tunnel." It encrypts network traffic, providing confidentiality and integrity, and is commonly used for secure remote login and file transfer.

6. a) Intrusion Detection System (IDS): An Intrusion Detection System (IDS) is a security control used to prevent unauthorized access to a network by monitoring and analyzing network traffic patterns. It detects and alerts on suspicious or malicious activity that may indicate an intrusion attempt.

7. a) Confidentiality: Confidentiality is a security concept that ensures data is protected from unauthorized disclosure or access. It involves measures such as encryption, access controls, and data classification to prevent unauthorized individuals from accessing sensitive information.

8. d) Smart Card Authentication: Smart Card Authentication is a secure method for authenticating and authorizing users by requiring them to provide something they have, such as a smart card. Smart cards store cryptographic keys and can be used to verify the identity of the user.

9. d) Web Application Firewall (WAF): A Web Application Firewall (WAF) is a security control used to prevent unauthorized access to a network by analyzing and filtering packets at the application layer. It specifically focuses on protecting web applications from common attacks and vulnerabilities.

10. a) Principle of least privilege: The Principle of least privilege is a security principle that states that a user should only have access to the information and resources necessary to perform their job functions. It minimizes the potential impact of a compromised account and limits unauthorized access.

11. c) Ransomware: Ransomware is a type of malware that encrypts a victim's files and demands a ransom to decrypt them. It restricts access to the files until the ransom is paid, posing a significant threat to data confidentiality and availability.

12. b) Biometric authentication: Biometric authentication is a security control that uses biometric characteristics, such as fingerprints or iris scans, to verify an individual's identity. It provides a high level of assurance as biometric traits are unique to each individual.

13. d) Non-repudiation: Non-repudiation is a security principle that ensures individuals cannot deny their actions or transactions. It provides evidence that a specific action or transaction occurred and that the parties involved cannot later deny their involvement.

14. b) Firewall: A firewall is a security control used to prevent unauthorized access to a network by identifying and blocking known malicious IP addresses. It monitors incoming and outgoing traffic and can be configured to block IP addresses associated with malicious activity.

15. a) HTTPS (Hypertext Transfer Protocol Secure): HTTPS is a cryptographic protocol used to provide secure communication over an untrusted network. It encrypts the communication between a client and a server, ensuring confidentiality and integrity of the data transmitted.

16. a) Account lockout: Account lockout is a security control used to detect and prevent unauthorized access attempts by repeatedly entering different passwords. After a certain number of failed login attempts, the account is locked, preventing further login attempts.

17. a) Phishing: Phishing is a social engineering attack that involves an attacker pretending to be a trusted individual or entity to deceive victims. The goal is to trick individuals into revealing sensitive information, such as passwords or credit card numbers.

18. a) Role-Based Access Control (RBAC): Role-Based Access Control is a security control that assigns specific privileges and permissions to users based on their roles within an organization. Users are granted access based on their job responsibilities, ensuring they have appropriate access rights.

19. b) Security Information and Event Management (SIEM): Security Information and Event Management (SIEM) is a security control used to monitor and record events occurring within a system or network for later analysis. It collects and analyzes data from various sources to detect and respond to security incidents.

20. c) Integrity: Integrity is a security principle that ensures data is accurate and has not been modified or tampered with. It involves measures such as data validation, checksums, and digital signatures to detect and prevent unauthorized modifications to data.

21. a) Denial of Service (DoS): Denial of Service (DoS) is a type of attack that involves overwhelming a target system or network with a flood of requests to disrupt its normal operation. By exhausting the system's resources, the attacker can render the target inaccessible to legitimate users.

22. a) WPA2 (Wi-Fi Protected Access 2): WPA2 is a security control that encrypts data transmitted over a wireless network to prevent unauthorized interception. It uses encryption algorithms to protect the confidentiality of data transmitted between devices connected to the wireless network.

23. b) Availability: Availability is a security concept that ensures that resources and services are accessible and usable when needed. It involves implementing measures, such as redundancy, fault tolerance, and disaster recovery plans, to minimize downtime and prevent disruptions to critical systems.

24. c) Antivirus software: Antivirus software is a security control used to detect and prevent malicious software from infecting a system or network. It scans files and processes for known malware signatures or suspicious behavior and takes actions to quarantine or remove the detected threats.

25. c) SHA (Secure Hash Algorithm): SHA is a cryptographic algorithm used to securely hash passwords or data. It takes an input and generates a fixed-size hash value, which is unique to the input data. The hash function is designed to be computationally difficult to reverse, providing data integrity and password storage security.

26. b) Firewall: A firewall is a security control used to monitor and filter network traffic based on predefined rules. It can inspect packets at the network and application layers and enforce access control policies to allow or block specific network connections, protecting the network from unauthorized access and threats.

27. b) Defense in depth: Defense in depth is a security principle that involves implementing multiple layers of security controls to protect against various threats. It recognizes that no single security measure is foolproof and that a combination of measures, such as firewalls, intrusion detection systems, encryption, and employee training, provides a stronger overall defense.

28. b) Spamming: Spamming is a type of attack that involves sending unsolicited messages or requests to a large number of recipients. The messages are typically unwanted and may contain advertisements, scams, or malicious links. Spamming can overload email servers and disrupt communication.

29. b) PKI (Public Key Infrastructure): PKI is a security control that validates the integrity and authenticity of digital documents or communications. It uses cryptographic techniques to issue, manage, and verify digital certificates, which bind public keys to individuals or entities, ensuring secure communication and data integrity.

30. b) Firewall: A firewall is a security control used to prevent unauthorized access to a network by blocking certain types of network traffic. It examines packets at the network and application layers and applies predefined rules to allow or deny traffic based on criteria such as source/destination IP addresses, port numbers, and protocols.

31. c) PGP (Pretty Good Privacy): PGP is a cryptographic protocol used to secure email communication by encrypting the message content. It uses public-key cryptography to encrypt the message with the recipient's public key, ensuring confidentiality, and can also provide digital signatures for message integrity and authentication.

32. a) Account lockout: Account lockout is a security control that limits the number of login attempts a user can make within a certain time period. After a specified number of failed login attempts, the account is temporarily locked, preventing further login attempts and protecting against brute-force attacks.

33. a) Phishing: Phishing is a type of attack that involves sending deceptive emails or messages to trick recipients into revealing sensitive information. The attacker typically impersonates a trusted individual or entity and tricks the recipient into providing passwords, credit card numbers, or other confidential information.

34. a) Certificate Authority (CA): A Certificate Authority (CA) is a security control that verifies the integrity and authenticity of digital certificates. CAs are trusted entities that issue digital certificates to individuals or organizations after validating their identity. The CA's digital signature on the certificate ensures its authenticity.

35. a) Intrusion Detection System (IDS): An Intrusion Detection System (IDS) is a security control that monitors and analyzes network traffic in real time to detect and block suspicious or malicious activities. It can detect patterns or signatures of known attacks or anomalous behavior that may indicate an ongoing security incident.

36. a) Principle of least privilege: The Principle of least privilege is a security principle that states that a user should only have access to the information necessary to perform their job functions. It minimizes the potential impact of a compromised account by limiting privileges and access rights to essential resources.

37. a) Trojan horse: A Trojan horse is a type of malware that disguises itself as legitimate software to deceive users into installing it. Once installed, it can perform various malicious actions, such as stealing sensitive information, providing unauthorized access to the attacker, or damaging the system.

38. d) Password authentication: Password authentication is a security control that verifies the identity of individuals accessing a network by requiring them to provide something they knowsuch as a password. It is a common method of authentication where users prove their identity by entering a password that matches the one stored in the system's database. The system compares the entered password with the stored password hash to validate the user's identity.

39. d) Web Application Firewall (WAF): A Web Application Firewall (WAF) is a security control used to prevent unauthorized access to a network by inspecting and filtering packets at the application layer. It is specifically designed to protect

web applications from common attacks, such as SQL injection, cross-site scripting (XSS), and cross-site request forgery (CSRF).

40. a) AES (Advanced Encryption Standard): AES is a cryptographic algorithm used to securely encrypt data and ensure its confidentiality. It is widely adopted as a symmetric encryption algorithm and is used to protect sensitive data at rest or in transit. AES operates on fixed-size blocks of data and supports key lengths of 128, 192, or 256 bits.

41. d) Time-of-Day Restrictions: Time-of-Day Restrictions is a security control that restricts access to certain resources based on the time of day or week. It allows organizations to define specific time periods during which users are allowed or denied access to particular resources. This control is commonly used to enforce security policies and limit access to sensitive information during non-business hours or specific time windows.

42. a) SSH (Secure Shell): SSH is a secure method for transmitting data over an untrusted network by creating a secure "tunnel." It provides encrypted communication between the client and server, ensuring confidentiality and integrity of the transmitted data. SSH is commonly used for secure remote login, file transfer, and command execution on remote systems.

43. a) Intrusion Detection System (IDS): An Intrusion Detection System (IDS) is a security control used to prevent unauthorized access to a network by monitoring and analyzing network traffic patterns. It detects and alerts administrators about potential security incidents or policy violations. IDS can identify known attack signatures or anomalous behavior, helping to protect the network from unauthorized access or malicious activities.

44. a) Confidentiality: Confidentiality is a security concept that ensures that data is protected from unauthorized disclosure or access. It involves implementing measures, such as encryption and access controls, to prevent unauthorized individuals from accessing sensitive information. Confidentiality aims to maintain the privacy and secrecy of data, protecting it from unauthorized disclosure or interception.

45. d) Smart Card Authentication: Smart Card Authentication is a secure method for authenticating and authorizing users by requiring them to provide something they have, such as a smart card. Smart cards contain embedded chips that store cryptographic keys and personal credentials. Users must physically possess the

smart card and provide a correct PIN or biometric authentication to access secure systems or resources.

46. b) Firewall: A firewall is a security control used to prevent unauthorized access to a network by analyzing and filtering packets at the network layer. It examines network traffic based on predefined rules and policies and allows or blocks traffic based on factors such as source and destination IP addresses, port numbers, and protocols. Firewalls act as a barrier between internal and external networks, protecting the network from unauthorized access and potential threats.

47. a) Principle of least privilege: The Principle of least privilege is a security principle that states that a user should only have access to the information and resources necessary to perform their job functions. It aims to minimize the potential impact of a compromised account by limiting privileges and access rights to essential resources. By adhering to the principle of least privilege, organizations can reduce the attack surface and mitigate the risks associated with unauthorized access or misuse of resources.

48. c) Ransomware: Ransomware is a type of malware that encrypts a victim's files and demands a ransom to decrypt them. It typically infiltrates a system through malicious email attachments, infected websites, or vulnerabilities in software. Once the files are encrypted, the attacker demands payment, often in cryptocurrency, in exchange for the decryption key. Ransomware attacks can cause significant data loss and financial damage to individuals and organizations.

49. b) Biometric authentication: Biometric authentication is a security control that uses biometric characteristics, such as fingerprints or iris scans, to verify an individual's identity. Biometric data is unique to each individual and difficult to forge, providing a higher level of security compared to traditional authentication methods. Biometric authentication systems capture and compare biometric traits to stored templates to grant or deny access to systems or resources.

50. d) Non-repudiation: Non-repudiation is a security principle that ensures that individuals cannot deny their actions or transactions. It provides evidence that a particular action or transaction took place and that the involved parties cannot later deny their involvement. Non-repudiation techniques, such as digital signatures or audit trails, provide cryptographic proof of the integrity and authenticity of data or transactions, preventing individuals from disowning their actions.

51. d) IP blacklist: An IP blacklist is a security control used to prevent unauthorized access to a network by identifying and blocking known malicious IP addresses. It maintains a list of IP addresses that have been associated with suspicious or malicious activities, and incoming traffic from those addresses is denied or subjected to additional scrutiny. IP blacklists are commonly used in firewalls or intrusion prevention systems to enhance network security.

52. a) Security Information and Event Management (SIEM): Security Information and Event Management (SIEM) is a security control that monitors and analyzes system activities and events to detect and respond to potential security incidents. It collects and correlates log data from various sources, such as network devices, servers, and applications, to provide real-time visibility into security events. SIEM systems enable organizations to detect and investigate security breaches, generate alerts, and facilitate incident response.

53. c) Integrity: Integrity is a security principle that ensures that data remains complete, accurate, and unmodified. It involves implementing controls and measures to prevent unauthorized alteration or tampering of data. Integrity mechanisms, such as checksums, digital signatures, and access controls, protect data from unauthorizedmodification and maintain its reliability and trustworthiness.

54. d) Hashing: Hashing is a technique used to verify the integrity and authenticity of a message by generating a fixed-size hash value. A hash function takes an input (message or data) and produces a unique hash value, often referred to as a digest or fingerprint. The hash value is used to verify that the message has not been altered during transmission or storage. Even a small change in the input will result in a completely different hash value, making it highly improbable for two different inputs to produce the same hash value.

55. d) Data Diode: A Data Diode is a security control that enforces restrictions on data transfers between different security domains or networks. It allows data to flow in one direction while preventing any flow in the opposite direction. This unidirectional flow ensures that information from a high-security network can be accessed by a lower-security network or system, but information cannot be transferred from the lower-security network to the higher-security network, reducing the risk of unauthorized access or data exfiltration.

56. b) Availability: Availability is a security concept that ensures that data and services are available and accessible to authorized users when needed. It involves implementing measures to prevent or minimize disruptions, downtime, or denial

of service. Availability measures include redundancy, fault tolerance, backup systems, disaster recovery plans, and proactive monitoring to ensure that systems and resources remain operational and accessible to users.

57. b) Firewall: A firewall is a security control used to prevent unauthorized access to a network by examining and filtering packets based on their source and destination IP addresses. It acts as a barrier between different networks, allowing or blocking traffic based on specified rules and policies. By inspecting packet headers, firewalls can enforce access controls, protect against malicious traffic, and ensure network security.

58. b) Defense in depth: Defense in depth is a security principle that advocates for implementing multiple layers of security controls to protect systems and data. It involves using a combination of preventive, detective, and corrective measures at different layers of an infrastructure. This approach ensures that even if one layer of defense is breached, there are additional layers that can provide protection and mitigate the impact of an attack. Defense in depth includes measures such as firewalls, intrusion detection systems, access controls, encryption, and employee training.

59. a) Encryption: Encryption is a technique used to protect sensitive information by converting it into an unreadable format. It involves using cryptographic algorithms and keys to transform plaintext data into ciphertext, which can only be decrypted back into plaintext with the appropriate decryption key. Encryption provides confidentiality and ensures that even if the encrypted data is intercepted, it remains secure and unreadable to unauthorized individuals.

60. d) Certificate-based authentication: Certificate-based authentication is a security control used to prevent unauthorized access to a network by authenticating and authorizing users based on their digital certificates. Digital certificates are issued by trusted Certificate Authorities and contain a user's public key and other identifying information. The certificates are used to verify the identity of users and facilitate secure communication. Certificate-based authentication enhances security by leveraging the principles of asymmetric cryptography and ensuring the authenticity and integrity of user identities.

61. d) Non-repudiation: Non-repudiation is a security concept that ensures that actions and transactions cannot be denied by the parties involved. It provides evidence to prove that a particular action or transaction took place and that the parties involved cannot deny their involvement.

62. b) Firewall: A firewall is a security control used to prevent unauthorized access to a network by examining and filtering packets at the transport layer. It acts as a barrier between the internal network and external networks, allowing only authorized traffic to pass through while blocking unauthorized traffic.

63. c) Separation of duties: Separation of duties is a security principle that advocates for dividing responsibilities among multiple individuals to prevent fraud and misuse of privileges. By separating critical tasks and assigning them to different individuals, it becomes more difficult for a single person to carry out malicious activities without detection.

64. b) Rootkit: A rootkit is a type of malware that remains hidden on a system and provides unauthorized access to an attacker. It is designed to conceal its presence and grant the attacker administrative-level control over the compromised system, making it difficult to detect and remove.

65. b) Biometric authentication: Biometric authentication is a security control used to prevent unauthorized access to a network by authenticating and authorizing users based on their unique physical characteristics, such as fingerprints, iris patterns, or facial features. It provides a higher level of security compared to traditional password-based authentication methods.

66. c) Integrity: Integrity is a security concept that ensures that data cannot be altered without detection. It involves protecting the accuracy and completeness of data throughout its lifecycle, preventing unauthorized modifications, and detecting any unauthorized changes that may occur.

67. b) Firewall: A firewall is a security control used to prevent unauthorized access to a network by examining and filtering packets based on their protocol and port numbers. It acts as a barrier between the internal network and external networks, enforcing security policies to allow or block network traffic based on predetermined rules.

68. c) Antivirus software: Antivirus software is a security control used to detect and block known malicious software from infecting a system. It scans files and programs for patterns or signatures of known malware and takes appropriate action to prevent the malware from causing harm.

69. a) Principle of least privilege: The principle of least privilege is a security principle that requires individuals to have a legitimate need to access specific information or resources. It aims to minimize the level of access rights and privileges granted

to users, limiting their capabilities to only what is necessary to perform their job functions.

70. c) Identity verification system: An identity verification system is a security control used to protect against social engineering attacks by verifying the identity of individuals before disclosing sensitive information. It may involve verifying personal information, such as a government-issued ID or biometric data, to ensure that the person making the request is who they claim to be.

71. c) Availability: Availability is a security concept that ensures data is consistently available and accessible by authorized users. It involves implementing measures to prevent disruptions to systems and networks, such as redundant infrastructure, backup systems, and disaster recovery plans, to ensure continuous access to data and services.

72. b) Intrusion Prevention System (IPS): An Intrusion Prevention System (IPS) is a security control used to prevent unauthorized access to a network by monitoring and controlling incoming and outgoing network traffic based on predetermined security policies. It can detect and block suspicious or malicious activity in real-time, providing proactive protection against network-based attacks.

73. C) Flooding a network or website with excessive traffic to disrupt its availability: A distributed denial-of-service (DDoS) attack involves flooding a network or website with excessive traffic to disrupt its availability. The attack overwhelms the target's resources, such as bandwidth or server capacity, making it difficult for legitimate users to access the network or website.

74. C) Something the user is: Something the user is, such as biometric characteristics (e.g., fingerprints, iris patterns), is considered the strongest authentication factor. Biometric authentication provides a high level of assurance because the user's physical traits are unique and difficult to forge or replicate compared to something the user knows (e.g., password) or something the user has (e.g., token).

75. A) AES (Advanced Encryption Standard): AES is commonly used for securing wireless networks. It is a symmetric encryption algorithm that provides strong security and performance. AES has become the industry standard for encrypting sensitive data, including wireless network traffic, due to its efficiency and resistance to cryptographic attacks.

Test 3

1. Which of the following authentication methods provides the HIGHEST level of security?
   A. Password-based authentication
   B. Biometric authentication
   C. Single-factor authentication
   D. Token-based authentication

2. Which of the following BEST describes the purpose of a firewall in a network security infrastructure?
   A. To prevent unauthorized access to the network
   B. To encrypt data transmitted over the network
   C. To monitor network traffic for malicious activities
   D. To detect and remove malware from network devices

3. A security administrator wants to implement a control that prevents employees from connecting unauthorized devices to the corporate network. Which of the following would be the MOST effective control to achieve this?
   A. Intrusion Detection System (IDS)
   B. Network Access Control (NAC)
   C. Virtual Private Network (VPN)
   D. Data Loss Prevention (DLP)

4. Which of the following BEST describes the concept of social engineering?
   A. Exploiting vulnerabilities in software or hardware
   B. Manipulating individuals to disclose sensitive information
   C. Gaining unauthorized access to a network through wireless means
   D. Using cryptographic algorithms to protect data in transit

5. Which of the following encryption algorithms is considered the MOST secure for protecting sensitive data?
   A. DES (Data Encryption Standard)
   B. AES (Advanced Encryption Standard)
   C. RSA (Rivest-Shamir-Adleman)
   D. RC4 (Rivest Cipher 4)

6. A company wants to ensure that data transmitted between its branch offices over the internet is secure. Which of the following protocols should be used?
   A. IPsec (Internet Protocol Security)
   B. FTP (File Transfer Protocol)

C. SNMP (Simple Network Management Protocol)

D. ICMP (Internet Control Message Protocol)

7. Which of the following BEST describes the purpose of a vulnerability assessment?

A. To identify and exploit vulnerabilities in a system

B. To simulate an attack on a system to test its security

C. To identify and assess weaknesses in a system's security

D. To monitor and analyze network traffic for suspicious activities

8. Which of the following is an example of a physical security control?

A. Intrusion Detection System (IDS)

B. Firewall

C. Biometric access control

D. Antivirus software

9. A security administrator wants to implement a control that prevents employees from using weak or easily guessable passwords. Which of the following would be the MOST effective control to achieve this?

A. Account lockout policy

B. Password complexity requirements

C. Two-factor authentication

D. Role-based access control

10. Which of the following BEST describes the purpose of a security incident response plan?

A. To prevent security incidents from occurring

B. To detect and respond to security incidents in a timely manner

C. To recover from security incidents and restore normal operations

D. To assess the security posture of an organization and identify vulnerabilities

11. Which of the following is an example of a preventive control in information security?

A. Intrusion Detection System (IDS)

B. Firewall

C. Incident response plan

D. Security awareness training

12. A company wants to securely store passwords for user authentication. Which of the following would be the BEST method to achieve this?

A. Storing passwords in plain text

B. Using symmetric encryption to encrypt passwords

C. Utilizing a hash function to store password hashes

D. Implementing biometric authentication instead of passwords

13. Which of the following is an example of a network-based security control?
    A. Antivirus software
    B. Host-based intrusion detection system
    C. Secure Sockets Layer (SSL) certificate
    D. Network segmentation

14. A security administrator wants to ensure that employees can only access certain resources based on their job roles. Which of the following access control models would be the MOST appropriate to implement?
    A. Mandatory Access Control (MAC)
    B. Role-Based Access Control (RBAC)
    C. Discretionary Access Control (DAC)
    D. Rule-Based Access Control (RBAC)

15. Which of the following is a security principle that is focused on ensuring that only authorized individuals have access to resources?
    A. Integrity
    B. Availability
    C. Confidentiality
    D. Non-repudiation

16. A company wants to protect sensitive data stored on its laptops in case of theft or loss. Which of the following would be the BEST control to implement?
    A. Full disk encryption
    B. Intrusion Prevention System (IPS)
    C. Virtual Private Network (VPN)
    D. Password complexity requirements

17. Which of the following BEST describes the purpose of penetration testing in information security?
    A. To identify and exploit vulnerabilities in a system
    B. To simulate an attack on a system to test its security
    C. To monitor and analyze network traffic for suspicious activities
    D. To implement security controls to prevent unauthorized access

18. A security administrator wants to ensure that all network traffic is encrypted to protect sensitive data. Which of the following protocols would be the BEST choice to achieve this?

A. HTTP (Hypertext Transfer Protocol)

B. FTP (File Transfer Protocol)

C. SSH (Secure Shell)

D. Telnet

19. Which of the following is an example of a technical control in information security?
    A. Security awareness training
    B. Incident response plan
    C. Biometric access control
    D. Acceptable use policy

20. A company wants to implement a control that can detect and prevent unauthorized access attempts by analyzing patterns and behaviors. Which of the following would be the MOST appropriate control to implement?
    A. Intrusion Detection System (IDS)
    B. Firewall
    C. Security information and event management (SIEM)
    D. Access control lists (ACLs)

21. Which of the following is an example of a preventive control in information security?
    A. Intrusion Detection System (IDS)
    B. Firewall
    C. Incident response plan
    D. Security awareness training

22. A company wants to securely store passwords for user authentication. Which of the following would be the BEST method to achieve this?
    A. Storing passwords in plain text
    B. Using symmetric encryption to encrypt passwords
    C. Utilizing a hash function to store password hashes
    D. Implementing biometric authentication instead of passwords

23. Which of the following is an example of a network-based security control?
    A. Antivirus software
    B. Host-based intrusion detection system
    C. Secure Sockets Layer (SSL) certificate
    D. Network segmentation

24. A security administrator wants to ensure that employees can only access certain resources based on their job roles. Which of the following access control models would be the MOST appropriate to implement?
   A. Mandatory Access Control (MAC)
   B. Role-Based Access Control (RBAC)
   C. Discretionary Access Control (DAC)
   D. Rule-Based Access Control (RBAC)

25. Which of the following is a security principle that is focused on ensuring that only authorized individuals have access to resources?
   A. Integrity
   B. Availability
   C. Confidentiality
   D. Non-repudiation

26. A company wants to protect sensitive data stored on its laptops in case of theft or loss. Which of the following would be the BEST control to implement?
   A. Full disk encryption
   B. Intrusion Prevention System (IPS)
   C. Virtual Private Network (VPN)
   D. Password complexity requirements

27. Which of the following BEST describes the purpose of penetration testing in information security?
   A. To identify and exploit vulnerabilities in a system
   B. To simulate an attack on a system to test its security
   C. To monitor and analyze network traffic for suspicious activities
   D. To implement security controls to prevent unauthorized access

28. A security administrator wants to ensure that all network traffic is encrypted to protect sensitive data. Which of the following protocols would be the BEST choice to achieve this?
   A. HTTP (Hypertext Transfer Protocol)
   B. FTP (File Transfer Protocol)
   C. SSH (Secure Shell)
   D. Telnet

29. Which of the following is an example of a technical control in information security?
   A. Security awareness training
   B. Incident response plan
   C. Biometric access control

D. Acceptable use policy

30. A company wants to implement a control that can detect and prevent unauthorized access attempts by analyzing patterns and behaviors. Which of the following would be the MOST appropriate control to implement?
A. Intrusion Detection System (IDS)
B. Firewall
C. Security information and event management (SIEM)
D. Access control lists (ACLs)

31. Which of the following is an example of a social engineering attack?
A. Brute-force password cracking
B. SQL injection
C. Phishing
D. Cross-site scripting (XSS)

32. A company wants to ensure that data sent between its headquarters and remote offices is protected from eavesdropping. Which of the following protocols would be the BEST choice to achieve this?
A. SSL/TLS (Secure Sockets Layer/Transport Layer Security)
B. POP3 (Post Office Protocol 3)
C. SNMP (Simple Network Management Protocol)
D. SMTP (Simple Mail Transfer Protocol)

33. Which of the following is an example of a security control that focuses on ensuring the availability of resources and services?
A. Firewall
B. Backup and recovery procedures
C. Intrusion Detection System (IDS)
D. Access control lists (ACLs)

34. A security administrator wants to limit the exposure of internal network resources to external threats. Which of the following would be the BEST control to implement?
A. DMZ (Demilitarized Zone)
B. VLAN (Virtual Local Area Network)
C. NAT (Network Address Translation)
D. IPSec (Internet Protocol Security)

35. Which of the following is an example of a technical control that can prevent unauthorized access to a network?

A. Security awareness training
B. Biometric authentication
C. Incident response plan
D. Security policy review

36. A company wants to ensure that data stored on its servers cannot be accessed by unauthorized individuals, even if the servers are physically stolen. Which of the following would be the BEST control to implement?
A. Data encryption
B. Intrusion Prevention System (IPS)
C. Two-factor authentication
D. Network segmentation

37. Which of the following is an example of a security control that can help detect and prevent network-based attacks?
A. Antivirus software
B. Data loss prevention (DLP) system
C. Intrusion Prevention System (IPS)
D. Virtual Private Network (VPN)

38. A security administrator wants to implement a control that can detect and block malicious network traffic based on predefined rules. Which of the following would be the BEST control to achieve this?
A. Firewall
B. Intrusion Detection System (IDS)
C. VPN concentrator
D. Load balancer

39. Which of the following is an example of a security control aimed at protecting against data leakage?
A. Firewall
B. VPN (Virtual Private Network)
C. DLP (Data Loss Prevention) system
D. Intrusion Prevention System (IPS)

40. A company wants to ensure that employees can only access specific areas within a building based on their job roles. Which of the following would be the BEST control to implement?
A. Video surveillance
B. Proximity card access
C. Security guard patrols

D. Biometric access control

41. Which of the following is an example of a security control that can help protect against phishing attacks?
A. Email filtering
B. Intrusion Detection System (IDS)
C. Firewall
D. Network segmentation

42. A company wants to ensure that data stored in its database is protected from unauthorized access. Which of the following would be the BEST control to implement?
A. Role-Based Access Control (RBAC)
B. Intrusion Prevention System (IPS)
C. VPN (Virtual Private Network)
D. Data encryption

43. Which of the following is an example of a security control that can help detect and prevent unauthorized access attempts at the network perimeter?
A. Intrusion Detection System (IDS)
B. Firewall
C. Antivirus software
D. Two-factor authentication

44. A security administrator wants to implement a control that can detect and block network traffic that violates predefined security policies. Which of the following would be the MOST appropriate control to implement?
A. Intrusion Prevention System (IPS)
B. Network Access Control (NAC)
C. Data loss prevention (DLP) system
D. Virtual Private Network (VPN)

45. Which of the following is an example of a security control that can help protect sensitive information stored on a laptop in case of theft or loss?
A. Full disk encryption
B. Intrusion Detection System (IDS)
C. Firewall
D. Security awareness training

46. A company wants to ensure that only authorized individuals can access certain areas within its premises. Which of the following would be the BEST control to implement?
    A. Biometric access control
    B. Security guard patrols
    C. Video surveillance
    D. Intrusion Prevention System (IPS)

47. Which of the following is an example of a security control that can help prevent data leakage through email?
    A. Email encryption
    B. Intrusion Detection System (IDS)
    C. Network segmentation
    D. Access control lists (ACLs)

48. A security administrator wants to implement a control that can monitor and analyze network traffic for suspicious activities and potential security incidents. Which of the following would be the BEST control to achieve this?
    A. Security information and event management (SIEM) system
    B. Firewall
    C. Intrusion Prevention System (IPS)
    D. Data loss prevention (DLP) system

49. Which of the following is an example of a security control that can help protect against Distributed Denial of Service (DDoS) attacks?
    A. Load balancer
    B. Intrusion Detection System (IDS)
    C. VPN (Virtual Private Network)
    D. Biometric access control

50. A company wants to ensure that data backups are securely stored and can be easily recovered in case of data loss or system failure. Which of the following would be the BEST control to implement?
    A. Regular backup and recovery procedures
    B. Intrusion Prevention System (IPS)
    C. Network segmentation
    D. Two-factor authentication

51. Which of the following is an example of a security control that can help protect against phishing attacks?
    A. Email filtering

B. Intrusion Detection System (IDS)

C. Firewall

D. Network segmentation

52. A company wants to ensure that data stored in its database is protected from unauthorized access. Which of the following would be the BEST control to implement?

A. Role-Based Access Control (RBAC)

B. Intrusion Prevention System (IPS)

C. VPN (Virtual Private Network)

D. Data encryption

53. Which of the following is an example of a security control that can help detect and prevent unauthorized access attempts at the network perimeter?

A. Intrusion Detection System (IDS)

B. Firewall

C. Antivirus software

D. Two-factor authentication

54. A security administrator wants to implement a control that can detect and block network traffic that violates predefined security policies. Which of the following would be the MOST appropriate control to implement?

A. Network Access Control (NAC)

B. Intrusion Prevention System (IPS)

C. Data loss prevention (DLP) system

D. Virtual Private Network (VPN)

55. Which of the following is an example of a security control that can help protect sensitive information stored on a laptop in case of theft or loss?

A. Firewall

B. Intrusion Detection System (IDS)

C. Full disk encryption

D. Security awareness training

56. A company wants to ensure that only authorized individuals can access certain areas within its premises. Which of the following would be the BEST control to implement?

A. Biometric access control

B. Security guard patrols

C. Video surveillance

D. Intrusion Prevention System (IPS)

57. Which of the following is an example of a security control that can help prevent data leakage through email?
A. Access control lists (ACLs)
B. Intrusion Detection System (IDS)
C. Network segmentation
D. Email encryption

58. A security administrator wants to implement a control that can monitor and analyze network traffic for suspicious activities and potential security incidents. Which of the following would be the BEST control to achieve this?
A. Firewall
B. Security information and event management (SIEM) system
C. Intrusion Prevention System (IPS)
D. Data loss prevention (DLP) system

59. Which of the following is an example of a security control that can help protect against Distributed Denial of Service (DDoS) attacks?
A. VPN (Virtual Private Network)
B. Intrusion Detection System (IDS)
C. Load balancer
D. Biometric access control

60. A company wants to ensure that data backups are securely stored and can be easily recovered in case of data loss or system failure. Which of the following would be the BEST control to implement?
A. Regular backup and recovery procedures
B. Intrusion Prevention System (IPS)
C. Network segmentation
D. Two-factor authentication

61. Which of the following is an example of a security control that can help protect against social engineering attacks?
A. Network segmentation
B. Intrusion Detection System (IDS)
C. Firewall
D. Security awareness training

62. A company wants to ensure that only authorized users can access a computer system. Which of the following would be the BEST control to implement?
A. Intrusion Prevention System (IPS)

B. User authentication

C. Virtual Private Network (VPN)

D. Data encryption

63. Which of the following is an example of a security control that can help prevent unauthorized modification of data?

A. Access control lists (ACLs)

B. Intrusion Detection System (IDS)

C. Firewall

D. Data backup

64. A security administrator wants to implement a control that can monitor and block malicious software attempting to enter the network through email attachments. Which of the following would be the MOST appropriate control to implement?

A. Data loss prevention (DLP) system

B. Intrusion Prevention System (IPS)

C. Network Access Control (NAC)

D. Email filtering

65. Which of the following is an example of a security control that can help protect against insider threats?

A. Firewall

B. Intrusion Detection System (IDS)

C. User access audit logs

D. Network segmentation

66. A company wants to ensure that data transmitted between its headquarters and branch offices is encrypted and secure. Which of the following technologies would be the BEST choice to achieve this?

A. Intrusion Prevention System (IPS)

B. Virtual Private Network (VPN)

C. Network Address Translation (NAT)

D. Two-factor authentication

67. Which of the following is an example of a security control that can help protect against brute-force password cracking attacks?

A. Account lockout policies

B. Intrusion Detection System (IDS)

C. Firewall

D. Data encryption

68. A security administrator wants to implement a control that can detect and block unauthorized access attempts by monitoring and analyzing user behavior. Which of the following would be the MOST appropriate control to implement?
A. Two-factor authentication
B. Intrusion Prevention System (IPS)
C. Network Access Control (NAC)
D. User behavior analytics (UBA)

69. Which of the following is an example of a security control that can help protect against web application vulnerabilities, such as cross-site scripting (XSS) attacks?
A. Network segmentation
B. Intrusion Detection System (IDS)
C. Web application firewall (WAF)
D. Data encryption

70. A company wants to ensure that its sensitive data is securely destroyed when it is no longer needed. Which of the following would be the BEST control to implement?
A. Secure data erasure
B. Intrusion Prevention System (IPS)
C. Network Access Control (NAC)
D. Data encryption

71. Which of the following is an example of a security control that can help protect against man-in-the-middle attacks?
A. Intrusion Detection System (IDS)
B. Transport Layer Security (TLS)
C. Firewall
D. Network segmentation

72. A company wants to ensure that user passwords are stored securely and cannot be easily compromised. Which of the following would be the BEST control to implement?
A. Data encryption
B. Intrusion Prevention System (IPS)
C. Virtual Private Network (VPN)
D. Password hashing

73. Which of the following is an example of a security control that can help protect against data exfiltration?
A. Firewall

B. Intrusion Detection System (IDS)
C. Data loss prevention (DLP) system
D. Network segmentation

74. A security administrator wants to implement a control that can detect and block malicious software attempting to exploit vulnerabilities in the operating system. Which of the following would be the MOST appropriate control to implement?
A. Host-based intrusion prevention system (HIPS)
B. Intrusion Prevention System (IPS)
C. Network Access Control (NAC)
D. Two-factor authentication

75. Which of the following is an example of a security control that can help protect against insider data theft?
A. Role-based access control (RBAC)
B. Intrusion Detection System (IDS)
C. Firewall
D. Data encryption

Answers

1. B) Biometric authentication: Biometric authentication provides the highest level of security as it relies on unique physical or behavioral traits, making it very difficult for unauthorized individuals to replicate or spoof.

2. A) To prevent unauthorized access to the network: The primary purpose of a firewall is to prevent unauthorized access to a network by controlling and filtering incoming and outgoing traffic.

3. B) Network Access Control (NAC): Network Access Control (NAC) is the most effective control to prevent employees from connecting unauthorized devices to the corporate network. It enforces policies and checks to ensure only authorized devices can connect.

4. B) Manipulating individuals to disclose sensitive information: Social engineering involves manipulating individuals to reveal confidential information, such as passwords, by exploiting human psychology rather than technical vulnerabilities.

5. B) AES (Advanced Encryption Standard) - AES is widely recognized as the most secure encryption algorithm for protecting sensitive data due to its strength and widespread adoption.

6. A) IPsec (Internet Protocol Security): IPsec is used to secure data transmitted over the internet, ensuring data confidentiality and integrity, making it ideal for securing data between branch offices.

7. C) To identify and assess weaknesses in a system's security: A vulnerability assessment is conducted to identify and assess weaknesses in a system's security, helping organizations address potential vulnerabilities.

8. C) Biometric access control: Biometric access control is a physical security control that uses unique biological traits, like fingerprints or retinal scans, for authentication.

9. B) Password complexity requirements: Implementing password complexity requirements is the most effective control to prevent employees from using weak or easily guessable passwords.

10. B) To detect and respond to security incidents in a timely manner: A security incident response plan's main purpose is to detect and respond to security incidents promptly to minimize their impact.

11. B) Firewall: Firewalls are network-based security controls designed to monitor and control traffic, preventing unauthorized access to the network.

12. C) Utilizing a hash function to store password hashes: Storing password hashes using a secure hash function is a recommended practice for protecting user passwords.

13. D) Network segmentation: Network segmentation is used to separate a network into segments or zones, restricting access based on job roles or responsibilities.

14. C) Confidentiality: Confidentiality in information security ensures that only authorized individuals have access to resources, preventing unauthorized access.

15. A) Full disk encryption: Full disk encryption is an effective control to protect sensitive data stored on laptops in case of theft or loss by encrypting the entire disk.

16. A) To identify and exploit vulnerabilities in a system: Penetration testing is conducted to identify and exploit vulnerabilities in a system, helping organizations improve their security measures.

17. C) SSH (Secure Shell): SSH is a protocol used to encrypt network traffic, providing secure communication between systems, making it suitable for securing data transmission.

18. C) Biometric access control: Biometric access control is a technical control that uses biological traits, such as fingerprints, for access authorization.

19. C) Security information and event management (SIEM): SIEM systems analyze patterns and behaviors to detect and prevent unauthorized access attempts and other security events, making them suitable for this purpose.

20. A) Intrusion Detection System (IDS): Intrusion Detection Systems (IDS) are designed to detect and alert on suspicious activities or potential security breaches in a network or system. They are used for monitoring and analysis, rather than access control or prevention.

21. B) Firewall: A firewall is a preventive control that helps protect a network by filtering and controlling incoming and outgoing traffic based on security policies.

22. C) Utilizing a hash function to store password hashes: Storing password hashes using a secure hash function is a recommended method for securely storing passwords, preventing plain text exposure.

23. D) Network segmentation: Network segmentation is a network-based security control that separates and isolates different parts of a network, limiting the potential impact of security breaches.

24. B) Role-Based Access Control (RBAC): Role-Based Access Control (RBAC) is an access control model that allows users to access resources based on their job roles, making it suitable for ensuring employees can only access specific resources.

25. C) Confidentiality: Confidentiality in information security ensures that only authorized individuals have access to resources, preventing unauthorized access.

26. A) Full disk encryption: Full disk encryption is an effective control to protect sensitive data stored on laptops, ensuring that even if a laptop is stolen, the data remains encrypted and inaccessible.

27. B) To simulate an attack on a system to test its security: Penetration testing involves simulating an attack on a system to identify vulnerabilities and assess its security, helping organizations improve their defenses.

28. C) SSH (Secure Shell): SSH is a secure protocol used to encrypt network traffic and is the best choice for ensuring that all network traffic is encrypted to protect sensitive data.

29. C) Biometric access control: Biometric access control uses unique physical or behavioral traits for authentication, making it a technical control that enhances security.

30. A) Intrusion Detection System (IDS): Intrusion Detection Systems (IDS) can detect and prevent unauthorized access attempts by analyzing patterns and behaviors, making them suitable for this purpose.

31. C) Phishing: Phishing is a social engineering attack that involves manipulating individuals to disclose sensitive information, often through deceptive emails or websites.

32. A) SSL/TLS (Secure Sockets Layer/Transport Layer Security): SSL/TLS protocols are used to encrypt data transmitted between locations to protect against eavesdropping.

33. B) Backup and recovery procedures: Backup and recovery procedures are security controls that focus on ensuring the availability of resources and services by providing redundancy and recovery mechanisms.

34. A) DMZ (Demilitarized Zone): A DMZ is a security control that limits the exposure of internal network resources to external threats by placing them in a separate, less trusted zone.

35. B) Biometric authentication: Biometric authentication is a technical control that can prevent unauthorized access to a network by requiring unique biological traits for authentication.

36. A) Data encryption: Data encryption is a security control that ensures data on servers cannot be accessed by unauthorized individuals, even if the servers are physically stolen.

37. C) Intrusion Prevention System (IPS): An Intrusion Prevention System (IPS) is a security control that can help detect and prevent network-based attacks by blocking malicious traffic based on predefined rules.

38. B) Intrusion Detection System (IDS): Intrusion Detection Systems (IDS) detect and block malicious network traffic based on predefined rules, making them suitable for this purpose.

39. C) DLP (Data Loss Prevention) system: A Data Loss Prevention (DLP) system is a security control aimed at protecting against data leakage by monitoring and preventing unauthorized data transfers.

40. D) Biometric access control: Biometric access control can be used to control access to specific areas within a building based on individual authentication, making it suitable for this purpose.

41. A) Email filtering: Email filtering is an effective security control for protecting against phishing attacks. It can identify and block phishing emails, reducing the likelihood of users falling for phishing scams by preventing such emails from reaching their inboxes.

42. D) Data encryption: Data encryption is the best control to implement when a company wants to protect data stored in its database from unauthorized access. Encryption ensures that even if an unauthorized person gains access to the database, they cannot make sense of the encrypted data without the proper decryption keys.

43. D) Two-factor authentication: Two-factor authentication is an effective control for detecting and preventing unauthorized access attempts at the network perimeter. It requires users to provide two forms of authentication, such as a password and a one-time code, making it more challenging for unauthorized users to gain access.

44. A) Intrusion Prevention System (IPS): An Intrusion Prevention System (IPS) is the most appropriate control for detecting and blocking network traffic that violates predefined security policies. It actively prevents potential threats by identifying and blocking malicious activities in real-time.

45. A) Full disk encryption: Full disk encryption is a security control that can help protect sensitive information stored on a laptop in case of theft or loss. It encrypts the entire contents of the laptop's hard drive, rendering the data inaccessible without the proper decryption key or passphrase.

46. A) Biometric access control: Biometric access control is the best control for ensuring that only authorized individuals can access specific areas within a company's premises. Biometric systems use unique physical traits, such as fingerprints or retinal scans, for authentication, making it difficult for unauthorized individuals to gain access.

47. A) Email encryption: Email encryption is a security control that helps prevent data leakage through email. It ensures that the content of emails is encrypted, so even if an email is intercepted, the sensitive information remains confidential and secure.

48. A. Security information and event management (SIEM) system: A Security Information and Event Management (SIEM) system is the best control for monitoring and analyzing network traffic for suspicious activities and potential security incidents. It collects and correlates data from various sources to provide insights into network security events.

49. A) Load balancer: Load balancers can help protect against Distributed Denial of Service (DDoS) attacks by distributing network traffic across multiple servers. This helps prevent overloads on individual servers, ensuring the availability of services during a DDoS attack.

50. A) Regular backup and recovery procedures: Implementing regular backup and recovery procedures is the best control for ensuring that data backups are securely stored and easily recoverable in case of data loss or system failure. This control enhances data availability and provides a means for data recovery in emergencies.

51. A) Email filtering: Email filtering is an effective security control against phishing attacks. It can identify and filter out phishing emails, reducing the risk of users falling victim to phishing scams.

52. D) Data encryption: Data encryption is the best control for protecting a company's database from unauthorized access. It ensures that even if an unauthorized person gains access to the database, the data remains encrypted and inaccessible without the appropriate decryption keys.

53. D) Two-factor authentication: Two-factor authentication is the best control for detecting and preventing unauthorized access attempts at the network perimeter. It adds an extra layer of security by requiring users to provide two forms of authentication, typically something they know (like a password) and something they have (like a mobile device).

54. B) Intrusion Prevention System (IPS): An Intrusion Prevention System (IPS) is the most appropriate control for detecting and blocking network traffic that violates predefined security policies. It actively prevents potential threats by identifying and blocking malicious activities in real-time.

55. C) Full disk encryption: Full disk encryption is a security control that helps protect sensitive information on a laptop in case of theft or loss. It encrypts the entire contents of the laptop's hard drive, making the data inaccessible without the proper decryption key.

56. A) Biometric access control: Biometric access control is the best control to ensure that only authorized individuals can access specific areas within a company's premises. Biometric systems use unique physical traits, such as fingerprints or retinal scans, for authentication, making it challenging for unauthorized individuals to gain access.

57. D) Email encryption: Email encryption is a security control that helps prevent data leakage through email. It ensures that email content is encrypted, maintaining the confidentiality of sensitive information in transit.

58. B) Security information and event management (SIEM) system: A Security Information and Event Management (SIEM) system is the best control for monitoring and analyzing network traffic for suspicious activities and potential security incidents. SIEM systems collect, correlate, and analyze data from various sources to identify and respond to security threats.

59. C) Load balancer: A load balancer is a security control that helps protect against Distributed Denial of Service (DDoS) attacks. It distributes incoming network traffic across multiple servers, preventing any single server from being overwhelmed by a DDoS attack.

60. A) Regular backup and recovery procedures: Implementing regular backup and recovery procedures is the best control to ensure that data backups are securely stored and easily recoverable in the event of data loss or system failure. This

control enhances data availability and provides a means for data recovery in case of emergencies.

61. D) Security awareness training: Security awareness training is a key security control to help protect against social engineering attacks. It educates employees and users to recognize and respond to various social engineering tactics, reducing the risk of falling victim to such attacks.

62. B) User authentication: User authentication is the best control to ensure that only authorized users can access a computer system. It verifies the identity of users before granting access to the system.

63. A) Access control lists (ACLs): Access control lists (ACLs) are a security control that helps prevent unauthorized modification of data. ACLs define which users or systems have access to specific resources and what actions they are allowed to perform.

64. D) Email filtering: Email filtering is the most appropriate control to monitor and block malicious software attempting to enter the network through email attachments. It can detect and filter out potentially harmful attachments, reducing the risk of malware infections.

65. C) User access audit logs: User access audit logs are a security control that can help protect against insider threats. By monitoring and logging user activities, organizations can detect and investigate suspicious behavior or unauthorized access by insiders.

66. B) Virtual Private Network (VPN): To ensure secure and encrypted data transmission between headquarters and branch offices, a Virtual Private Network (VPN) is the best choice. It establishes a secure, encrypted communication channel over the public internet, protecting data in transit.

67. A) Account lockout policies: Account lockout policies are a security control that helps protect against brute-force password cracking attacks. They automatically lock user accounts after a certain number of failed login attempts, preventing further login attempts by attackers.

68. D) User behavior analytics (UBA): User behavior analytics (UBA) is the most appropriate control for detecting and blocking unauthorized access attempts by monitoring and analyzing user behavior. UBA systems can identify unusual or suspicious activities and respond to them.

69. C) Web application firewall (WAF): A Web Application Firewall (WAF) is a security control that can help protect against web application vulnerabilities, such as cross-site scripting (XSS) attacks. It filters and monitors web traffic to detect and block malicious input or code.

70. A) Secure data erasure: Secure data erasure is the best control to ensure that sensitive data is securely destroyed when it is no longer needed. It ensures that data is permanently and irrecoverably removed from storage devices.

71. B) Transport Layer Security (TLS): Transport Layer Security (TLS) is a security control that helps protect against man-in-the-middle attacks. It encrypts data during transmission and ensures the integrity and authenticity of the communication.

72. D) Password hashing: Password hashing is the best control to securely store user passwords and prevent easy compromise. Hashing transforms passwords into irreversible, hashed values, making it difficult for attackers to recover the original passwords.

73. C) Data loss prevention (DLP) system: A Data Loss Prevention (DLP) system is a security control that helps protect against data exfiltration. It monitors, detects, and prevents unauthorized data transfers or leaks, whether intentional or accidental.

74. A) Host-based intrusion prevention system (HIPS): A host-based intrusion prevention system (HIPS) is the most appropriate control to detect and block malicious software attempting to exploit vulnerabilities in the operating system. HIPS monitors and protects the host system from various threats and vulnerabilities.

75. A) Role-based access control (RBAC): Role-based access control (RBAC) is a security control that can help protect against insider data theft. RBAC assigns specific roles and permissions to users based on their job responsibilities, limiting their access to sensitive data and reducing the risk of data theft.

Conclusion

As you've journeyed through this study guide, you've equipped yourself with valuable knowledge and skills essential for the CompTIA Security+ SY0-601 exam. You've delved into the intricate world of information security, understood network vulnerabilities, and mastered security principles that will serve as your armor in the digital realm.

Now, as you prepare to embark on the challenge of the certification exam, remember that the knowledge you've gained, the countless hours of studying, and the determination that brought you here will be your greatest allies! With each chapter, each practice question, and every moment of focused learning, you've built a solid foundation.

As you enter the examination room, stay calm and confident. Know that you are well-prepared! Trust your instincts, and remember to read each question carefully. Recall the concepts you've absorbed from this guide and approach each question with a clear and analytical mind.

I want to extend my heartfelt wishes to you as you tackle the CompTIA Security+ SY0-601 exam. May your hard work, dedication, and knowledge shine brightly, propelling you toward success! I have all the confidence that you will rise to the challenge and emerge victorious.

Good luck on your exam, and may your future in the world of cybersecurity be as bright as your dedication and effort deserve. You've got this!

GET YOUR BONUSES

Dear reader,

First and foremost, thank you for purchasing my book! Your support means the world to me, and I hope you find the information within valuable and helpful in your journey.

As a token of my appreciation, I have included some exclusive bonuses that will greatly benefit you. My hope is that this nudges you to give an authentic review. Remember, it only takes a brief moment, and it's invaluable for small publishers.

To access these bonuses, scan the QR Code with your phone:

Once again, thank you for your support, and I wish you the best of luck in your Exam. I believe these bonuses will provide you with the tools and knowledge to excel.

If you want to leave an honest review/ rating, here's the link for direct access, it would be very helpful and it takes less than 30 seconds:

Scan this QR Code below

CONTACT THE AUTHOR

I always strive to make this guide as comprehensive and helpful as possible, but there's always room for improvement. If you have any questions, suggestions, or feedback, I would love to hear from you. Hearing your thoughts helps me understand what works, what doesn't, and what could be made better in future editions.

To make it easier for you to reach out, I have set up a dedicated email address: epicinkpublishing@gmail.com

Feel free to email me for:

- Clarifications on any topics covered in this book

- Suggestions for additional topics or improvements

- Feedback on your experience with the book

- Any problem (getting your bonuses etc)

Your input is invaluable. I read every email and will do my best to respond in a timely manner.

Thank you once again for entrusting me with a part of your educational journey.

BOOK 2

COMPTIA A+ Study Guide

Chapter 1: Hardware Fundamentals

1.1 Personal Computer Components

The central processing unit (CPU) is often called the brain of a computer system. It performs most of the operations and calculations essential for the computer to function. The CPU is responsible for executing instructions and controlling the overall operation of the computer system.

The main function of the CPU is to fetch instructions from the memory, determine what operation needs to be performed, and then complete it. This is called the fetch-execute cycle. This process is repeated continuously until the computer is turned off.

The CPU also manages and coordinates the activities of other hardware components in the computer system. It communicates with the memory, input/output devices, and other peripherals to ensure that data is transferred correctly and instructions are carried out as intended.

Furthermore, the CPU contains a set of registers – small, high-speed storage areas – that hold data and instructions temporarily during execution. These registers play a crucial role in the performance of the CPU, as they provide quick access to information frequently accessed during operations.

Overall, the CPU is responsible for the essential functions of a computer, including performing calculations, executing instructions, coordinating with other hardware components, and managing data flow. Without a CPU, a computer system count not perform tasks or process data.

The motherboard is the main circuit board of a computer system and acts as a platform that connects and allows communication between various hardware components. It serves as a central hub, providing power, data transfer, and connectivity to all the other parts of the computer. The working parts of the motherboard are essential to know and understand.

The CPU socket is the area where the central processing unit (CPU) is installed. The socket is designed to match the specific CPU type and allows for communication and power delivery to the CPU.

Random access memory (RAM) slots are used to install memory modules that provide temporary storage for data and instructions. The number of slots determines the maximum amount of memory installed on the motherboard.

The PCI-Express slots allow for the installation of graphics cards, sound cards, network cards, and other expansion cards. These slots are crucial for expanding the capabilities of the system and enabling high-speed data transfer.

The Serial ATA (SATA) ports are used to connect hard drives, solid-state drives (SSDs), and optical drives. These ports facilitate data transfer between the storage devices and the motherboard at high speeds.

The universal serial bus (USB) ports are used for connecting various external devices, such as keyboards, mice, printers, and external storage devices. Motherboards usually have multiple USB ports for increased connectivity options. This is also the most commonly used port.

The ethernet port enables a wired network connection, allowing the computer to connect to a local area network (LAN) or the internet. However, most computers and laptops no longer come with an ethernet port unless specifically ordered. With the advancements in technology, wireless internet is the most commonly used source of connectivity.

The motherboard has power connectors that receive power from the power supply unit (PSU) and distribute it to different components, ensuring the smooth functioning of the entire system. If the PSU is disconnected suddenly, systems can fail and data become lost.

The Basic input/output system (BIOS) chip stores the firmware responsible for initializing and configuring hardware components during the boot-up process. A small battery provides power to the CMOS (Complementary Metal-Oxide-Semiconductor) chip, which stores basic system configuration information, such as date, time, and BIOS settings, even when the computer is turned off.

These are just a few of the essential components and connections found on a motherboard. Additionally, there may be audio jacks, fans and heatsinks, headers for connecting front panel buttons and LEDs, along with various other connectors and slots specific to the motherboard model and features.

There are several types of RAM (Random Access Memory), each with its own characteristics and capabilities. The most common types are DRAM, SDRAM, and SRAM.

Dynamic Random Access Memory (DRAM) is the most widely used type of RAM. It is volatile memory, which means it requires constant refreshing of its data to retain information. DRAM is relatively slower compared to other types but offers high-density storage capacity at a lower cost. It is used in systems like desktop computers and laptops.

Synchronous Dynamic Random Access Memory (SDRAM) is a type of DRAM that synchronizes its operations with the clock speed of the computer's bus system. It operates at a higher speed than regular DRAM and is commonly used in desktop computers. SDRAM has been further improved with advancements like DDR (Double Data Rate) and DDR2, DDR3, DDR4, and DDR5, which increase the data transfer rates and bandwidth.

Static Random Access Memory (SRAM) is a faster and more expensive type of RAM compared to DRAM. It does not require refreshing, making it faster and more dependable. SRAM is used in cache memory, CPU registers, and other applications where speed is critical.

There are also DRAM-based memory modules. These modules help with keeping and storing vital information. It's important to note the difference between each one to ensure the proper one is used on your device.

The dual in-line memory module (DIMM) is the most commonly used in desktop computers and servers. It has separate pins on both sides and provides a high capacity with multiple RAM chips on a single module. A small outline dual in-line memory module (SODIMM) is a smaller version of DIMM. It is commonly used in laptops, mini-PCs, and other small form factor systems. It has a smaller physical size and fewer pins compared to a DIMM. Micro-DIMM modules are used in laptops and other small devices where size is a constraint. They are smaller than SODIMM modules and are often used in specific laptop models.

A term you may have heard often is flash memory. This memory module is a non-volatile type of memory commonly used in devices like USB drives, SSDs, and memory cards. It retains data even when power is turned off. Flash memory is slower than RAM but provides a higher capacity for long-term storage.

It's important to note that different types of RAM are not interchangeable. Motherboards have specific slots and compatibility requirements for the type and generation of RAM they support. It is essential to check the motherboard's specifications to ensure compatibility before upgrading or installing RAM.

There are also several types of storage devices available. Two of the most popular ones are hard disk drives (HDDs) and solid-state drives (SSDs).

HDDs have been the traditional and most commonly used storage devices for many years. They consist of one or more spinning magnetic disks coated with a thin layer of magnetic material. Data is written and read using a read/write head that moves across the spinning disks.

They offer higher storage capacities compared to other storage devices, ranging from several hundred gigabytes to multiple terabytes. HDDs are generally cheaper per unit of storage compared to SSDs. However, HDDs do have their faults. They are generally slower than SSDs in terms of read/write speeds and access times. They are also more susceptible to physical damage due to their moving parts.

SSDs have gained popularity in recent years due to their significant performance improvements over HDDs. Unlike HDDs, SSDs use flash memory to store data electronically. They offer significantly faster reading and writing speeds and access times compared to HDDs. This makes them ideal for tasks that require quick data retrieval, such as booting up the operating system or loading applications.

SSDs have no moving parts, making them more resistant to physical damage from shocks and vibrations. They are generally more reliable and durable compared to HDDs. SSDs also consume less power compared to HDDs, making them more energy-efficient and suitable for portable devices like laptops and smartphones.

While SSDs are available in various capacities, ranging from a few hundred gigabytes to multiple terabytes, their high capacity can be more expensive compared to HDDs.

Hybrid drives, also known as SSHDs (Solid-State Hybrid Drives), combine the features of both HDDs and SSDs. They have a traditional spinning disk for large storage capacity and a smaller portion of solid-state memory for frequently accessed data. The data stored in the solid-state memory is automatically managed by the drive, providing improved performance for frequently used files while still offering higher overall storage capacities.

However, HDDs and SDDS are not the only storage devices available. There are network-attached storage (NAS) devices that connect to a network and allow multiple users to access and store data. USB flash drives are portable storage devices that connect to a computer's USB port. These devices are popular for data transfer on the go. There are also optical drives. These storage devices, such as CD and DVD drives, use lasers to read and write data on optical discs.

The choice of storage device a person chooses depends on factors like budget, performance requirements, capacity needs, and specific use cases. SSDs are generally recommended for improved speed, reliability, and performance, while HDDs still offer cost-effective high-capacity storage. Hybrid drives can be a compromise between the two, offering a blend of storage capacity and faster performance.

What about expanding storage and features on the motherboard? There's a card for that too. Expansion cards are hardware components that are installed into slots on the motherboard to expand the functionality of a computer system. They provide additional features or capabilities that are not built into the motherboard itself.

The graphics card, also known as a video card or GPU (Graphics Processing Unit), is responsible for rendering images, videos, and 3D graphics on a computer display. It has its own processor, memory, and cooling system. These cards are essential for gaming, graphic design, video editing, and other visually intensive tasks.

The network adapter, also called a network interface card (NIC), enables a computer to connect to a network. It provides the necessary hardware to connect to Ethernet cables or wireless networks for internet access or communication with other devices on a network. Network adapters are commonly used in desktop computers to provide wired or wireless networking capabilities.

A sound card is responsible for processing audio signals and providing sound output on a computer. It enhances audio quality and provides features such as surround sound, audio recording, and playback. Sound cards are particularly useful for gaming, multimedia production, and music enthusiasts who require high-quality sound reproduction.

A RAID (Redundant Array of Independent Disks) controller card is used to manage multiple hard drives or SSDs in a RAID configuration. It provides enhanced data protection, improved performance, or both by combining multiple drives into a logical unit. RAID controller cards are often used in servers and high-performance workstations.

TV tuner cards allow a computer to receive and display television signals. These cards allow users to watch live TV, record shows, and even pause, rewind, or schedule recordings. TV tuner cards are commonly used in desktop computers for media centers or to add TV functionality to a computer.

USB expansion cards provide additional USB ports that can be used to connect various USB devices to a computer. They are useful for systems with limited USB ports or for adding USB ports with specific features such as fast charging or USB 3.0 compatibility. These cards are often used by gamers.

A modem card is used to connect a computer to a telephone line or broadband connection to access the internet. While integrated modems are common in laptops, desktop computers may require a separate modem card for internet connectivity. In today's society, people do not typically have to worry about modem cards, but they are still available.

Each expansion card typically requires a compatible slot on the motherboard, such as PCI (Peripheral Component Interconnect), PCIe (Peripheral Component Interconnect Express), or AGP (Accelerated Graphics Port). It's important to ensure compatibility with the motherboard and the operating system when installing expansion cards.

1.2 Peripheral Device

With all the time we spend on screens, it's nice to have different display options. There are several types of displays available, but two of the most commonly used ones are LCD (Liquid Crystal Display) and LED (Light-Emitting Diode) monitors as they provide the best quality display.

LCD monitors work based on the concept of blocking and allowing light to pass through liquid crystal pixels. The monitor has a layer of liquid crystal material sandwiched between two glass plates, which is manipulated to block or allow light to pass through. The crystals align to control the amount of light emitted by individual pixels.

LCDs also require a separate light source, known as a backlight, positioned behind the liquid crystal display. Common backlight sources include CCFLs (Cold Cathode Fluorescent Lamps) or fluorescent tubes. This lighting helps with the good image quality LCDs can offer. However, they may suffer from limited viewing angles and slower response times in comparison to other display technologies like OLED (Organic Light-Emitting Diode).

The power consumption of LCD monitors is known to be power-efficient compared to older display technologies like CRT (Cathode Ray Tube) screens. This is why they are commonly used in devices like computer monitors, televisions, laptops, and smartphones.

The other display mentioned was the LED. LED monitors share the same underlying display technology as LCD monitors but use light-emitting diodes (LEDs) as their backlight source. LEDs are more energy-efficient and allow for better control of brightness levels compared to CCFLs.

With a thinner design and energy efficiency, LED monitors have become popular in the market. Their high-resolution screens, vibrant colors, and sharp images give the LED an appeal one cannot deny. These monitors are widely used in computer monitors, televisions, outdoor displays, digital signage, and other applications where lower power consumption and enhanced visual quality are desired.

Overall, both LCD and LED monitors have their advantages and disadvantages. Both are extensively used in various fields, ranging from consumer electronics to professional applications.

Outside of motherboards and displays are input devices. These are essential peripherals that allow users to interact with electronic devices. A lot of these devices we already know but may not know their full functions. In the following section, I will discuss their components and full uses.

First, if the keyboard. Keyboards are used for entering text, commands, and other data into the computer. They consist of a set of keys, including alphanumeric keys, function keys, modifier keys (Shift, Alt, Ctrl), and special purpose keys (Enter, Backspace, Delete). Keyboards can be wired or wireless, and there are various keyboard layouts available.

A mouse is a pointing device that allows users to move a graphical cursor or pointer on the computer screen. By moving the mouse along a surface, the cursor on the screen moves correspondingly. Mouse actions, such as clicking, dragging, and right-clicking, enable users to interact with graphical user interfaces easily.

Then there's the touchpad. It is a pointing device commonly found on laptops and is similar to a mouse. It responds to finger movements on its surface, allowing users to move the cursor and perform various actions. Touchpads support gestures like tapping, scrolling, and pinch-to-zoom for multi-touch input on the device.

Ever heard of a trackball? It is a pointing device that consists of a ball mounted on top of the device. Users roll the ball with their fingers or palm, which translates into cursor movements on the screen. Trackballs are often used as an alternative to traditional mice, offering precision and reduced hand movement. They are perfect for people with limited desk space, debilitating staring injuries, or painful arthritis.

Ah, the joystick. While primarily used for gaming and controlling machinery, it is another input device worth mentioning. They typically have a handle that users can tilt or move in different directions to control on-screen movements or simulate various actions. Joysticks often include additional buttons or triggers for additional inputs, depending on your need for one.

If you are a gamer, I'm sure you have heard of gamepads or controllers. These input devices are designed specifically for gaming. They usually feature an array of buttons, triggers, analog sticks, and directional pads to provide precise control over game characters or environments. Different game consoles have independent controller designs.

A touchscreen is a display that can detect touch gestures and inputs directly on its surface. Touchscreens can be found on smartphones, tablets, laptops, and interactive kiosks. It eliminates the need for separate input devices like keyboards or mice, as users can interact with the device by touching or tapping directly on the screen.

These are just a few examples of input devices. There are many more available depending on your specific needs or applications. Each input device serves a distinct purpose in facilitating user interactions with computers and electronic devices.

Wait, that's not all. There are also output devices too. These devices are peripherals that display or reproduce information from a computer or other electronic devices. Namely, the printer.

Printers are devices that produce hard copies of digital documents or images on various media, such as paper, plastic, or fabric. There are different types of printers including inkjet, laser, and 3D. Which you use will depend on your needs.

Inkjet printers use tiny nozzles to spray droplets of ink onto the paper. They are versatile and capable of producing high-quality color prints and text documents. Inkjet printers are best for pictures, graphics, flyers, brochures, etc.

Also used for high-production, top-quality prints is the laser printer. Laser printers use a laser beam to create an electrostatic image on a drum, which attracts and fuses toner onto the paper. They are faster and more suitable for high-volume printing. For that reason, they are often found in large office environments.

Lastly, there's the 3D printer. These specialized printers build physical objects layer by layer from a digital model using materials such as plastic, metal, or resin. They are commonly used in prototyping, manufacturing, and various industries.

Printers connect to computers via USB, Ethernet, or Wi-Fi. They can print documents, images, or even labels and stickers. Additionally, features like duplex printing (printing on both sides of the paper) and wireless connectivity are common in modern printers.

Another output device is speakers, which are commonly used by all ages. Speakers are audio output devices that produce sound generated by computers or other electronic devices. They convert electrical signals into sound waves, allowing users to hear audio.

Speakers can vary in size and complexity, from simple built-in speakers in laptops and smartphones to multi-channel surround sound systems. Some commonly used types of speakers are stereo speakers, soundbars, and surround sound.

Stereo speakers use two audio channels to create a sense of depth and directionality in the sound. They are commonly used for general audio playback on computers, televisions, and music systems. If there's music, there's stereo speakers.

Soundbars are elongated speakers that generate high-quality audio for televisions. They provide better sound quality compared to built-in TV speakers and often include multiple audio drivers to produce virtual surround sound. These are great if you have a large room and the built-in speakers for your television struggle to produce good sound.

Surround sound systems consist of multiple speakers placed around a room to create an immersive audio experience. They typically include a combination of front, center, rear, and subwoofer speakers for detailed audio reproduction and are commonly used in home theaters or gaming setups.

Speakers can connect to devices using wired connections such as auxiliary cables or digital connections like HDMI. Additionally, wireless options like Bluetooth and Wi-Fi are available to provide flexible audio streaming without the need for physical cables. In recent years, Bluetooth has become the favored option.

Both printers and speakers play a significant role in enhancing user experiences by providing tangible outputs in the form of documents or audio. They are widely used in homes, offices, educational institutes, and various professional settings.

How might all these devices work together? There's a device for that. The modem and router are devices used for network connectivity. They play a crucial role in establishing and managing communication between devices within a network and the internet. Let's take a look at the differences between the two and the different options available with each.

A modem, short for modulator-demodulator, is a device that connects a computer or network to an internet service provider (ISP) by converting digital signals from the computer into analog signals that can be transmitted over a telephone line or cable line. There are three distinct kinds of modems: DSL, cable, and fiber.

DSL (Digital Subscriber Line) modems connect to a phone line and use DSL technology to transmit data over existing copper telephone lines. They are commonly used in homes or businesses with DSL internet connections. However, this modem has started to phase out over the last decade due to cable and fiber.

Cable modems use coaxial cables to connect to the internet. They are typically used with cable TV networks and provide high-speed internet access. While cable is preferred over DSL, it still does not compare to fiber advantages.

Fiber modems are used with fiber optic networks that transmit data using light signals. These modems convert those light signals into digital data, providing high-speed internet access. Fiber optic advantages have helped spread the use of high-speed internet in rural areas that did not have the option before.

Now that we've discussed modems and the different types available, let's take a glance at routers and their features.

A router is a networking device that enables devices within a network to communicate with each other and also facilitates connectivity to the internet. Routers receive data packets from devices in the network and forward them to the appropriate destination. They perform functions like routing, forwarding, and managing network traffic.

Routers have multiple Ethernet ports to connect devices within a local network, such as computers, printers, or gaming consoles. This is known as a local area network (LAN) connectivity. Similar to that is wide area network (WAN) connectivity. WAN connects to the modem, allowing the network to access the internet.

With all this connectivity, there is a way to make your network private. Routers use NAT to assign private IP addresses to devices within the local network and translate them to a single public IP address provided by the ISP.

Routers also can use wireless capabilities. This allows users to connect to multiple devices on the same network via Wi-Fi. You may have a router in your home that everyone connects with and then different tasks can be completed by each person. It's a great benefit to a router with wireless capabilities.

Routers also provide additional features such as firewall protection, port forwarding, Quality of Service (QoS) settings, and guest networks. They function as a central point for network management, enabling devices to communicate locally and access the internet simultaneously.

Modems and routers work together to establish network connectivity and internet access for devices. Modems establish the connection to the ISP, while routers manage internal network communication and provide internet access to multiple devices in a network.

1.3 Hardware Troubleshooting

Now that you have a general idea of the hardware, what do you do if issues arise? We will go through some typical problem-solving approaches you can try at home.

Step 1: Identify the problem.

Start by gathering as much information as possible about the hardware issue. Determine if the problem is related to a specific component or if it affects the entire system.

Step 2: Isolate the issue.

If possible, try to replicate the problem or narrow it down to a specific area of the hardware. This could involve disconnecting and reconnecting cables, swapping components, or using diagnostic tools. You can run a diagnostics test in the settings.

Step 3: Check the connections.

Ensure that all cables and connections are securely plugged in. Loose or faulty connections can cause hardware problems. If necessary, clean the connectors and reseat the cables.

Step 4: Run diagnostics.

Many hardware issues can be diagnosed using built-in diagnostic tools. Check the manufacturer's website or documentation for specific diagnostic tests that can be run to identify the problem.

Step 5: Update drivers and firmware.

Outdated or incompatible drivers and firmware can cause hardware issues. Check the manufacturer's website for the latest updates and install them if necessary.

Step 6: Test the hardware in a different system.

If possible, try the suspect hardware on a different computer or device. This will help determine if the issue is with the hardware itself or with other components in the system.

Step 7: Remove unnecessary hardware.

If the problem persists, try removing any non-essential hardware components one by one to see if any of them are causing the issue. This includes expansion cards, external devices, and extra RAM.

Step 8: Check for overheating.

Hardware components can overheat, leading to performance issues and hardware failures. Ensure that cooling fans are working properly, clean out any dust or debris from the system, and consider using additional cooling solutions if necessary.

Step 9: Check for physical damage.

Inspect hardware components for any physical damage, such as bent pins, cracked circuits, or swollen capacitors. If any damage is found, it may need to be repaired or replaced.

Step 10: Seek professional help.

If the issue cannot be resolved through the above steps, it may be best to consult a professional technician or contact the manufacturer for further assistance. They may be able to provide additional troubleshooting steps or recommend repairs or replacements.

There are several common hardware troubleshooting tools available that can help diagnose and resolve hardware issues. In the next section, we will discuss some of these tools.

A multimeter is a versatile tool that measures electrical characteristics such as voltage, current, and resistance. It can be used to assess power supplies, check for faulty components, and troubleshoot electrical connections. They can be found at most hardware or electronics retail stores.

Many hardware manufacturers provide diagnostic software tools that can help identify and troubleshoot specific hardware issues. These programs run tests and generate reports to pinpoint problems, such as memory errors, hard drive issues, or CPU performance.

Thermal paste and thermal compound are used to ensure proper heat transfer between the CPU or GPU and the cooling device, such as a heat sink or a cooling fan. Applying new thermal paste can help resolve overheating issues by improving thermal conductivity.

Cable testers are used to check the integrity of cables, such as Ethernet cables or SATA cables. They can quickly identify if a cable is faulty or if there is a connectivity issue. Some cable issues are not visible, which is why a tester is good to use.

A power supply tester determines if a power supply is functioning correctly. By connecting it to the power supply's connectors, it can check if the voltage levels are within acceptable ranges, helping to diagnose power-related issues. Some modems require a higher voltage of power which may not be available in all outlets.

There are various diagnostic tools available that can be loaded onto a USB drive and booted from to run diagnostics on a computer system. These tools can test RAM, hard drives, CPU, and other components without the need for an operating system.

Loopback plugs are tools used to test ports on devices such as network interface cards (NICs) or serial ports. They "loop back" the outgoing signal to ensure that the port is functioning correctly.

Always have replacement hardware components on hand. Keeping spare hardware components on hand can be useful for troubleshooting purposes more efficiently. By swapping out suspect components with known working ones, you can identify if the issue lies in the hardware itself.

LED testers can help diagnose issues with power and signal indicators. They indicate whether LEDs are properly receiving power or if there are any problems with the connections.

Remember to always consult the documentation provided by the manufacturer and follow proper safety precautions when using any hardware troubleshooting tools. If you are not completely comfortable doing it yourself, find a service provider to help.

There are typical everyday problems that can be easily fixed at home. The following are some common hardware issues, along with their potential solutions to try.

The computer is not turning on. Check if the power cable is securely connected and the power outlet is working. If the power supply unit (PSU) fan is not spinning, it may be faulty and need replacement.

The device seems to be slower than usual. Ensure that the computer has sufficient RAM and storage space. Scan for malware and close unnecessary background programs. If the issue persists, consider upgrading the hardware components (e.g., adding more RAM or upgrading to a faster storage drive).

It's overheating. Clean out dust and debris from cooling fans and ensure proper airflow in the computer case. Check if the CPU cooler or graphics card fan is properly seated. Consider replacing the thermal paste on the CPU or GPU to improve heat dissipation.

Nothing is happening and you are staring at the blue screen of death (BSOD). Update device drivers and firmware. Run a memory test to check for RAM errors. If the problem continues, it might indicate a hardware failure such as a faulty hard drive, defective memory module, or overheating.

There is no display or distorted graphics. Ensure that the monitor is properly connected and powered on. Check the cables for any damage and try a different video cable or port. If using a discrete graphics card, reseat it securely in the PCIe slot. If integrated graphics, try using a graphics card to isolate the issue.

There is an unexpected system shutdown. Check for overheating issues and ensure proper ventilation. Verify if the power supply unit (PSU) is adequately powering the system. Run a disk scan to check for errors on the hard drive.

There's an unresponsive or malfunctioning peripheral. Ensure that the peripherals are properly connected. Try using them on different USB ports or with a different computer. Update the device drivers if necessary. If a peripheral is still not functioning, it may indicate a hardware failure, requiring repair or replacement.

There's no internet connectivity. Check if the network cables are properly connected and the router/modem is functioning correctly. Restart the router or modem if needed. Update network drivers and perform a network reset if necessary.

Unusual noises are coming from the device. Grinding or clicking sounds from a hard drive could indicate an imminent failure. Make sure to back up important data and consider replacing the hard drive. Loud fan noises might indicate a malfunctioning or obstructed fan that needs to be replaced.

BIOS does not recognize hardware. Ensure that the hardware components are properly connected and seated. Check for any available BIOS updates and apply them. Reset the BIOS to default settings if needed.

It is important to consult the manufacturer's documentation or seek professional assistance if you are unsure about diagnosing or resolving hardware problems.

Chapter 2: Networking

2.1 Network Fundamentals

Networking is a fundamental concept in computer science that involves the connection and communication between multiple devices or systems. It allows computers and other devices to share resources, transfer data, and collaborate. To understand networking, it is essential to be familiar with protocols, IP addressing, and subnetting.

Protocols are a set of rules and procedures that govern the exchange of data and communication between devices on a network. They ensure that data is transmitted accurately, efficiently, and securely. Some common protocols used in networking include TCP/IP (Transmission Control Protocol/Internet Protocol), HTTP (Hypertext Transfer Protocol), FTP (File Transfer Protocol), and DNS (Domain Name System).

An IP (Internet Protocol) address is a unique numerical identifier assigned to each device connected to a network. IP addressing allows devices to locate and communicate with each other within a network or across the internet. There are two main versions of IP addresses: IPv4 (Internet Protocol version 4) and IPv6 (Internet Protocol version 6). IPv4 addresses consist of four sets of numbers separated by periods (e.g., 192.168.0.1), while IPv6 addresses are written as eight sets of hexadecimal digits separated by colons (e.g., 2001:cdba:0000:0000:0000:0000:3257:9652).

Subnetting is the process of dividing a network into smaller subnetworks or subnets. It helps in the efficient utilization of IP addresses and improves network performance and security. Subnetting involves borrowing bits from the host portion of an IP address to create subnets. Each subnet has its range of IP addresses, which allows for better organization and management of devices within the network.

In summary, protocols define the rules for communication, IP addressing provides a unique identification for devices, and subnetting allows for the division of a network into smaller subnets. These concepts form the building blocks of networking and are crucial for understanding how devices connect and interact in a networked environment.

There are various types of networks, each designed to suit specific requirements and scale. Three common types of networks are LAN (Local Area Network), WAN (Wide Area Network), and wireless networks.

A LAN is a network that connects devices within a limited geographical area, such as a home, office building, or campus. It typically comprises computers, servers, printers, and other devices connected using wired technologies like Ethernet cables or switches. LANs offer high-speed communication and allow for resource sharing, file sharing, and collaboration within the local environment. They are commonly used for small-scale networks within a single location.

A WAN spans a larger geographical area, connecting devices across different locations or cities. It utilizes public or private telecommunication infrastructures like leased lines, satellites, or the internet to interconnect LANs or other networks. WANs connect multiple LANs and enable communication and data transfer between geographically dispersed sites. They are commonly used by organizations with branch offices in various locations to establish seamless connectivity.

Wireless networks, also known as Wi-Fi networks, enable devices to connect and communicate without physical wired connections. They use radio waves to transmit data between devices and access points. Wireless networks offer flexibility and mobility, allowing devices to connect and access the network within the range of the wireless signal. They are widely used in homes, offices, public places, and other environments where wired connections may be impractical or inconvenient.

Additionally, there are other network types such as MAN (Metropolitan Area Network) that cover larger areas than LANs but smaller than WANs, PAN (Personal Area Network) that connects personal devices in proximity, and CAN (Campus Area Network) that interconnects LANs within a specific geographic area like a university campus.

Understanding different network types is essential for designing, implementing, and maintaining effective and efficient communication infrastructures that meet specific organizational needs and scale requirements. This understanding will help you narrow down which is best suitable for your lifestyle.

Switches, routers, and access points are key network devices that play distinct roles in networking. They help connect networks and keep devices functioning.

Switches operate at the data link layer (Layer 2) of the OSI (Open Systems Interconnection) model. They connect multiple devices within a LAN and facilitate communication by directing data packets to their intended destinations within the local network.

Switches receive data packets and forward them to the appropriate destination based on the MAC (Media Access Control) address of the devices connected to the switch. They maintain an internal MAC address table, allowing them to efficiently forward packets only to the intended recipient, reducing network congestion.

Switches also support the creation of VLANs, which enable logical segmentation and isolation of network traffic. Many offer features like access control lists (ACLs) and port security to enhance network security by controlling access and preventing unauthorized devices from connecting.

Routers operate at the network layer (Layer 3) of the OSI model. They connect multiple networks, including LANs or WANs, and determine the optimal path for data packets to travel from the source to the destination network.

They use protocols like RIP (Routing Information Protocol), OSPF (Open Shortest Path First), or BGP (Border Gateway Protocol) to determine the best path for forwarding packets based on IP addresses. Routers use these IP addresses to identify and route packets between different networks.

Routers can prioritize traffic, implement Quality of Service (QoS) policies, and incorporate features like traffic shaping or packet filtering for better network performance. They allow for the creation of separate IP subnets, enabling network segmentation and isolation of traffic for security or performance purposes.

Access points (APs) are devices that enable wireless connectivity. They serve as a central point for wireless devices to connect to a wired network. Access points provide network identification through Service Set Identifiers (SSIDs), allowing users to select and connect to the desired wireless network.

They also implement wireless security standards like WPA2 (Wi-Fi Protected Access II) or WPA3 to protect the network from unauthorized access. Access points in larger networks with multiple APs enable seamless roaming, allowing devices to switch between access points without interruptions.

Understanding the roles and functions of switches, routers, and access points is crucial for designing and maintaining effective and efficient networks, whether wired or wireless, to enable reliable connectivity and data transfer within and between networks.

Diagnosing and resolving network connectivity issues can be a complex task, but by following a systematic approach, you can efficiently identify and fix the problem. Here's a step-by-step guide:

1. Identify the Problem:

Talk to the user or gather information about the issue, including specific symptoms, affected devices, and recent changes to the network. Determine if the problem is specific to a single device or affects multiple devices on the network.

2. Check Physical Connections:

Ensure that all network cables are properly connected and not damaged. This includes cables connecting to routers, switches, and modems. Verify power connections for network devices and ensure they are powered on.

3. Restart Devices:

Rebooting network devices such as routers, switches, and modems can often resolve temporary issues. Power off the devices, wait for a few seconds and then power them back on.

4. Test Connectivity:

Determine if the issue is limited to a specific device or affects the entire network. Try accessing different websites or services from different devices to verify connectivity.

5. Check IP Configuration:

Verify that devices have been assigned valid IP addresses either through DHCP or manual configuration. Use the command prompt or network settings to check IP addresses, subnet masks, default gateways, and DNS servers.

6. Perform Network Troubleshooting:

Use network diagnostic tools like ping, traceroute, or nslookup to identify potential issues. Ping the default gateway or external IP addresses to check for connectivity and latency. Perform a traceroute to identify the network path and pinpoint potential failures. Use nslookup to verify DNS settings and check if domain names can be resolved.

7. Check Firewall and Security Settings:

Ensure that firewalls or security software on devices or routers aren't blocking network traffic. Review firewall logs or security settings to identify any potential restrictions or misconfigurations.

8. Update Firmware and Software:

Check for firmware updates for routers, switches, and modems, and update them if available. Ensure that devices have the latest network drivers or software updates installed.

9. Seek Expert Assistance:

If you're unable to resolve the issue, consider consulting with network administrators, Internet Service Providers (ISPs), or IT professionals specializing in networking.

Remember, this is a general guide, and specific troubleshooting steps may vary depending on your network setup and equipment.

Now, let's talk about network troubleshooting tools that can help diagnose and resolve connectivity issues. These tools are commonly used and each has its purpose with advantages and disadvantages.

Ping (Packet Internet Groper) is a widely used tool that sends ICMP echo requests to a specified IP address or hostname. It measures round-trip time (RTT) and checks if a remote host is reachable. Ping can help identify network connectivity problems, packet loss, and latency issues.

A traceroute (or tracers on Windows) tracks the path packets take from your device to a target destination. It provides a list of intermediate routers or hops along the way and measures the time taken for packets to reach each hop. Traceroute can help pinpoint network congestion, routing problems, or bottlenecks.

The nslookup (Name Server Lookup) tool is used to query DNS (Domain Name System) servers and retrieve information about domain names, IP addresses, and other DNS records. It helps verify DNS resolutions and troubleshoot DNS-related issues, such as incorrect or missing DNS entries.

Netstat (Network Statistics) is a command-line tool that displays active network connections, open ports, and routing information on a device. It provides insights into network traffic, listening ports, and established connections. Netstat can help identify processes or services consuming bandwidth or potential security threats.

Wireshark is a powerful packet analyzer that captures and analyzes network traffic in real-time. It allows detailed inspection of network packets and can help identify the source of network problems, including packet loss, protocol errors, or suspicious activity. Wireshark is commonly used for advanced troubleshooting in complex network environments.

Port scanning tools, such as Nmap (Network Mapper), are used to discover open ports on a target device or network. Port scanners help identify services or applications running on specific ports, check for open or closed ports, and detect potential security vulnerabilities.

Network monitoring software, such as Nagios, Zabbix, or SolarWinds, continuously monitor network devices, bandwidth utilization, server availability, and other metrics. These tools provide comprehensive visibility into network performance and can alert administrators about potential issues.

Using these tools, network administrators can gather valuable information, diagnose connectivity problems, and implement appropriate solutions to ensure smooth network operation.

What about network problems? There are plenty of those, most of which you can troubleshoot at home. The following are some basic network issues and their solutions.

A slow or intermittent internet connection. First, check for bandwidth-consuming applications or downloads and limit their usage. Next, restart your modem, router, and devices. Upon startup, make sure your router's firmware is updated. If you are still having issues, check for signal interference from nearby devices or appliances. If all else fails, contact your Internet Service Provider (ISP) to troubleshoot potential line or service issues.

The Wi-Fi signal is weak or there are coverage issues. First, reposition your router to a central location for better coverage. Adjust the antenna orientation if applicable. Consider using Wi-Fi range extenders or additional access points if you feel it is too far. If this fails, upgrading to a more powerful router may be necessary.

The network device cannot connect to Wi-Fi. Ensure that Wi-Fi is enabled on the device. Verify the correct Wi-Fi network name (SSID) and password. Disable MAC address filtering on the router if enabled. Reset network settings on the device and reconnect to Wi-Fi.

There's a DNS resolution failure. Restart your router or modem. Use the command prompt or terminal to flush the DNS cache. Manually configure DNS servers, such as using Google DNS (8.8.8.8 and 8.8.4.4) or Cloudflare DNS (1.1.1.1 and 1.0.0.1). Check the router's DNS settings and ensure they are correct.

There's limited or no network connectivity. Verify cable connections and replace or reseat cables if necessary. Restart networking devices, including routers and switches. Disable and re-enable network adapters on affected devices. Update network drivers on devices if available. Run network diagnostic tools like ping or traceroute to identify potential issues.

There's an IP address conflict. Check if multiple network devices have the same static IP address. Set affected devices to obtain IP addresses automatically (DHCP). Configure DHCP server settings on the router to avoid IP conflicts.

A firewall or security software program is blocking network connections. Review firewall or security software settings to allow necessary network traffic. Temporarily disable the firewall or security software to test connectivity. Whitelist or create exceptions for network applications or services.

Inability to access a domain or website. Check if the website or domain is down for everyone using online tools or alternate devices. Clear browser cache and cookies. Flush DNS cache. Contact the website administrator if the issue persists.

Remember, network issues can have various causes and troubleshooting steps may vary. If you're unable to resolve the problem, consider seeking assistance from network administrators or IT professionals.

Chapter 3: Operating Systems and Software

3.1 Operating System Fundamentals

Windows 95 is an operating system developed by Microsoft and released in August 1995. It was a significant advancement over its predecessor, Windows 3.1, and introduced several new features, including the Start menu, taskbar, and plug-and-play functionality. Although Windows 95 is now considered outdated, it played a pivotal role in the history of personal computing.

Windows XP is an operating system developed by Microsoft and released in October 2001. It was the successor to Windows 2000 and was designed to provide a more user-friendly interface and improved stability. Windows XP introduced several significant features, including the new Start menu layout, the taskbar with quick access to commonly used programs, faster boot-up and shutdown times, and enhanced multimedia capabilities.

Windows XP was widely popular and remained in use for a long time, even after the release of its successors, Windows Vista, Windows 7, and Windows 8. It was known for its stability and compatibility with a wide range of software and hardware. However, Microsoft officially ended support for Windows XP on April 8, 2014, which means that it no longer receives security updates or technical assistance from Microsoft.

Windows 7 is an operating system developed by Microsoft and released in October 2009. It was the successor to Windows Vista and was designed to improve upon the criticisms and issues faced by its predecessor. Windows 7 introduced several notable features and enhancements, making it one of the most widely used Windows operating systems.

Some key features of Windows 7 include a redesigned taskbar with improved functionality and the introduction of Aero Peek, which allows users to preview open windows by hovering over the taskbar icons. It also included native support for touchscreens, improved performance and stability, enhanced security features such as BitLocker encryption, and the integration of Internet Explorer 8 as the default web browser.

Windows 7 gained popularity for its intuitive user interface, better hardware compatibility compared to Vista, and improved performance over previous versions of Windows. It remained a prevalent choice for many users until the release of Windows 8 in 2012.

Microsoft ended mainstream support for Windows 7 on January 13, 2015, and extended support on January 14, 2020. This means that Windows 7 no longer receives security updates and technical assistance from Microsoft. It is generally recommended to upgrade to a more recent and supported version of Windows, such as Windows 10.

Windows 8 and Windows 8.1 are operating systems developed by Microsoft and released in October 2012 and October 2013, respectively. They were the successors to Windows 7 and aimed to provide a more touch-centric user interface and enhanced performance.

One of the most notable changes in Windows 8 was the introduction of the Start screen, which replaced the traditional Start menu with a full-screen interface consisting of tiles. These tiles could display live updates and were designed to be easily navigated on touch-enabled devices, such as tablets.

Windows 8 also included various improvements under the hood, including faster boot times, improved energy efficiency, and better security features, such as Windows Defender antivirus software built-in by default.

Windows 8.1 was an update released a year later, which addressed some of the criticisms and feedback received from users regarding the initial release of Windows 8. It reintroduced the Start button, although it still led to the Start screen instead of a menu and allowed users to boot directly to the desktop environment. Windows 8.1 also included several updates and performance enhancements.

Despite the improvements, Windows 8 and 8.1 received mixed reviews and were met with some resistance due to the significant changes in the user interface. Many users found the full screen Start screen disruptive on traditional desktop computers. As a result, Windows 8 and 8.1 adoption rates were relatively slower compared to previous versions of Windows.

Microsoft ended mainstream support for both Windows 8 and 8.1 in January 2018 and extended support in January 2023. It is generally recommended to upgrade to a more recent and supported version of Windows, such as Windows 10.

Windows 10 is an operating system developed by Microsoft and released in July 2015. It is the successor to Windows 8.1 and aims to combine the best features of Windows 7 and Windows 8 while introducing new functionality and improvements.

Some key features of Windows 10 include a redesigned Start menu that incorporates elements from both Windows 7's Start menu and Windows 8's Start screen. It also includes the virtual assistant Cortana, Microsoft Edge as the default web browser, and the ability to create multiple virtual desktops for better organization.

Windows 10 introduced the concept of "universal apps," which are applications that can run on all devices using Windows 10, including PCs, tablets, and smartphones. It also introduced the Windows Store, which allows users to download applications, games, and other content directly onto their devices.

In terms of security, Windows 10 includes features such as Windows Hello for biometric authentication, improved Windows Defender antivirus software, and regular security updates delivered through Windows Update.

Windows 10 has been well-received and is currently the most widely used operating system globally. Microsoft continues to release regular updates and feature enhancements for Windows 10 to improve functionality and security.

Windows 11 is the latest major release of Microsoft's Windows NT operating system, released on October 5, 2021. It succeeded Windows 10 and is available for free for any Windows 10 devices that meet the new Windows 11 system requirements.

Windows 11 features major changes to the Windows shell influenced by the canceled Windows 10X, including a redesigned start menu, the replacement of its live tiles with a separate widgets panel on the taskbar, the ability to create tiled sets of windows that can be minimized and restored from the taskbar as a group, and new gaming technologies inherited from Xbox Series X and Series S such as Auto HDR and DirectStorage on compatible hardware.

Internet Explorer (IE) has been replaced by the Chromium-based Microsoft Edge as the default web browser, like its predecessor, Windows 10, and Microsoft Teams is integrated into the Windows shell. Microsoft also announced plans to allow more flexibility in software that can be distributed via the Microsoft Store and to support Android apps on Windows 11 (including a partnership with Amazon to make its app store available for the function).

Windows has always been about helping you work how you want, by offering flexibility of multiple windows and the ability to snap apps side by side. New in Windows 11, are the introductions of Snap Layouts, Snap Groups, and Desktops to provide an even more powerful way to multitask and stay on top of what you need to get done. Windows 11 also delivers the best PC gaming experiences yet and a faster way to get the information you care about.

Another operating system is macOS. The macOS is the operating system developed by Apple Inc. for their line of Macintosh computers. It was originally introduced in 1984 as Macintosh System Software and has undergone several major revisions since then. macOS provides a graphical user interface and a wide range of features and applications for users.

Some notable features of macOS include a clean and intuitive interface, seamless integration with other Apple devices and services, built-in security measures, and a robust ecosystem of productivity and creative software. macOS also supports features such as Siri, the voice-controlled virtual assistant, and iCloud, Apple's cloud storage and syncing service.

macOS has gone through multiple iterations, each with a different naming convention. Recent versions include macOS Mojave, macOS Catalina, macOS Big Sur, and macOS Monterey. These updates have brought new features, improvements, and performance enhancements to the operating system.

MacOS is specifically designed to run on Apple's Mac hardware, and it is not compatible with non-Apple computers or devices. It offers a visually appealing and user-friendly interface known for its sleek design and intuitive navigation. It includes the Dock, which provides easy access to applications, and the Finder, which functions as a file manager.

MacOS includes Siri, a voice-activated virtual assistant similar to those found on other platforms. Siri can perform various tasks, such as searching the web, answering questions, setting reminders, sending messages, and launching applications.

MacOS provides Continuity features that allow seamless integration between Apple devices. For example, you can start a task on your iPhone or iPad and continue it on your Mac. Handoff enables you to switch between devices while working on the same document or browsing session.

MacOS integrates with iCloud, Apple's cloud storage and synchronization service. iCloud enables users to store files, photos, and other data in the cloud and access them seamlessly from multiple devices.

It also features built-in backup software that allows users to easily back up their entire system or specific files to an external storage device. Time Machine enables easy recovery of files or the entire system in case of data loss or hardware failure.

MacOS places a strong emphasis on security and privacy. It includes features like Gatekeeper, which verifies the authenticity of apps, and FileVault, which encrypts your data. macOS also supports features like Intelligent Tracking Prevention and App Store sandboxing to enhance privacy.

MacOS provides a range of features to enhance multitasking and productivity. These include Mission Control, which provides a bird's eye view of all open windows and spaces, and Split View, which allows you to work with multiple apps side-by-side.

MacOS benefits from a diverse ecosystem of software applications. It supports a wide range of productivity apps, creative tools, video editing software, and more. The Mac App Store provides a centralized location to discover and download applications.

Another operating system is Linus. Linux is a family of open-source operating systems built on the Linux kernel, which was created by Linus Torvalds in 1991. Linux operating systems are popular among developers, server administrators, and tech enthusiasts due to their flexibility, stability, security, and ability to be customized.

Linux is free and open source, which means developers have access to its source code. This allows communities to contribute to its development, fix bugs, and improve the overall system. Linux is available in various distributions or distros, which are assortedflavors or versions of the operating system. Examples of popular Linux distros include Ubuntu, Fedora, Debian, CentOS, and Arch Linux. Each distribution may have different default software, user interfaces, package management systems, and philosophies, catering to diverse needs and user preferences.

Linux provides a powerful command-line interface where users can interact with the system directly through commands. The terminal allows for precise system control, automation, and scripting. Users can execute commands, manage files, install software, modify settings, and initiate system tasks using the CLI.

Linux uses package managers to install, update, and manage software packages. Package managers like apt-get (used in Debian-based distributions) and yum/dnf (used in Red Hat-based distributions) handle dependencies, resolve conflicts and simplify the process of software installation and maintenance. Linux follows a standardized file system hierarchy known as the Filesystem Hierarchy Standard (FHS). It organizes files and directories in a hierarchical structure, such as /home for user home directories, /etc for system configuration files and /var for variable data such as log files.

Security and Permissions: Linux provides robust security features and an access control system based on permissions. Each file and directory has permission settings for the owner, group, and others. Administrators can set read, write, and execute permissions, ensuring fine-grained control over system access and security. Linux is known for its stability and ability to handle multitasking efficiently. It supports true multitasking, allowing multiple processes to run simultaneously. Linux can efficiently manage system resources, allocate them to applications, and handle memory and process management, resulting in a reliable and stable system.

Linux is widely used as a server operating system due to its stability, security, and scalability. Many web servers, database servers, cloud infrastructure, and supercomputers run Linux. Additionally, Linux is prevalent in embedded devices, smartphones, routers, and IoT devices.

Linux encompasses a vast ecosystem with many variations and configurations, so this overview covers the general basics. Specific features can vary depending on the distribution and version of Linux.

3.2 Software Troubleshooting

Like with devices and other programs, there are step-by-step approaches with diagnosing and resolving software issues. The following describes some easy at home tips to try.

Step 1: Identify the problem.

Clearly understand and define the issue that you are experiencing. Gather as much information as possible about the symptoms, error messages, and any specific circumstances or actions that lead to the problem.

Step 2: Reproduce the problem.

Try to replicate the issue by following the same steps or triggering the same conditions that caused it initially. This will help you analyze the problem more effectively and determine the root cause.

Step 3: Check for common causes.

Review common causes for software issues such as incorrect input or configurations, software conflicts, outdated software, insufficient system resources, or hardware-related problems. Verify that all prerequisites and dependencies are met.

Step 4: Review error messages and logs

Examine any error messages, warnings, or logs related to the problem. These can provide valuable information about the cause of the issue or point you towards a specific component or code segment that needs attention.

Step 5: Conduct a system check.

Perform a comprehensive system check to ensure that all hardware components, drivers, and operating system settings are functioning correctly. Utilize appropriate system diagnostic tools to identify any underlying hardware or operating system problems.

Step 6: Update software.

Ensure that all involved software components are up to date. Check for available patches, bug fixes, or newer versions that might address the issue you are facing. Update the software and retest the problem.

Step 7: Validate configurations.

Verify that all software configurations and settings are accurate and in line with the recommended requirements. Pay special attention to network configuration, security settings, and access permissions.

Step 8: Test in a controlled environment

If possible, create a controlled environment to isolate the issue. This could involve using a test or staging environment with identical or similar configurations as the production environment. By testing in a controlled environment, you can eliminate variables and identify whether the issue is specific to the production environment or occurs elsewhere.

Step 9: Revert recent changes

If the issue started occurring after a recent change or update, consider reverting those changes to see if the problem resolves. This could involve rolling back updates, undoing configuration changes, or removing newly installed software.

Step 10: Seek online resources and support

Consult relevant online forums, knowledge bases, documentation, and support resources. Often, there are dedicated forums or communities where users share similar experiences and offer solutions or workarounds. Consider reaching out to the software vendor's support channels for assistance if necessary.

Step 11: Trial-and-error troubleshooting

If previous steps have not resolved the issue, you may need to try different troubleshooting techniques. This includes systematically disabling or enabling different components, modules, or integrations to identify the cause of the issue.

Step 12: Escalate and document

If you are unable to resolve the issue independently, escalate it to a higher level of support or involve subject matter experts. Provide detailed documentation of the steps you have taken, any error messages or logs encountered, and the expected versus actual behavior observed. This will help expedite the resolution process.

Remember that software issues can vary greatly in complexity and may require further expertise or collaboration to resolve. If you are not confident in completing the steps above or believe it is something complicated, it's always best to seek expert advice.

If you do attempt to troubleshoot your software, it is a good idea to familiarize yourself with some common software troubleshooting tools.

A task manager is a built-in utility in Windows that allows you to monitor and manage running processes, applications, and system performance. It provides information about CPU and memory usage, disk activity, and network performance. Task Manager is useful for identifying resource-intensive processes that may be causing software issues or slowing down the system. It also allows you to end unresponsive applications or processes.

An event viewer is another built-in Windows tool that records system events and error messages. It provides detailed logs and information about software and hardware issues, including application crashes, system startup failures, and driver problems. Event viewer helps in diagnosing software issues by analyzing error codes, warnings, and system events related to the problem.

Performance monitor, also known as PerfMon, is a Windows tool that monitors and analyzes system performance over time. It provides real-time and historical data on various performance counters, such as CPU usage, memory usage, disk activity, and network performance. Performance monitor allows you to identify performance bottlenecks or resource utilization issues that may be causing software problems.

Network Diagnostics Tools: Network diagnostics tools, such as Ping, Traceroute, and Network Monitor, help diagnose network-related software issues. Ping tests network connectivity by sending a signal to a specific IP address or domain. Traceroute traces the route network packets take to reach a destination, helping identify network hops causing latency or packet loss. Network Monitor captures and analyzes network traffic, enabling you to identify network-related issues or conflicts.

A dependency walker is a tool for diagnosing problems with missing or incorrect dependencies in executable files or DLLs. It scans the file's dependencies, verifying their existence and compatibility. This is useful when encountering errors related to missing or mismatched DLL files, which can cause software crashes or failures.

Debugging tools, such as gdb (GNU Debugger) for Linux or WinDbg for Windows, enable developers and advanced users to trace and debug software issues at a low level. These tools allow for step-by-step execution, setting breakpoints, inspecting variables, and analyzing memory dumps. Debugging tools are especially valuable for identifying and resolving complex software bugs or crashes.

System File Checker (SFC) is a built-in Windows tool that scans and repairs corrupted or missing system files. It checks the integrity of critical system files and replaces any corrupt files with a cached copy from the system. Running the SFC scan can help resolve software issues caused by corrupt system files, such as DLL errors or system crashes.

These are just a few examples of common software troubleshooting tools. The specific tools to use may vary depending on the operating system, the software being used, and the nature of the problem.

What can cause these software problems? There are a few different things, which can easily be checked and fixed.

The program is performing slowly. The solution is to check for excessive resource usage by using task manager or activity monitor to identify resource-intensive processes. Close unnecessary applications and consider upgrading hardware components like RAM or storage if needed. Perform regular system maintenance tasks like disk cleanup and defragmentation.

The application crashes. Ensure that your software is up to date, including any available patches or updates. Check for compatibility issues with the operating system or other software. Disable any conflicting plugins or extensions. If the problem persists, reinstall the software or contact the software vendor for support.

If there are software compatibility issues. Ensure that all system requirements, such as operating system version, hardware specifications, and software dependencies, are met. Update the software to the latest version, which may have addressed compatibility issues. Consider using virtualization or compatibility mode for older software. Reach out to the software developer or vendor for assistance if required.

When you get an error message. Read and understand the error message to gather information about the issue. Search for the error message online to find relevant solutions or troubleshooting steps provided by the software community or the vendor. Update the software to the latest version as it might include error fixes. If the problem persists, contact the software support team for further assistance.

There's a network connectivity issue. Check network cables, routers, and modem connections for physical faults. Restart your modem and router. Verify that the network settings are correct, such as IP address, DNS server, and proxy settings. Use network diagnostic tools such as Ping or Traceroute to identify any network issues. Contact your internet service provider (ISP) if the problem persists.

What if data become corrupted? Implement regular backups to protect against data loss. Use reliable storage media and ensure proper handling of files. Scan the storage device for errors using disk checking utilities. Use data recovery software to attempt recovery from corrupted files. Consider using file integrity checking tools to detect any changes in critical files.

Security vulnerabilities become a concern. Keep your software and operating system up to date with the latest security patches. Use reputable antivirus and antimalware software and keep them updated. Be cautious with downloading and installing software from untrusted sources. Enable firewalls and secure network connections. Regularly scan your system for malware and perform security audits.

You are notified of a licensing error. Ensure that you have a valid license for the software. Double-check that the license key or activation code is entered correctly. Check the software's licensing terms and verify that you are within the allowed usage period. Contact the software vendor if you are encountering activation errors or need assistance with licensing.

If you encounter persistent software problems that cannot be resolved using the suggested solutions, it is recommended to seek assistance from software support channels, such as forums, help documentation, or contact the software vendor directly.

Chapter 4: Mobile Devices

4.1 Mobile Device Hardware

Smartphones have become an essential part of our daily lives, offering a wide range of components and features that make them versatile and powerful devices. We use them from leisure to business to connecting with friends and family. But what makes smartphones work?

Smartphones run on operating systems such as Android or iOS, which provide the platform for all the features, apps, and services. These systems are updated often to accommodate changes and newer app features. These updates also extended the screen displays.

The display is a crucial component of a smartphone. It is usually an LCD or OLED screen, though OLED screens have become firmly established in the smartphone market. These displays range in size from around 4 to 7 inches or more, offering vibrant colors and high resolution for a great visual experience.

The processor, often referred to as the CPU (Central Processing Unit), is responsible for executing tasks and running applications. It determines the speed and efficiency of the smartphone. It's typically integrated into one larger chip called a SoC that handles many other key functions.

Like a computer, a smartphone also has memory chips that help keep these key functions saved. There are two types of memory for smartphones. RAM (Random Access Memory) which enables the device to multitask efficiently, while internal storage stores all your apps, files, and media. Additional storage capacity can be expanded through external microSD cards.

Let's discuss the battery. While battery life was once short-lived in a smartphone, now we have longer sustainability. Battery capacity is measured in milliampere-hours (mAh) and determines how long the smartphone can last on a single charge. Lithium-ion batteries are used in most of our modern-day smartphones.

Cameras have also changed. When we once had only rear cameras for capturing photos and videos, we now have front and various angle views. The quality and features of smartphone cameras have improved significantly, with multiple lenses, optical zoom, image stabilization, and advanced software for enhanced photography. With these improvements, DSLR cameras are becoming obsolete when compared to smartphones.

You will need ways to connect to the internet to use the greatest features offered. Smartphones offer various connectivity options, including Wi-Fi, Bluetooth, NFC (Near Field Communication), and cellular network connectivity for calls, messaging, and internet access. If you don't have access at home, a lot of businesses and public city buildings offer free internet.

What if you can't find your phone? What if you get lost? No worries. Smartphones come equipped with various sensors, such as GPS (Global Positioning System) for location tracking, accelerometer for screen rotation and motion detection, gyroscope for orientation tracking, proximity sensor for auto screen-off during calls, and ambient light sensor for adjusting screen brightness accordingly.

With all these technical abilities, one might worry about their security if their device is stolen. Many smartphones now incorporate biometric security measures like fingerprint sensors or facial recognition scanners to unlock the device securely. These extra measures have helped keep information safe from prying eyes.

The availability of a wide range of apps and software is a key feature of smartphones. Users can access various productivity apps, social media platforms, entertainment apps, games, and much more. Storage is a key component as to how many apps your phone can handle. However, there are external options available to help combat this.

Keep in mind that the above components and features may vary across different smartphone models. Manufacturers often differentiate their devices by introducing additional features like waterproofing, wireless charging, stereo speakers, and more. Be sure to do your research before buying a smartphone to ensure it is the one for you.

Smartphones aren't the only mobile device available. There are tablets. Tablets are portable devices that offer a larger screen size compared to smartphones while being more compact and lightweight than laptops. The hardware of a tablet also differs in some ways but is the same in others.

Tablets feature LCD or OLED displays with sizes ranging from around 7 to 13 inches, or even larger in some cases. The larger screen provides a more immersive experience for tasks like watching videos, gaming, or reading. The large screen does make it harder to type quickly or reply to large messages such as emails. A Bluetooth keyboard or voice-to-text is recommended.

Tablets are equipped with processors similar to those in smartphones, typically ARM-based chips or in some cases, Intel or AMD processors. These processors determine the speed and overall performance of the device.

Tablets have both RAM and internal storage. RAM allows for smooth multitasking, while internal storage is used to store apps, files, photos, and videos. Some tablets also offer expandable storage via microSD cards. These cards can be transferred to computers, laptops, and other devices to retrieve the information if needed.

A tablet battery should last longer, right? That's not necessarily true. While tablets include larger batteries compared to smartphones, the battery life varies and can be the same as a smartphone. This will depend on usage, but tablets are designed to provide extended usage time for tasks like web browsing, media consumption, and productivity.

What about the camera quality? Tablets usually have front and rear cameras, similar to smartphones. While the camera specifications may not be as advanced as those in high-end smartphones, they are sufficient for video calls, capturing photos, and recording videos.

Like smartphones, Tablets support various connectivity options, including Wi-Fi and Bluetooth. Additionally, some tablets offer cellular connectivity (3G/4G/5G) options, enabling them to access the internet and make calls without relying solely on Wi-Fi.

Tablets also feature sensors like GPS for location tracking, accelerometers for screen rotation and motion sensing, ambient light sensors for automatic brightness adjustment, and gyroscopes for orientation tracking. Some tablets may also include biometric sensors like fingerprint readers or facial recognition for secure device unlocking.

A tablet's interface depends on its operating system. Tablets run on operating systems like Android, iOS, or Windows, providing a user interface and access to apps and services specific to the platform. If you have a smartphone and tablet that run on the same system they can be connected to stay updated together.

Tablets include built-in speakers for audio playback. Some may even have stereo speakers for a more immersive sound experience. They also feature audio jacks or Bluetooth connectivity to connect external headphones or speakers.

Tablets generally have connectivity ports like USB-C or micro USB for charging, data transfer, and connecting peripherals. Some tablets may also include HDMI ports or SD card slots. Smartphones do not have these options.

It's important to remember that the features and specifications of tablets can vary across different models and manufacturers. Additionally, some tablets may offer additional features like stylus support, water and dust resistance, or detachable keyboards for enhanced productivity. Doing your research is important when considering purchasing a tablet.

There's more! Wearables are electronic devices that are designed to be worn on the body. They offer various functionalities and features to enhance user convenience and provide useful information.

Many wearables come with built-in displays, ranging from small LED or OLED screens to full-color touchscreens. The display provides visual feedback and allows users to interact with the device and view information such as time, notifications, and health data.

Here's where a lot of differences between smartphones, tablets, and wearables exist... sensors. Wearables incorporate a range of sensors to collect data and provide useful insights for your health and routine. The following are some features commonly found with most smartwatches:

- Accelerometer: Measures movement, orientation, and gestures.
- Gyroscope: Tracks rotation and orientation.
- Heart Rate Monitor: Measures the user's heart rate.
- GPS: Enables location tracking and navigation.
- Barometer: Measures atmospheric pressure and altitude.
- Ambient Light Sensor: Adjusts display brightness based on the surrounding light conditions.
- Thermometer: Measures body temperature or ambient temperature.
- Sleep Tracker: Monitors sleep patterns and quality.
- ECG (Electrocardiogram): Used to monitor heart activity.

These sensors have helped many people stay active and be mindful of their health. It also provides easy information to give to your healthcare provider about matters of sleep, heart, and activity. A smartphone and tablet cannot do this.

How do they stay connected? Wearable devices often offer wireless connectivity options, allowing them to connect and sync with smartphones, tablets, or computers. Bluetooth is commonly used for connecting to other devices, and some wearables may also have Wi-Fi or cellular connectivity for independent functionality.

A wearable's battery life varies. They have built-in batteries providing power for their operation. The battery life depends on the device and usage patterns. Some wearables need to be charged frequently, while others can last for several days or even weeks on a single charge.

The user interface of wearables can vary. Some devices use touchscreens for interaction, while others rely on physical buttons, rotating bezels, or voice commands. The interface allows users to navigate menus, access features, and interact with notifications and apps.

Notifications from connected smartphones can also be displayed on wearables, such as incoming calls, messages, emails, and social media updates. They can also provide vibrating alerts for alarms, reminders, and notifications without the need to check the connected device.

Some wearables offer smart features like music playback control, remote camera control, voice assistant integration (such as Siri or Google Assistant), and the ability to install and use third-party apps. These features enhance the overall functionality and convenience of the wearable device.

Wearable devices come in various forms such as smartwatches, fitness bands, smart glasses, smart rings, and even smart clothing. The design and form factors vary, allowing users to choose the one that best suits their preferences and requirements.

It's important to note that the specific components and functionalities of wearables may vary depending on the manufacturer, model, and intended use of the device. Newer wearables are constantly being developed, introducing innovative features and expanding the capabilities of these devices over time.

4.2 Mobile Device Operating Systems

The Android operating system is a mobile operating system developed by Google. It is designed to power a wide range of mobile devices such as smartphones, tablets, smartwatches, and televisions.

Androids offer a customizable and intuitive user interface. Users can personalize their home screens, widgets, wallpapers, and organize apps according to their preferences. They have a vast app ecosystem through Google Play Store, where users can download and install millions of applications for various purposes such as productivity, entertainment, communication, gaming, and more.

Android also allows multitasking, enabling users to run multiple apps simultaneously. It features a comprehensive notification system that alerts users about incoming messages, updates, and other events from installed applications.

Android devices are deeply integrated with various Google services, including Google Search, Google Maps, Gmail, Google Drive, Google Photos, and more. Google assistant, a virtual assistant that helps users perform tasks, answer questions, provide recommendations, and control various aspects of their device through voice command is also available. This integration enhances the overall functionality of Android devices, including wearables.

Want to make the device reflect your personality? No problem. Android offers extensive customization options, allowing users to personalize their devices to suit their preferences. Users can customize themes, icons, launchers, and even install custom ROMs for a unique user experience. And with multiple connectivity options, such as Wi-Fi, Bluetooth, and cellular networks, it's easy to keep all your Android devices synced.

With all these features, the designers knew they had better have strong security. Android incorporates various security measures to protect users' data and privacy. It includes features like app permissions, secure lock screen options, encryption, Google Play Protect (malware detection), and regular security updates. Security measures are continuously updated as providers are constantly looking at security advancements.

These are just a few of the many features and functionalities offered by the Android operating system. It is important to note that the exact set of features and functionalities may vary depending on the version of Android and the device manufacturer.

Another operating system is iOS. iOS is the mobile operating system developed by Apple for its range of devices such as iPhones, iPads, and iPod Touch. While their features are very similar to Android, they do differ some.

iOS offers a clean and user-friendly interface known for its simplicity and ease of use. The home screen consists of app icons. Users can swipe between screens to access their apps. iOS also has a dedicated app store that offers a wide selection of applications curated specifically for Apple devices.

iOS couldn't be outdone by Google Assist. Siri is Apple's virtual assistant integrated into iOS devices. Users can interact with Siri using voice commands to perform tasks, ask questions, set reminders, make calls, send messages, and more. Users can make Siri personal by choosing her accent and sexuality, giving it a unique experience.

Apple's cloud storage service, iCloud, is tightly integrated with iOS. It allows users to backup and sync their devices, store files, photos, and videos, and access them across multiple Apple devices seamlessly. Transferring data has never been easier.

With iOS, multitasking enables users to run multiple apps simultaneously. They can switch between apps quickly, use Split View and Slide Over to view multiple apps side by side, and even access a dock for easy app switching.

Ever forgot your wallet at home and had no money? No worries anymore if you are an iOS user. With the creation of Apple Pay, iOS devices support a contactless payment system that allows users to make secure transactions using their devices. With Face ID or Touch ID authentication, users can easily pay for goods and services in stores or within apps.

iOS is known for its strong security measures. It provides features like Face ID, Touch ID, and passcodes to protect devices from unauthorized access. Additionally, iOS consistently focuses on user privacy by implementing privacy controls and restrictions on data access by apps.

iOS devices offer seamless integration with other Apple devices through features like AirDrop and Continuity. AirDrop allows users to share files wirelessly between devices, while Continuity enables the continuity of tasks like picking up calls or transferring activities between devices.

Another excellent feature of iOS devices is their accessibility. iOS includes a comprehensive set of accessibility features to ensure that users with disabilities can use their devices effectively. It includes features like VoiceOver, AssistiveTouch, Magnifier, and more.

Like with all other devices, it's important to remember that iOS and its features may vary depending on the version of the operating system and the specific device model. When choosing a device, be sure to consult with a specialist if looking for specific features.

4.3 Mobile Device Troubleshooting

Like with all programs, even mobile devices can have their moments of trouble. Before taking it to the repair store, there are a few things you can do to troubleshoot it yourself.

Step 1: Identify the Problem

Begin by understanding the specific issue or symptom the mobile device is experiencing. Is it a software problem, hardware failure, or connectivity issue? Gather as much information as possible from the user regarding the symptoms, error messages, and when the issue started.

Step 2: Restart the Device

Many minor glitches and temporary software issues can be resolved by simply restarting the device. Ask the user to power off the device and then turn it back on after a few seconds. This can often resolve common issues like frozen screens or unresponsive apps.

Step 3: Update Software

Ensure that the mobile device's operating system, as well as all installed apps, are up to date. Outdated software can lead to compatibility problems and performance issues. Check for software updates in the device's settings and encourage the user to install any available updates.

Step 4: Clear Cache and Data

If a specific app is causing issues, clearing its cache and data can often resolve the problem. In the device's settings, locate the app causing trouble, go to its storage, and clear the cache and data. Note that this may log the user out of the app, so make sure they have any necessary login credentials.

Step 5: Check Storage Space

Insufficient storage space can lead to slow performance and crashes. Verify how much available storage the device has in the settings. If the storage is nearly full, suggest removing unnecessary files, apps, or media to free up space.

Step 6: Disable Unnecessary Apps

Sometimes, background apps or poorly optimized apps can cause performance problems. Ask the user to review and disable any unnecessary apps running in the background. This can be done through the device's app settings or using a task manager app.

Step 7: Test on Airplane Mode

If the issue is related to connectivity, test the device in airplane mode. This will help determine if the problem is with the mobile network or Wi-Fi connection. If the issue is resolved in airplane mode, the user may need to troubleshoot their network settings or contact their service provider.

Step 8: Perform a Factory Reset

If all else fails and the issue persists, a factory reset can help resolve persistent software problems. However, this should be the last resort, as it erases all data and settings on the device. Encourage the user to back up their important data before proceeding with the factory reset.

Step 9: Contact Support

If the above steps don't solve the problem, advise the user to contact the device manufacturer's support or their service provider for further assistance. They may be able to provide specific troubleshooting steps or recommend repair options.

Discuss common mobile device troubleshooting tools, such as device diagnostics and recovery modes.

Each device has troubleshooting tools to help diagnose and resolve issues. These tools were designed by the programmers for users to have more access to problem-solving. Technology can be a complicated beast, but it can also be as simple as a button push.

Many mobile devices have built-in diagnostic tools or apps that can perform tests on various hardware components like the display, battery, sensors, and connectivity. These diagnostics tools can provide insights into potential hardware problems and help identify the root cause of issues.

Recovery mode is a special bootable partition available on most mobile devices that allows users to perform advanced troubleshooting and system maintenance tasks. It provides options to wipe cache partitions, perform a factory reset, update firmware, or even install custom software or firmware. Accessing recovery mode differs among devices, but common methods involve holding specific buttons during device startup.

Safe mode is a troubleshooting mode that starts the device with only essential system apps and services, disabling all third-party apps. It helps determine if the issue is caused by a specific app or conflicts between apps. To enter safe mode, typically press and hold the power button, then long-press the "restart" option on the screen and confirm entering safe mode.

External diagnostic tools are hardware devices specifically designed to diagnose and repair mobile devices. These tools often offer more advanced testing capabilities, such as checking voltage, analyzing circuit boards, or measuring signal strength. They are commonly used by professional technicians or repair centers.

Android Debug Bridge (ADB) is a command-line tool used primarily for Android devices. It enables communication between a computer and an Android device, allowing for advanced troubleshooting, debugging, and even installing or uninstalling apps outside the regular user interface. ADB commands can be used to perform tasks like resetting a device, installing firmware updates, or accessing log files.

Mobile operating systems generate system logs that record information about device activities, errors, and events. Accessing system logs can provide valuable insights into software crashes, error messages, and resource usage. Various apps or tools are available to view and analyze system logs, such as Logcat for Android or Console for iOS.

Remember that some of these tools and methods may require technical knowledge or expertise. It's essential to follow proper instructions, consult documentation or guides specific to the device, and proceed with caution to avoid any accidental data loss or further damage to the device.

Other issues can be caused by settings, too many apps being open, or an array of other things. Here are some basic troubleshoots for common problems.

If your mobile device's battery drains quickly, there are a few different things you can try. Start by reducing the screen brightness and timeout duration. Limit background app refresh and push notifications. Disable unnecessary connectivity features like Wi-Fi, Bluetooth, or GPS when not in use. Close all unused apps running in the background. Consider replacing an old or faulty battery if the problem persists.

If your mobile device is slow or laggy, consider doing the following. Clear app cache and data for specific apps. Remove unused apps or files to free up storage space. Restart the device to clear temporary system files. Update the device's operating system and apps to the latest versions. After backing up important data, perform a factory reset as a last resort.

What if your device is overheating? Close power-hungry apps or games running in the background. Remove any protective cases that may block heat dissipation. Keep the device in a cooler environment and avoid direct sunlight. Disable unnecessary features or connectivity options. Perform a factory reset if the problem persists, as it could be due to a software issue.

For connectivity problems, attempt some of the following. Restart the device and the Wi-Fi router/modem. Verify that Wi-Fi is enabled and the correct network is selected. "Forget" and re-enter Wi-Fi network credentials. Move closer to the Wi-Fi router to ensure a stable signal. Reset network settings or perform a factory reset if all else fails.

If certain apps crash frequently or freeze update the app to the latest version available. Clear the app cache and data in the device settings. Uninstall and reinstall the app. Restart the device to clear any temporary system issues. Contact the app developer for support if the problem persists.

When the touchscreen becomes unresponsive clean the screen using a microfiber cloth to remove any smudges or dirt. Remove screen protectors or cases that might interfere with touch sensitivity. Restart the device or perform a soft reset. Update the device's firmware or operating system. Contact service or support if the problem persists or if it is a hardware issue.

If the above solutions don't resolve the problem, it may be necessary to seek professional assistance from the device manufacturer's support team or a qualified technician.

Chapter 5: Security

5.1 Security Fundamentals

Security threats and vulnerabilities can pose significant risks to computer systems, networks, and data. With so much information on our devices, it is important to stay on top of the latest security threats and how to combat them. The next section discusses common terms you may hear when researching security and ways to combat them.

Malware is malicious software such as viruses, worms, trojans, and ransomware. It can infect systems, disrupt operations, compromise data, and steal sensitive information. Hackers use malware to steal data and destroy computers.

Phishing attacks involve tricking users into revealing sensitive data like passwords, credit card information, or personal details by posing as a trustworthy entity. These attacks most commonly come in the form of fraudulent emails, websites, or text messages. What may appear real could be an easy fraud. It's always best to double-check the source if in doubt, especially when asked for sensitive information.

Denial-of-Service (DoS) attacks aim to overwhelm or exhaust system resources, such as computing power, network bandwidth, or application capacity. This causes a disruption or renders systems unavailable to legitimate users. This cyberattack keeps the legitimate host from accessing their information.

Cross-site scripting (XSS) is a vulnerability that occurs when malicious actors inject and execute malicious scripts into web pages viewed by users. This potentially leads to the theft of sensitive information or unauthorized account access.

SQL injection attacks exploit security vulnerabilities in web applications that process user-provided data to execute unauthorized SQL commands. This allows the attacker to manipulate databases, steal data, or gain unauthorized access.

You can never be careful with the people around you. Insider threats arise daily, whether from an employee or internal individual misusing their privileges or accessing sensitive information for personal gain, sabotage, or inadvertently causing security breaches. Always be sure to monitor your information and who you decide to share it with. Insider threats happen often and are the least expected from the victim.

Poorly implemented or weak password policies, including the absence of multi-factor authentication (MFA), can make it easier for attackers to gain unauthorized access to systems and sensitive data. The more complicated the password, the better. Most systems will inform you if your password is strong enough or not. Some may not even let you use a weak password at all.

Social engineering involves manipulating individuals through psychological manipulation or deception to trick them into revealing sensitive information, granting access, or performing actions that compromise security. This happens often when threats of stolen information are sent out and the receiver is asked to confirm their identity for protection. Once the receiver enters their information it is no longer safe.

Software vulnerabilities occur due to programming errors, design flaws, or outdated software versions. Attackers can exploit it to gain unauthorized access, disrupt services, or execute malicious code. It is always best to update software programs when they become available. Most updates offer a new security measure or may have an update to fix an old issue.

Failure to encrypt sensitive data, both at rest and in transit, increases the risk of unauthorized access or interception by attackers. It's essential for organizations to implement a comprehensive security strategy with measures such as regular software updates, robust access controls, employee training, network monitoring, and incident response plans to mitigate these threats and vulnerabilities effectively.

Security practices are crucial for both individuals and organizations to protect their systems, networks, and data. Individuals must know how to protect themselves. Businesses have to stay on top of security advancements to protect their customers.

The following are some tips individuals can do to protect themselves. Use a strong and unique password. Create complex passwords and avoid reusing them across multiple accounts. Consider using a password manager to securely store and generate passwords. If you write your passwords down make sure to keep them somewhere safe where others cannot see them.

Enable multi-factor authentication whenever possible to add an extra layer of security to your accounts by requiring additional verification beyond just a password. These authenticators are easy to use individually or for business. Also keep your operating systems, applications, and devices up to date with the latest security patches and updates. Enable automatic updates whenever possible.

Exercise caution with email and online communications. Be vigilant against phishing emails, spear-phishing, and suspicious attachments or links. Verify the sender's identity before sharing sensitive information. Although some of these communications seem legit it's always important to air on the side of caution.

Avoid using public wi-fi networks for transactions involving sensitive information. Open networks are an invitation for others to intrude on your system. If it is absolutely necessary, use a virtual private network (VPN) to create a secure connection.

Be sure to regularly back up your important files and data to an external storage device or a cloud service. This helps in case of data loss due to ransomware, hardware failure, or other incidents. The more you backup your files the less you are liable to lose.

Always install antivirus and anti-malware software. Use reputable security software to protect your devices from viruses, malware, and other malicious threats. Like with all devices, keep these programs updated. Antivirus companies are continuously updating their security to fight off attackers.

If you own an organization, or would like to know what type of security measures your company has, here are some common measures to a good security plan.

First, develop a comprehensive security policy. This should be established within the company's procedures. A strong security policy defines guidelines, procedures, and responsibilities to ensure a consistent approach to security across the organization. All employees should understand and implement these security measures at all times.

Educate and train all employees. Conduct regular security awareness training sessions to educate employees about security threats, best practices, and how to identify and respond to potential risks. A lot of companies will send out fake phishing emails to test employee. A lot of times if you click on the link within the email you will have to take the training again.

Also, restrict user access and privileges. Assign access rights and privileges based on the principle of least privilege (PoLP). Regularly review and revoke unnecessary access to prevent unauthorized actions. If access is needed for a guest, have a separate network for guests only.

As we've discussed before, regularly back up and test data. Implement automated and frequent data backups. Regularly test data restoration processes to ensure backups are accurate and functional. Use firewalls to monitor and control incoming and outgoing network traffic. Deploy intrusion detection/prevention systems to detect and respond to potential threats.

Conduct vulnerability assessments and penetration testing in your systems and networks. Perform penetration testing to identify weaknesses and simulate real-world attacks to strengthen defenses. Implement robust monitoring systems to track network traffic and log activity. Analyze logs and monitor for unusual or suspicious behavior that may indicate a security breach.

Always have a structured plan outlining the steps to be taken in response to a security incident. Regularly review and update the plan to adapt to new threats. Remember, security is an ongoing process, and it's crucial to stay informed about the latest threats, vulnerabilities, and best practices to ensure the highest level of protection.

5.2 Security Procedures and Data Disposal

Security procedures, such as incident response and user access control, are essential for maintaining the confidentiality, integrity, and availability of data and systems. It's good to understand these terms and when they are implemented.

Incident response refers to the set of procedures and practices followed in response to a security incident. It aims to minimize the impact of the incident, investigate its root cause, and prevent future occurrences. Incident response typically involves the following steps:

Step 1: Establishing an incident response team, defining roles and responsibilities, and creating an incident response plan.

Step 2: Monitor systems for signs of incidents, analyze alerts, and investigate potential security breaches.

Step 3: Isolate affected systems or networks to prevent further damage and limit the impact.

Step 4: Identify the source of the incident, remove any malicious components, and restore affected systems to a secure state.

Step 5: Restore normal operations, recover data, and implement measures to prevent similar incidents in the future.

Step 6: Reviewing the incident response process, identifying areas for improvement, and updating security controls and policies accordingly.

User access control involves managing and regulating user access to resources, systems, and data based on their roles, responsibilities, and authorization levels. It aims to prevent unauthorized access and ensure that users only have access to the resources they need to perform their tasks. There are several elements to access control.

Verifying the identity of users through usernames, passwords, biometrics, or multi-factor authentication methods. Assigning appropriate access privileges to users based on their roles, responsibilities, and the principle of least privilege.

Access management is always a good idea. Periodically reviewing and updating user access rights, disabling or removing access for terminated employees or individuals who no longer require it. Leaving old users with access is not only a risk, but it also takes up unnecessary storage. It's also important to implement additional controls and monitor privileged accounts since they have elevated access rights.

Also, log and audit user activities, record access attempts, and generate audit logs for security and compliance purposes. Organizations need to establish comprehensive security procedures, continuously monitor and improve them, and educate users about their roles and responsibilities in maintaining a secure environment.

Proper data disposal techniques are crucial to ensure data security and prevent unauthorized access or misuse of sensitive information. When organizations no longer require certain data, they must follow appropriate methods to dispose of it securely. There are certain types of recommendations.

For certain types of data storage, such as physical hard drives, tapes, or other media, physical destruction is the most reliable method. This can be achieved through methods like shredding, pulverizing, or incinerating the storage devices, rendering the data irretrievable. For digital data stored on electronic devices like hard drives, solid-state drives (SSDs), or USB drives, secure erasure techniques should be employed. This involves using specialized software that overwrites the data multiple times to make it virtually unrecoverable.

Degaussing is a method primarily used for magnetic media, erasing data by subjecting the media to a strong magnetic field. This process permanently removes the data, rendering it unreadable. This is a quick way to erase sensitive information at a lower cost.

Another method is data wiping which involves securely deleting data from a storage device using specialized software or utilities that overwrite the existing data with random information. Multiple passes of data overwriting may be used to ensure complete eradication. If sensitive data is encrypted, the secure disposal process can be simplified. Instead of relying solely on disposal methods, organizations can securely delete the encryption keys, making the encrypted data effectively unreadable.

Organizations can engage certified professional disposal services that specialize in data destruction. These services adhere to industry best practices, conform to security standards, and provide necessary documentation certifying the secure disposal. It is crucial to have clear data disposal policies and procedures in place within an organization. These policies should outline the steps to be followed when disposing of data and provide instructions on proper techniques. Documentation of the disposal process and records of which data was disposed of, when, and how is essential for audit purposes and regulatory compliance.

It is important to note that different types of data and storage media may require specific disposal methods. Organizations should always consult relevant laws, regulations, and industry best practices to determine the most appropriate data disposal techniques for their specific needs.

5.3 Security Troubleshooting

Some troubleshooting tasks can be related to issues within the network or system. The following is a step-by-step guide to finding security issues on your own.

Step 1: Identify the Issue

Gather information and evidence related to the security issue. Review logs, reports, and any available data. Determine the nature and scope of the security issue.

Step 2: Prioritize and Escalate

Evaluate the severity of the security issue. Determine the potential impact if left unresolved. Notify relevant stakeholders and escalate the issue as needed.

Step 3: Contain the Issue

Isolate affected systems, devices, or networks. Disable compromised accounts or privileges. Limit the potential for further damage or spread of the issue.

Step 4: Investigate and Analyze

Conduct a thorough investigation of the incident. Analyze logs, network traffic, and system behavior. Identify the root cause and any vulnerabilities exploited.

Step 5: Remediate and Patch

Develop and implement a plan to resolve the security issue. Apply patches, updates, or fixes to affected systems. Address the root cause and vulnerabilities identified.

Step 6: Monitor and Test

Implement monitoring tools or security solutions. Continuously monitor for any unusual or malicious activities. Conduct regular security testing and assessments.

Step 7: Communicate and Educate

Notify internal and external stakeholders about the incident and resolution. Provide guidance on best practices to prevent similar issues. Offer security awareness training and education initiatives.

Step 8: Learn and Improve

Document the incident and lessons learned. Review and update security policies, procedures, and controls. Continually improve security measures based on the incident.

Remember, depending on the specific security issue, you may need to involve security experts, forensic teams, or other specialists to assist with the diagnosis and resolution process.

There are common security tools, such as antivirus software and firewalls to help with security troubleshooting. These programs are highly recommended for securing your system.

Antivirus software is designed to detect and remove malicious software, such as viruses, worms, and Trojans, from computers and networks. It scans files, emails, and web pages for known patterns or behaviors commonly associated with malware.

Antivirus software often includes real-time protection that monitors system activity and alerts users if any suspicious or malicious activities are detected. Some popular antivirus software includes Norton, McAfee, Avast, and Bitdefender.

Firewalls act as a barrier between a trusted internal network and external networks, controlling incoming and outgoing network traffic based on predefined security rules. Firewalls can be either software-based or hardware-based.

They inspect network packets, filter traffic based on IP addresses, port numbers, and protocols, and can be configured to allow or deny certain types of network connections. Firewalls help protect against unauthorized access, network attacks, and data breaches. Examples of firewalls include Windows Firewall, Cisco ASA, and pfSense.

Intrusion Detection Systems (IDS) and Intrusion Prevention Systems (IPS) are security tools designed to detect and prevent unauthorized access, intrusion attempts, or malicious activities within a network. IDS monitors network traffic, analyzes patterns, and generates alerts for suspicious activities. IPS, in addition to detection, actively blocks or mitigates intrusions by taking preventative actions.

These tools play a vital role in identifying and responding to various types of attacks like DoS, DDoS, and port scans. Snort, Suricata, and Sourcefire are examples of popular IDS/IPS tools.

Vulnerability scanners scan networks or systems for potential security vulnerabilities and provide reports on identified weaknesses. They identify outdated software, misconfigurations, weak passwords, and other security flaws that could be exploited by attackers. Popular vulnerability scanning tools include Nexpose, OpenVAS, and Nessus.

Log analysis tools collect, analyze, and visualize log data from various sources, such as operating systems, applications, and network devices. These tools help in monitoring and identifying security events, anomalous behavior, and potential security incidents. Examples of log analysis tools include Splunk, ELK Stack (Elasticsearch, Logstash, and Kibana), and Graylog.

Network analyzers capture and analyze network traffic to investigate and troubleshoot security issues. They decode and inspect packets, allowing for the identification of network attacks, malware infections, and suspicious activities. Wireshark is a commonly used network analyzer.

It's important to keep in mind that while these tools can help troubleshoot security issues, they are not foolproof, and a layered approach to security, including regular updates, strong access controls, and user awareness, is essential for comprehensive security protection.

What can cause these security problems? Several common issues have solutions that are easy for the user to figure out. The next few paragraphs discuss these measures.

The first one we will discuss is weak passwords. Weak passwords make it easier for attackers to gain unauthorized access to systems or accounts. What's the solution? Enforce strong password policies, including minimum length, complexity requirements, and regular password updates. Implement multi-factor authentication (MFA) to add an extra layer of security.

Another security problem is phishing attacks. Phishing attacks deceive users into revealing sensitive information, such as usernames, passwords, or financial details. What's the solution to protect yourself? Educate users about recognizing and avoiding phishing emails or websites. Implement email filtering and anti-phishing software to detect and block malicious emails. Regularly update and patch software to fix any vulnerabilities that attackers could exploit.

Next are malware infections. Malware infections can damage systems, steal data, or provide attackers with backdoor access. What is the solution? Maintain up-to-date antivirus software and regularly scan systems for malware. Engage in safe browsing practices, avoid opening suspicious email attachments, and be cautious when downloading files from untrusted sources.

Another threat we've discussed is insider threats. Employees can cause insider threats intentionally or accidentally, compromising security. How can you protect yourself? Implement access controls and user permissions to restrict unauthorized access to sensitive data. Conduct regular employee training on security policies, emphasizing the significance of data protection and the consequences of insider threats. Monitor and audit user activities to identify any abnormal behaviors.

There's also unpatched software. Unpatched software can contain known vulnerabilities that attackers exploit to gain access or execute malicious activities. What's the solution? Have a regular patch management process in place to apply software updates, security patches, and bug fixes promptly. Use vulnerability scanners to identify unpatched software and prioritize patching based on criticality.

Lack of data encryption is another risk. Data transmitted and stored without encryption is vulnerable to interception or unauthorized access. What can you do? Utilize encryption technologies such as SSL/TLS for secure communication over networks. Encrypt sensitive data at rest using techniques like full-disk encryption or database-level encryption. Implement secure protocols and algorithms to safeguard data during transmission.

Weak network perimeter security is our next risk. Insufficient network perimeter security can allow unauthorized access, intrusions, or network-based attacks. What's the solution? Deploy firewalls, intrusion detection systems (IDS), and intrusion prevention systems (IPS) to monitor, filter, and block malicious network traffic. Implement strong access control mechanisms, such as virtual private networks (VPNs) and secure remote access protocols, to protect network boundaries.

A lack of security awareness can also be a problem. Insufficient security awareness among employees can lead to accidental security breaches or failure to recognize suspicious activities. What's the solution? Conduct regular security awareness training programs to educate employees about best practices, such as identifying phishing attacks, using strong passwords, and understanding social engineering tactics. Promote a culture of security awareness and encourage reporting of potential security incidents.

It's crucial to know that security is an ongoing process, and a proactive approach involving regular monitoring, risk assessments, updates, and user education is essential for maintaining a secure environment.

Chapter 6: Operational Procedures

6.1 Professionalism and Communication

Professionalism plays a crucial role in the IT industry, as it helps maintain a high standard of behavior, ethics, and quality of work. IT professionals often work with clients who rely on their expertise to solve complex technical issues and implement solutions. Demonstrating professionalism, such as being reliable, communicating effectively, and meeting deadlines, inspires trust and confidence in clients, leading to long-term relationships and repeat business.

In the IT industry, a professional reputation is highly valued. Professionals who conduct themselves with integrity, maintain confidentiality, and follow ethical practices build a strong reputation over time. This reputation not only attracts clients but also fosters collaboration and networking within the industry.

IT professionals are entrusted with sensitive data, company systems, and network security. Adhering to professional standards ensures compliance with legal and industry regulations, safeguarding against data breaches, cyber-attacks, and other security risks. Professionals who prioritize security demonstrate a commitment to protecting the interests of their clients and employers.

The IT industry is constantly evolving, with new technologies and methodologies emerging regularly. IT professionals who embody professionalism recognize the importance of ongoing learning and development to stay abreast of these changes. By investing time in professional growth, they can remain competent, adaptable, and valuable assets to their organizations.

IT projects often require collaboration among teams, both within and across organizations. Professionals who exhibit professionalism are more likely to engage in respectful communication, actively listen to others, and embrace teamwork. Such behavior fosters a positive work environment, enhances productivity, and encourages innovative problem-solving.

Professionalism encompasses more than just technical skills. It encompasses both technical competence and behavioral attributes, including effective communication, accountability, adaptability, and a commitment to quality. Overall, professionalism is crucial for building trust, maintaining ambitious standards, and driving success in the IT industry.

Effective communication is crucial for IT professionals as it facilitates collaboration, problem-solving, and understanding among team members, clients, and stakeholders. IT professionals deal with technical concepts and jargon that may be unfamiliar to others. Use clear and simple language to explain complex ideas, avoiding unnecessary technical terms. Break down information into digestible chunks and provide examples or analogies to enhance understanding.

Actively listening to others is vital for effective communication. Pay full attention to the speaker, ask clarifying questions, and paraphrase what you've understood before responding. This helps ensure that you correctly grasp the information being conveyed and show respect for the speaker.

Adapt your communication style and language to suit the audience you are addressing. Understand their level of technical knowledge and adjust your terminology accordingly. For non-technical stakeholders, use layman's terms to explain technical concepts and their implications.

When discussing technical solutions or changes, focus on the benefits and impact rather than solely on the technical details. Explain how the solution will address specific business needs, enhance efficiency, or improve user experience to engage the audience and garner support.

Incorporate visual aids such as diagrams, flowcharts, or presentations to support your communication. Visual representations help clarify complex ideas and can be valuable tools for conveying technical information effectively.

Keep all relevant parties informed of project progress, changes, or roadblocks in a timely and transparent manner. Regular updates through emails, meetings, or project management tools help manage expectations, foster trust, and maintain open lines of communication.

Clearly articulate roles, responsibilities, and expectations to minimize misunderstandings. Provide detailed instructions, documentation, or visual guides when necessary, ensuring that everyone understands their tasks and deliverables.

Pay attention to non-verbal cues, both in-person and virtual, as they contribute to effective communication. Maintain appropriate eye contact, use facial expressions, and adopt open body language during conversations or meetings. In virtual settings, utilize tools like video conferencing to enhance visual communication.

Offer and receive feedback constructively to improve communication within teams. Provide specific and actionable feedback while maintaining a supportive and respectful tone. Actively seek feedback from others to enhance your communication skills.

Create an environment where individuals feel comfortable approaching you with questions or concerns. Foster a culture of open communication, actively listening to others' perspectives, and demonstrating patience in addressing issues or challenges.

Remember, effective communication is a continuous process that requires practice, adaptability, and a willingness to refine and improve your skills over time.

6.2 Documentation and Change Management

Documentation plays a crucial role in software development and various domains to communicate information effectively. Documentation helps in transferring knowledge and information to different stakeholders, such as developers, users, and maintainers. It ensures that everyone involved can understand and utilize the project effectively, even if the original creator is no longer available.

Good documentation fosters collaboration among team members by providing a shared and accessible source of information. It allows team members to understand each other's work, contribute effectively, and solve problems collectively. Documentation aids in maintaining and extending codebases. It enables developers to comprehend the existing codebase and make changes without causing unintended side effects. It also helps in identifying obsolete or redundant code that can be removed.

Well-documented code and processes significantly reduce the likelihood of errors and bugs. Clear documentation allows developers to understand the code's intended behavior, resulting in better testing, debugging, and fewer issues during the development and maintenance phases.

Documentation serves as a valuable resource for onboarding new team members and enabling them to get up to speed quickly. It provides a structured overview of the project, its architecture, dependencies, and coding conventions, reducing the learning curve and promoting efficient knowledge acquisition.

Documentation helps users understand and utilize a product or system effectively. It provides instructions, FAQs, troubleshooting steps, and examples that can guide users in resolving issues independently. Clear and detailed documentation contributes to better user experience, customer satisfaction, and reduced support requests.

In regulated industries, documentation is often required to meet legal and compliance standards. Properly documented processes, data handling procedures, security measures, and privacy policies facilitate audits and certifications.

To ensure the effectiveness of documentation, following best practices is essential. Maintaining a consistent format, style, and structure throughout the documentation enhances readability and ease of navigation. Documentation should be clear, concise, and comprehensive. It should provide sufficient detail to guide users and developers effectively without overwhelming them.

Documentation should be kept up to date as the project evolves. Regular reviews and revisions allow for capturing changes, bug fixes, new features, and improvements. Ensure that documentation is easily accessible and searchable. Consider using a central repository or a knowledge base that is readily available to all team members and users.

By recognizing the importance of documentation and adhering to best practices, teams can promote effective knowledge sharing, enhance productivity, and build robust and maintainable projects.

Change management processes and procedures are crucial for organizations to effectively plan, implement, and manage changes in their operations, systems, policies, or procedures. Change management ensures that transitions are managed smoothly, minimizing risks and disruptions.

The change management process begins by identifying the need for change. This could be driven by internal factors such as process inefficiencies, external factors like technological advancements or market demands, or compliance requirements. Once the need for change is identified, change proposals are created. These proposals outline the objectives, scope, expected outcomes, and required resources for the change. It is important to involve relevant stakeholders during this stage for their input and feedback.

Before implementing any change, it is crucial to assess its potential impact on various aspects of the organization, such as processes, systems, employees, customers, and finances. This assessment helps in understanding the risks, benefits, and feasibility of the proposed change.

The next step involves creating a detailed plan for implementing the change. This plan should include a timeline, resource allocation, communication strategy, training needs, and a clear roadmap for executing the change. It should also consider potential contingencies and risk mitigation strategies.

Effective communication is essential throughout the change management process. Stakeholders, including employees, customers, and relevant external parties, should be informed and engaged to gain their support and facilitate a smooth transition. Regular updates and two-way communication channels help address concerns and manage expectations.

Depending on the nature of the change, training programs might be necessary to equip employees with the skills and knowledge required for the new processes or systems. Training should be well-planned, targeted, and delivered promptly to ensure a successful transition.

It is advisable to conduct testing or pilot programs before implementing changes on a wide scale. This allows organizations to identify and address issues or unforeseen consequences in a controlled environment. Feedback from the pilot phase helps fine-tune the change implementation strategy.

Once the testing phase is successful, the change is implemented across the organization. Monitoring should be done to ensure that the intended outcomes are achieved, and any issues or deviations are promptly addressed. Monitoring also helps in capturing lessons learned for future change initiatives.

After the change is implemented, it is important to evaluate its effectiveness and impact. This evaluation provides insights into the success of the change, identifies areas for improvement, and informs future change management efforts. Feedback loops and continuous improvement strategies should be established to adapt to evolving needs.

By following a systematic change management process, organizations can minimize resistance, navigate through uncertainties, and increase the likelihood of successful change implementation. Effective change management helps organizations remain agile, adapt to market dynamics, and stay ahead of competitors.

6.3 Safety Procedures

IT professionals play a critical role in ensuring the safety and security of data and systems within an organization. IT professionals implement access control mechanisms to restrict unauthorized access to sensitive systems and data. This involves assigning appropriate user privileges, implementing strong authentication mechanisms like multi-factor authentication, and regularly reviewing access permissions.

IT professionals enforce strong password policies that require employees to use complex passwords and regularly update them. They also encourage the use of password managers and provide education on password security best practices. They also implement firewalls, intrusion detection systems, and other network security measures to protect against unauthorized access and attacks. They regularly update and patch software and network devices to address vulnerabilities.

IT professionals establish regular data backup procedures to ensure that critical data can be recovered in the event of system failures, data corruption, or cyber-attacks. They also test the recovery process periodically to ensure its effectiveness. IT professionals conduct training sessions to educate employees about cybersecurity risks, common attack vectors, and best practices. They promote awareness about phishing emails, social engineering, and other techniques used by attackers to gain unauthorized access.

IT professionals develop incident response plans to respond to security incidents promptly and effectively. This includes procedures for detecting, responding, and mitigating incidents, as well as communication channels for reporting and escalation.

IT professionals ensure that all software and applications are regularly updated with the latest security patches and updates. This helps address known vulnerabilities and reduce the risk of exploitation. IT professionals implement tools and processes for continuous monitoring of systems and networks. This allows them to detect and respond to any suspicious activities or security breaches in real time.

IT professionals also address physical security concerns by restricting access to server rooms, data centers, and other critical IT infrastructure. They implement surveillance systems and access control mechanisms to prevent unauthorized physical access.

It's important to remember that safety procedures and protocols may vary depending on the organization's size, industry, and specific security requirements. IT professionals should continuously stay updated on the latest security trends and technologies to enhance safety measures.

Electrical safety practices and precautions are essential to prevent accidents, injuries, and even fatalities. Regular inspection and maintenance of electrical systems, including wires, circuits, outlets, and switches, is necessary to identify and address any potential hazards. This includes checking for frayed or damaged wires, loose connections, and overheating.

Electrical circuits and wiring should be installed and maintained by qualified professionals following local electrical codes and regulations. Proper grounding of electrical systems reduces the risk of electrical shocks and helps prevent electrical fires. Electrical circuits have a capacity limit, which should never be exceeded. Overloading can cause overheating, leading to fire hazards and damage to equipment. Avoid plugging too many appliances or devices into a single outlet or using extension cords excessively.

Always follow manufacturer instructions for the safe use of electrical equipment. Unplug devices when not in use, handle cords carefully to avoid damage, and never use equipment with worn-out or damaged cords or plugs.

Only authorized personnel should have access to electrical panels. Circuit breakers and fuses should be appropriately rated to protect against overcurrent and short circuits. Never tamper with or bypass circuit protection devices. Employees working with electrical systems or equipment should receive proper training in electrical safety practices, including understanding warning signs, using personal protective equipment (PPE), and responding to electrical emergencies.

Use of Ground Fault Circuit Interrupters (GFCIs) is crucial in areas where electricity and water can mix, such as kitchens, bathrooms, and outdoor spaces. GFCIs detect imbalances in electrical current and quickly shut off power to prevent electrical shocks.

When working on electrical systems or equipment, ensure proper lockout/tagout procedures are followed. This involves isolating and de-energizing equipment, locking it in the off position, and using tags to indicate that maintenance or repairs are in progress.

Have fire extinguishers readily available in areas with electrical equipment, and ensure employees are trained in their proper use. Avoid using water to extinguish electrical fires and instead use CO2 or dry chemical fire extinguishers.

Maintain a safe distance from overhead power lines to prevent accidental contact. Use caution when working near power lines and always assume the lines are energized. Remember, electrical safety is a shared responsibility, and everyone should actively participate in maintaining a safe environment. Regular safety audits, risk assessments, and compliance with local electrical codes are crucial to ensure electrical safety in both residential and professional settings.

Chapter 7: Practice Test

1. What does CPU stand for?
a) Central Processing Unit
b) Computer Processing Unit
c) Control Processing Unit

2. What is RAM short for?
a) Random Access Memory
b) Read-Only Memory
c) Random Algorithmic Memory

3. What is the purpose of an operating system?
a) To provide physical support for the computer
b) To manage hardware resources and provide a user interface
c) To prevent hackers from accessing the computer

4. Which programming language is used to create websites?
a) HTML
b) CSS
c) JavaScript

5. What is the function of a firewall?
a) To protect against viruses
b) To filter incoming and outgoing network traffic
c) To speed up internet connection

6. What is the purpose of a web browser?

a) To create websites
b) To search the internet
c) To regulate computer temperatures

7. What does HTML stand for?
a) Hyper Text Markup Language
b) Hyperlinks and Text Manipulation Language
c) Higher-Level Markup Language

8. What is the role of a modem?
a) To connect a computer to the internet
b) To store computer filcs
c) To display images on a monitor

9. What is a computer virus?
a) An electronic device that can infect computers
b) A type of malware that can replicate and cause harm
c) A physical damage to computer hardware

10. What is the function of an optical drive?
a) To read and write data from optical discs
b) To display images on a computer screen
c) To connect peripheral devices to a computer

11. What is the purpose of a motherboard?
a) To store and manage data
b) To provide power to the computer
c) To connect and communicate between all hardware components

12. What is the difference between ROM and RAM?
a) ROM is permanent memory, while RAM is temporary memory
b) ROM is faster than RAM
c) ROM is used for storage, while RAM is used for processing

13. What is the function of a graphics card?
a) To display images and videos on a monitor
b) To connect to the internet
c) To store computer files

14. What is an IP address used for?
a) To identify a specific computer or device on a network
b) To browse the internet
c) To send emails

15. What is the purpose of antivirus software?
a) To speed up your computer
b) To block unwanted incoming network traffic
c) To detect and remove malicious software

16. What is the difference between a hard disk drive (HDD) and a solid-state drive (SSD)?
a) HDD is faster than SSD
b) HDD has moving parts, while SSD is solid-state
c) HDD is used for temporary storage, while SSD is used for permanent storage

17. What is the function of a router?
a) To connect multiple computers to a network and provide internet access
b) To display images on a computer screen
c) To store computer programs

18. What is the purpose of a cache in a computer?
a) To store temporary data for quick access
b) To cool down the computer's temperature
c) To protect the computer from malware

19. What is the difference between LAN and WAN?
a) LAN is wireless, while WAN uses cables
b) LAN connects devices in a small area, while WAN connects devices across large distances
c) LAN is used for gaming, while WAN is used for internet browsing

20. What is the role of an operating system in a computer?
a) To provide physical support for the computer
b) To manage hardware resources and provide a user interface
c) To create and edit documents

21. What does SSD stand for in the context of computer storage?
a) Solid State Drive
b) System Storage Device
c) Software Storage Directory

22. What is the primary function of an input device?
a) To provide power to the computer
b) To display images and text
c) To enter data and instructions into the computer

23. What is the difference between software and hardware?
a) Software refers to physical components, while hardware refers to programs and applications
b) Software is intangible, while hardware refers to physical components
c) Software and hardware are essentially the same thing

24. What is the function of a wireless router?

a) To connect devices to the internet using cables
b) To transmit data wirelessly between devices on a network
c) To block unauthorized access to the network

25. What is the purpose of a spreadsheet program?
a) To create and edit text documents
b) To organize and analyze data in a tabular format
c) To create and edit images and graphics

26. Which of the following is a type of secondary storage in a computer?
a) Keyboard
b) Monitor
c) Hard Disk Drive (HDD)
d) CPU

27. What is the standard unit of measurement for data storage in computers?
a) Megahertz (MHz)
b) Gigabyte (GB)
c) Megabyte (MB)
d) Kilobyte (KB)

28. Which type of computer memory retains data even when the power is switched off?
a) RAM
b) ROM
c) CPU
d) GPU

29. Which type of computer port is used to connect external devices such as printers or keyboards?
a) USB (Universal Serial Bus) port
b) HDMI (High-Definition Multimedia Interface) port
c) Ethernet port
d) VGA (Video Graphics Array) port
30. Which of the following is an example of an output device?
a) Keyboard
b) Printer
c) Scanner
d) Mouse

31. Which device is responsible for converting digital signals into analog signals and vice versa?
a) Modem
b) Sound card
c) USB drive
d) Webcam

Answers:

1) A. Central Processing Unit
2) A. Random Access Memory
3) B. To manage hardware resources and provide a user interface
4) C. JavaScript
5) B. To filter incoming and outgoing network traffic
6) B. To search the internet
7) A. Hyper Text Markup Language
8) A. To connect a computer to the internet
9) B. A type of malware that can replicate and cause harm
10) A. To read and write data from optical discs
11) C. To connect and communicate between all hardware components
12) A. ROM is permanent memory, while RAM is temporary memory
13) A. To display images and videos on a monitor
14) A. To identify a specific computer or device on a network
15) C. To detect and remove malicious software
16) B. HDD has moving parts, while SSD is solid-state
17) A. To connect multiple computers to a network and provide internet access
18) A. To store temporary data for quick access
19) B. LAN connects devices in a small area, while WAN connects devices across large distances
20) B. To manage hardware resources and provide a user interface
21) A. Solid State Drive
22) C. To enter data and instructions into the computer
23) B. Software is intangible, while hardware refers to physical components
24) B. To transmit data wirelessly between devices on a network
25) B. To organize and analyze data in a tabular format
26) C. Hard Disk Drive (HDD)
27) B. Gigabyte (GB)
28) B. ROM
29) A. USB (Universal Serial Bus) port
30) B. Printer
31) A. Modem

Appendices:

ACLs: Access Control Lists

ADB: Android Debug Bridge

AGP: Accelerated Graphics Port

APs: Access Points

BGP: Border Gateway Protocol

BIOS: Basic Input/Output System

CAN: Campus Area Network

CCFLs: Cold Cathode Fluorescent Lamps

CMOS: Complementary Metal-Oxide-Semiconductor

CPU: Central Processing Unit

CRT: Cathode Ray Tube

DDR: Double Data Rate

DIMM: Dual In-Line Memory Module

DNS: Domain Name System

DoS: Denial-of-Service

DRAM: Dynamic Random Access Memory

DSL: Digital Subscriber Line

ECG: Electrocardiogram

ELK: Elasticsearch, Logstash, and Kibana

FHS: Filesystem Hierarchy Standard

FTP: File Transfer Protocol

GFCIs: Ground Fault Circuit Interrupters

GPS: Global Positioning System

GPU: Graphics Processing Unit

HDDs: Hard Disk Drives

HTTP: Hypertext Transfer Protocol

IDS: Intrusion Detection Systems

IP: Internet Protocol

IPS: Intrusion Prevention System

ISP: Internet Service Provider

LAN: Local Area Network

LCD: Liquid Crystal Display

LED: Light-Emitting Diode

MAC: Media Access Control

mAh: Milliampere-hours

MAN: Metropolitan Area Network

MFA: Multi-Factor Authentication

NAS: Network Attached Storage

NAT: Network Address Translation

NETSTAT: Network Statistics

NFC: Near Field Communication

NIC: Network Interface Card

Nmap: Network Mapper

OLED: Organic Light-Emitting Diode

OS: Operating System

OSI: Open Systems Interconnection

OSPF: Open Shortest Path First

PAN: Personal Area Network

PCI: Peripheral Component Interconnect

PCIe: Peripheral Component Interconnect Express

PING: Packet Internet Groper

PoLP: Principle of Least Privilege

PPE: Personal Protective Equipment

PSU: Power Supply Unit

QoS: Quality of Service

RAID: Redundant Array of Independent Disks

RAM: Random Access Memory

RIP: Routing Information Protocol

RTT: Round-Trip Time

SATA Ports: Serial ATA Ports

SDRAM: Synchronous Dynamic Random Access Memory

SFC: System File Checker

SODIMM: Small Outline Dual In-Line Memory Module

SRAM: Static Random Access Memory

SSDs: Solid-State Drives

SSHDs: Solid-State Hybrid Drives

SSIDs: Service Set Identifiers

TCP: Transmission Control Protocol

USB: Universal Serial Bus

VLAN: Virtual Local Area Network

VPN: Virtual Private Network

WAN: Wide Area Network

WPA2: Wi-Fi Protected Access II

XSS: Cross-Site Scripting

Glossary:

Accelerometer: Measures movement, orientation, and gestures.

Access Points: Access points are devices that enable wireless connectivity.

Ambient Light Sensor: Adjusts display brightness based on the surrounding light conditions.

Barometer: Measures atmospheric pressure and altitude.

Central Processing Unit (CPU): The CPU is often referred to as the "brain" of a computer system, as it performs most of the operations and calculations that are essential for the computer to function.

ECG: Used to monitor heart activity.

Enhanced Security: Many switches offer features like access control lists and port security to enhance network security by controlling access and preventing unauthorized devices from connecting.

Filtering and Forwarding: Switches maintain an internal MAC address table, allowing them to efficiently forward packets only to the intended recipient, reducing network congestion.

GPS: Enables location tracking and navigation.

Gyroscope: Tracks rotation and orientation.

Heart Rate Monitor: Measures the user's heart rate.

IP Addressing: An IP address is a unique numerical identifier assigned to each device connected to a network.

Local Area Network (LAN): A LAN is a network that connects devices within a limited geographical area, such as a home, office building, or campus.

Motherboard: The motherboard is the main circuit board of a computer system and acts as a platform that connects and allows communication between various hardware components.

Network Addressing: Routers use IP addresses to identify and route packets between different networks.

Network Segmentation: Routers allow for the creation of separate IP subnets, enabling network segmentation and isolation of traffic for security or performance purposes.

Packet Switching: Switches receive data packets and forward them to the appropriate destination based on the MAC address of the devices connected to the switch.

Protocols: Protocols are a set of rules and procedures that govern the exchange of data and communication between devices on a network.

Roaming Support: Access points in larger networks with multiple APs enable seamless roaming, allowing devices to switch between access points without interruptions.

Routers: Routers operate at the network layer of the OSI model.

Routing: Routers use protocols like RIP, OSPF, or BGP to determine the best path for forwarding packets based on IP addresses.

Security: Access points implement wireless security standards like WPA2 or WPA3 to protect the network from unauthorized access.

Sleep Tracker: Monitors sleep patterns and quality.

SSID Management: Access points provide network identification through SSIDs, allowing users to select and connect to the desired wireless network.

Subnetting: Subnetting is the process of dividing a network into smaller subnetworks or subnets.

Switches: Switches operate at the data link layer of the OSI model.

Thermometer: Measures body temperature or ambient temperature.

Traffic Management: Routers can prioritize traffic, implement Quality of Service policies, and incorporate features like traffic shaping or packet filtering for better network performance.

VLAN Support: Switches support the creation of VLANs, which enable logical segmentation and isolation of network traffic.

Wide Area Network (WAN): A WAN spans a larger geographical area, connecting devices across different locations and cities.

Wireless Connectivity: Access points create a wireless network by broadcasting a signal that allows devices like laptops, smartphones, or IoT devices to connect to the network.

Wireless Networks: Wireless networks, also known as Wi-Fi networks, enable devices to connect and communicate without physical wired connections.

GET YOUR BONUSES

Dear reader,

First and foremost, thank you for purchasing my book! Your support means the world to me, and I hope you find the information within valuable and helpful in your journey.

As a token of my appreciation, I have included some exclusive bonuses that will greatly benefit you.

To access these bonuses, scan the QR Code with your phone:

Once again, thank you for your support, and I wish you the best of luck in your Exam. I believe these bonuses will provide you with the tools and knowledge to excel.

Book 3

CompTIA Network+ Study Guide

Purpose of the Book

In the ever-evolving information technology landscape, networking forms the backbone of countless modern operations. As we delve into an era where connectivity is more crucial than ever, the significance of comprehensive and robust networking knowledge cannot be overstated. This is where the CompTIA Network+ certification gains prominence, standing as a testament to an individual's proficiency in understanding, maintaining, and troubleshooting various aspects of networking technology.

"CompTIA Network+ N10-008 Study Guide" is meticulously crafted with a singular objective: to provide an in-depth, easy-to-understand, and comprehensive guide for those aspiring to excel in the Network+ exam. This book is not just about passing an exam; it's a pathway to understanding the core concepts and practical applications of networking in the real world.

In the ever-evolving field of network technologies, staying updated is not just a choice but a necessity. The Network+ N10-008 exam has been updated to reflect these changing dynamics, focusing on contemporary networking technologies and practices. Our book comprehensively covers these new areas, ensuring that you are well-prepared not just for the exam but for a successful career in networking.

Whether you are an IT professional aiming to solidify your networking knowledge or a student stepping into the vast world of network technologies, this book guides you through the complexities and nuances of network concepts. It is designed to make learning engaging and effective, breaking down intricate topics into manageable sections that are easier to understand and remember.

We recognize the challenges learners face in retaining vast amounts of information and applying them in a high-pressure exam environment. Thus, this book is structured to facilitate easy learning, with each chapter dedicated to specific topics, filled with illustrations, real-world examples, and practical tips.

By the end of your journey through this book, you will not only be well-equipped to take on the Network+ N10-008 exam but also possess a solid foundation in network principles that will be invaluable in your professional life. Let this book be your companion in mastering the concepts necessary to become a certified network professional.

Welcome to your first step towards mastering the CompTIA Network+ N10-008. Let's embark on this journey together.

Introduction to CompTIA Network+ Certification

Certification Overview

The CompTIA Network+ certification is a pivotal milestone for professionals in information technology. This certification is not just a testament to one's knowledge; it's a gateway to understanding the core principles and practices of networking. In an industry where connectivity and network infrastructure play critical roles, having a Network+ certification showcases an individual's ability to manage, maintain, troubleshoot, and configure essential network infrastructure.

This certification is recognized globally and is often regarded as a foundational step in a networking career. It doesn't merely focus on a single vendor's hardware or software; instead, it provides a broad understanding of networking. This universal applicability makes the Network+ certification exceptionally valuable, ensuring that the knowledge gained is relevant across various platforms and technologies in the IT industry.

Benefits

The CompTIA Network+ certification opens numerous doors for IT professionals. One of the primary benefits is the enhancement of job opportunities. With this certification, you're not limited to a single role or industry. Network+ certified professionals are sought for roles such as network administrator, network analyst, IT consultant, and many more.

In terms of financial rewards, obtaining the Network+ certification can potentially lead to salary increases. As this certification demonstrates a robust understanding of network fundamentals and practices, employers often view Network+ certified professionals as valuable assets deserving higher compensation than their non-certified peers.

Additionally, this certification boosts professional credibility. It serves as an external validation of your skills and knowledge in networking, which can be a significant advantage in career growth and professional development.

Certification Path

The CompTIA Network+ certification is a stepping stone in the larger landscape of IT certifications. For many, it's the starting point for more advanced certifications and specialized roles in the IT industry. After achieving the Network+ certification, professionals often pursue higher-level certifications such as CompTIA Security+, CCNA, or specialized cloud computing or cybersecurity certifications.

Moreover, the Network+ certification fulfills prerequisites for other advanced certifications. It lays a solid foundation of networking knowledge essential for diving into more complex and specific areas of IT. In essence, it acts as a building block, enabling professionals to expand their expertise and advance their careers in various IT domains.

In conclusion, the CompTIA Network+ certification is more than just an exam; it's a key milestone in an IT professional's journey. It equips individuals with fundamental networking knowledge, opens up diverse career opportunities, and serves as a foundation for IT advancement.

Detailed Exam Structure

Understanding the structure of the CompTIA Network+ N10-008 exam is crucial for effective preparation and success. This section will explore the question formats, the scoring system, and provide targeted test-taking strategies.

Question Formats

The CompTIA Network+ exam incorporates a mix of question types to assess a wide range of skills and knowledge. The primary formats are:

Multiple-Choice Questions (MCQs): These are the most common and involve selecting the correct answer(s) from several options. They test your knowledge and understanding of networking concepts, principles, and best practices.
Example:
A network technician is setting up a subnet for four hosts. Which of the following subnet masks would provide the needed number of host addresses while minimizing waste?

A) 255.255.255.0
B) 255.255.255.192
C) 255.255.255.240
D) 255.255.255.248

Performance-Based Questions (PBQs): These interactive items test your problem-solving ability in a simulated environment. They may involve configuring network components, interpreting network configurations, or applying troubleshooting skills.
Example: You might be presented with a simulated network environment and asked to configure a router to meet specific network requirements.

Drag-and-Drop: In these questions, you need to place answers in the correct order or location. They often test your understanding of processes, sequences, or the categorization of components.
Example: Match the following networking protocols to their corresponding OSI layers by dragging and dropping the protocols to the appropriate layers.

Scoring

The CompTIA Network+ exam is scored on a scale of 100 to 900. To pass the exam, a candidate typically needs to score at least 720, although this number can vary slightly with different exam versions. It's important to note that CompTIA does not reveal how they weigh different questions, and some questions may be unscored pilot questions. Therefore, it's crucial to approach every question as if it counts toward your final score.

Test-Taking Strategies

When approaching the CompTIA Network+ exam, it's essential to have a strategy in place for managing the various types of questions you'll encounter. **Time Management** is crucial; allocate your time wisely during the exam. Performance-Based Questions (PBQs) are typically more time-consuming, so you might consider completing all the Multiple Choice Questions (MCQs) first. This approach ensures you cover as many questions as possible within the allotted time.

As you work through the exam, remember the importance of **Reading Questions Carefully**. Pay close attention to the details in each question. Often, keywords within the question can guide you to the correct answer. Being meticulous can significantly enhance your chances of selecting the right option.

It's important to keep **PBQ Strategies** in mind when taking the exam. Make sure you understand the task at hand before starting. For these performance-based questions, if you're unsure, it might be more strategic to move on and return to them later if time allows. This approach ensures that you don't spend too much time on one question at the expense of others.

Educated Guessing can be useful when you're unsure about an answer. Try to eliminate the options that are obviously incorrect. This method can significantly improve your chances of guessing correctly if you need to.

Make use of the exam's **Flag for Review** feature. This allows you to mark questions you are unsure about, making it easier to return to them later if you have additional time. It's a handy way to ensure you don't overlook any questions you might want to revisit.

Finally, it's important to **Stay Calm and Focused** throughout the exam. Maintaining a calm and positive mindset is crucial, as anxiety can impede your ability to recall information effectively. Remember that a clear mind is more likely to retrieve your studied information.

By understanding the exam structure and applying these strategies, you can approach the CompTIA Network+ exam with confidence, increasing your chances of success. Remember these tips, and you'll be well on your way to achieving a great result.

How to Use This Book

To maximize the benefits of the "CompTIA Network+ N10-008 Study Guide," it must be approached with a strategic plan. This section will guide you through creating an effective study plan, retention techniques to help you memorize and understand key concepts, and exam techniques to efficiently manage time and stress.

Study Strategies

When using this book to prepare for the CompTIA Network+ exam, a structured and strategic approach to studying is key to maximizing your understanding and retention of the material. To begin, **Create a Study Schedule**. Assess the time you have until your exam date and plan your study schedule accordingly. Break down your study time week by week, dedicating specific hours each day to study. It's crucial to ensure that your plan is realistic, allowing for breaks and time for revision. A well-structured schedule helps avoid last-minute cramming and ensures comprehensive material coverage.

Next, it's important to **Prioritize Topics**. Start with a self-assessment to identify your areas of strength and weakness. Focus more on the topics you're less familiar with while regularly revisiting those you are more comfortable with. This balanced approach helps reinforce your overall knowledge and boosts confidence in all areas.

As you dive into the book, adopt a **Chapter-by-Chapter Approach**. It's beneficial to tackle one chapter at a time. This book is structured to build your knowledge progressively. Following the order of the chapters ensures that you develop a strong foundation and understand the context of each topic.

To enhance your learning, **Combine Study Methods**. Don't rely solely on reading. Engage with the material in various ways, such as taking notes, watching instructional videos, participating in study groups, and utilizing flashcards. Different study methods cater to different learning styles and can help solidify your understanding.

Make sure to include **Regular Review Sessions** in your study plan. Regularly revisiting previously covered material is crucial for retention. These sessions help reinforce what you've learned and ensure that all topics remain fresh in your mind as you progress through the book.

Retention Techniques

To enhance your retention of the material as you prepare for the CompTIA Network+ exam, employing various retention techniques can be very beneficial. Firstly, **Active Reading** is a huge asset in memory retention. Engage deeply with the material as you read. This can involve highlighting key points, making notes in the margins, or summarizing each section in your own words. Active reading turns a passive activity into an interactive one, helping to cement your understanding of complex concepts.

Another effective method is the use of **Mnemonics**. Creating mnemonics can be a powerful tool for complex concepts or when you need to remember lists, models, or sequences. These memory aids simplify the process of recalling detailed information and can be a fun way to study.

A great way to solidify your understanding is to **Teach What You Learn**. Explaining the concepts you've learned to someone else not only reinforces your own understanding but also helps identify any areas that might need further clarification. Teaching is a way of learning twice.

Visualization can be particularly helpful, especially for subjects like networking. Creating diagrams or charts to visualize relationships between concepts is especially useful for understanding networking topologies and protocols. Visual aids can make complex information more accessible and easier to remember.

Exam Techniques

As you prepare for the CompTIA Network+ exam, it's not just about what you know; it's also about how you approach the exam. **Time Management** is a key factor. Developing a strategy for allocating your time during the exam is important. Since performance-based questions are typically more complex, plan to allocate more time for them. This ensures you have enough time to tackle these questions without rushing through the rest of the exam.

In addition to managing your time, it's equally important to manage stress. Learn and practice **Relaxation Techniques** such as deep breathing or mindfulness. These techniques can be very effective in managing stress before and during the exam, helping you maintain focus and composure.

Another crucial aspect is to **Simulate Exam Conditions** when taking practice tests. Try to make your practice as close to the actual exam as possible. This means timing yourself, limiting distractions, and following the same sequence as you would in the actual exam. Simulating the exam environment can help you adapt to the conditions of the exam day, reducing anxiety and improving performance.

Having a **Test-Day Plan** is also important. Be clear about the location of the exam center, understand what materials you need to bring, and be familiar with the exam's structure. Plan to arrive early to avoid any last-minute stress and to give yourself enough time to settle in.

Finally, have **Strategies for Tough Questions**. If you encounter a difficult question, avoid spending too much time on it. Instead, mark it for review and move on, then return to it if time allows. This approach ensures you don't miss out on answering questions you are confident about while still leaving time to address challenging ones.

By following these strategies and techniques, you can use this book to prepare for the CompTIA Network+ N10-008 exam. Remember, consistency and dedication are key to your success.

Chapter 1: Networking Concepts

Section 1: Networking Fundamentals

OSI Model

The Open Systems Interconnection (OSI) model is a conceptual framework for understanding network interactions in seven distinct layers. Each layer serves a specific function and communicates with the layers directly above and below it. Understanding the OSI model is incredibly important, as it helps in diagnosing network problems and designing efficient network solutions.

Physical Layer (Layer 1)

The Physical Layer, recognized as Layer 1 in the OSI model, plays a fundamental role in networking by dealing with the physical means of sending data over network devices. This layer is where the literal nuts and bolts of network communication reside, encompassing the tangible elements that constitute the backbone of any network.

At the Physical Layer, the focus is on hardware components and their specifications. This includes a wide array of equipment such as cables (like Ethernet cables and fiber optics), switches, hubs, and other physical means of data transmission. It's in this layer where the type of cabling, the layout of pins in connectors, and voltage levels are defined. The choice of medium can affect the speed, range, and reliability of data transmission, making this layer crucial for the overall network performance.

Additionally, this layer deals with devices like network adapters and host bus adapters, which are essential for interfacing computers with the network. The functionality of hubs and repeaters also falls under the purview of the Physical Layer. Hubs serve as basic data forwarding devices, transmitting data to all connected nodes without filtering or processing, while repeaters are used to regenerate and strengthen the signal over the same medium to extend the range of the network.

The Physical Layer is all about the electrical and physical representation of the system. It is the foundation upon which the higher layers of the OSI model are built. The effectiveness of this layer in accurately and efficiently translating data into signals and vice versa determines the quality of the communication over the network. Without a well-functioning Physical Layer, network reliability can be significantly compromised, leading to poor performance and connectivity issues. Therefore, understanding and ensuring the integrity of this layer is key to any robust and efficient network system.

Data Link Layer (Layer 2)

Layer 2 of the OSI model, known as the Data Link Layer, is pivotal in the networking framework. Its primary function revolves around node-to-node data transfer and error detection that originates in the physical layer. This layer takes the raw transmission facility provided by the Physical Layer and transforms it into a reliable link, ensuring that the data is transferred accurately and reliably.

One of the critical operations at the Data Link Layer is the framing of data. Framing involves encapsulating network layer data packets into frames and adding necessary headers and trailers for synchronization and error control. It's here that data packets are prepared for their journey across the network.

Additionally, the Data Link Layer manages MAC (Media Access Control) addressing. While the Physical Layer is concerned with transmitting bits over a medium, the Data Link Layer ensures that these bits are organized into frames and correctly addressed to their destination. MAC addresses are unique identifiers assigned to network interfaces, allowing for the identification of devices on the same physical network segment.

In terms of its role in networking, the Data Link Layer encompasses essential concepts like switching and MAC addresses. Switches, which primarily operate at this layer, use MAC addresses to forward data to the correct destination. Ethernet and PPP (Point-to-Point Protocol) operate at the Data Link Layer. Ethernet, for instance, is a core technology for local area networks, providing services at the Data Link Layer, such as frame transmission based on MAC addresses.

The efficiency and functionality of the Data Link Layer are crucial for the overall performance of the network. It ensures that data is not only accurately framed and addressed but also reliably transferred from one node to another. This layer acts as a bridge between the physical hardware and the more abstract layers above it, playing a key role in the actual implementation and operation of the network. Without a well-functioning Data Link Layer, data collisions and transmission errors could compromise network integrity and efficiency.

Network Layer (Layer 3)

Layer 3 of the OSI model, known as the Network Layer, is integral to the operation and efficiency of a network. Its primary function is to handle the routing of data across the network. This involves determining the best path for data transmission from source to destination, which is key for efficient and effective data communication, especially in large and complex networks.

A key aspect of the Network Layer is its responsibility for logical addressing. Unlike the Data Link Layer, which uses physical MAC addresses, the Network Layer utilizes logical addresses, such as IP addresses, to identify devices on a network. These addresses ensure that data packets are delivered to the correct destination, even when that destination is on a different network.

In the broader scope of networking, routers are the devices that primarily operate at the Network Layer. They are responsible for receiving, analyzing, and forwarding data packets based on their logical addressing. By doing so, routers play a pivotal role in directing traffic on the internet and within large corporate networks.

Additionally, the Network Layer encompasses various routing protocols, including IP (Internet Protocol) and ICMP (Internet Control Message Protocol). These protocols provide the rules and structures needed for routing data across networks. For instance, IP is responsible for defining how data packets are addressed and routed, while ICMP is used for sending error messages and operational information indicating success or failure in data transmission.

The Network Layer ensures that data reaches its intended destination across different networks. It decides the best path for data packets to traverse, considering network conditions, traffic load, and the distance between devices. This layer is where the network's ability to scale and handle complex routing decisions comes into play. Without an efficient Network Layer, the ability to send data across multiple networks - a cornerstone of modern networking - would be severely compromised.

Transport Layer (Layer 4)

Layer 4 of the OSI model, known as the Transport Layer, is crucial for facilitating end-to-end communication and efficient data transfer management in a network. Its primary function is ensuring data is transferred completely and accurately between systems. The Transport Layer achieves this through error checking and recovery mechanisms, playing a vital role in maintaining the integrity and reliability of data communication.

The Transport Layer is responsible for segmenting data from the system's application layer and reassembling it at the destination. This segmentation involves breaking down large data streams into smaller, manageable packets, which are then sent over the network and reassembled in the correct order at the receiving end. This process is essential for efficient network communication, especially when dealing with large amounts of data.

In terms of its role in networking, the Transport Layer includes critical protocols like TCP (Transmission Control Protocol) and UDP (User Datagram Protocol). TCP is known for its ability to provide reliable, ordered, and error-checked delivery of a stream of data between applications running on hosts on an IP network. It ensures that data packets are delivered in the correct order and retransmits lost packets. On the other hand, UDP is a simpler, connectionless protocol used for applications that require fast, efficient transmission, such as streaming audio and video. However, it does not guarantee delivery, order, or error checking.

The Transport Layer's management of data segments between the network and transport layers ensures reliable data transfer. It regulates the flow of data to prevent network congestion and uses error-checking mechanisms to verify that data is sent and received correctly. This layer is where you find the balance between speed and reliability in data transmission, making it a critical component in everyday internet usage and specialized applications.

The Transport Layer serves as a crucial link in the chain of data communication processes, ensuring that the applications on different computers can communicate in an error-free and efficient manner, regardless of the nature and state of the underlying network.

Session Layer (Layer 5)

Layer 5 of the OSI model, known as the Session Layer, is pivotal in network communication. Its fundamental function is to establish, manage, and terminate sessions between end-user applications. This layer is crucial for the smooth initiation and conclusion of communication sessions, facilitating effective and organized data exchange between applications running on different devices.

The Session Layer is responsible for managing dialog control between systems. This includes the control and synchronization of these dialogues or connections. It coordinates communication sessions, ensuring connections are established and maintained during the data exchange and properly terminated upon completion. This management includes tasks like authentication and reconnection after an interruption.

In a broader networking context, the Session Layer is vital in controlling computer dialogues. It oversees the establishment, management, and termination of connections for local and remote applications. For instance, when you log into a web application or start a file transfer, the Session Layer is involved in setting up and maintaining the session that allows these activities to occur. It ensures that each application receives the right information in a coordinated manner, maintaining the session's integrity.

Additionally, the Session Layer provides mechanisms for efficient data exchange, such as full-duplex, half-duplex, or simplex operation, and can establish checkpoints during a data transfer. In the event of transmission errors or interruptions, these checkpoints can resume data transmission from the last checkpoint rather than starting over.

The Session Layer is a critical component in the OSI model, facilitating seamless interaction and communication management between applications. Its ability to effectively establish, control, and terminate sessions directly impacts the reliability and efficiency of application-level communications across the network.

Presentation Layer (Layer 6)

Layer 6 of the OSI model, known as the Presentation Layer, plays a crucial role as the "translator" in the network communication process. Its core function is to format or present data in an understandable and usable way by the application layer. This layer is essentially responsible for the translation and transformation of data between the network and the application.

One of the key aspects of the Presentation Layer is its role in data encryption and decryption. It ensures that the data sent over the network is securely encrypted and that the received data is correctly decrypted into a usable format. This process is vital for maintaining data privacy and security across the network.

In addition to security, the Presentation Layer handles data compression and conversion. This includes tasks such as transforming data from one format to another (for example, from EBCDIC to ASCII) and compressing data to optimize transmission speed and bandwidth usage. By doing so, the Presentation Layer ensures that data is not only in the correct format but also optimized for efficient transmission.

The role of the Presentation Layer in networking is to act as a translator between the network and the applications. It converts network-formatted data into a format suitable for the application layer and vice versa. This layer ensures that the data received from the lower layers of the OSI model is in a format that the application layer can accept and use. For instance, when opening a JPEG image from the internet, the Presentation Layer translates the binary data from the network into a format that the image viewer application can interpret and display.

In summary, the Presentation Layer is essential in ensuring that data is correctly formatted, encrypted, decrypted, and compressed as needed. It bridges the gap between the application layer's requirements and the network's data format, playing an integral role in the smooth and secure communication between network systems and applications.

Application Layer (Layer 7)

Layer 7 of the OSI model, known as the Application Layer, is the layer closest to the end-user. It plays a pivotal role in network communication, where users interact directly with software applications. This layer essentially serves as the window through which users access network services, and it includes protocols and interfaces that applications use for communication.

The primary function of the Application Layer is to provide a set of interfaces and protocols that software applications can use to implement communication components. It facilitates the initiation of communication sessions, ensuring that user requests for network services are properly executed. This layer is where high-level data, such as documents, emails, or financial transactions, are processed into network communication.

The Application Layer provides network services directly to end-user applications in the broader networking context. It encompasses various standard communication protocols catering to different services and applications. For instance, HTTP (Hypertext Transfer Protocol) is used for web browsing, enabling users to access and interact with web pages. SMTP (Simple Mail Transfer Protocol) is used for sending and receiving email, and FTP (File Transfer Protocol) transfers files between systems.

The Application Layer is crucial because it provides the protocols and services used daily by businesses, consumers, and in various internet-based activities. It is the layer where network applications can access network services and perform user-oriented functions. These protocols are designed to be flexible and independent of the underlying network technologies, allowing the same application to function over different networks.

In essence, the Application Layer is where the network meets the user. It is responsible for handling user interface aspects and facilitating access to network services, making it an integral part of ensuring effective communication and data exchange in a networked environment.

Interaction Between Layers

In the OSI model, the interaction between layers is a dynamic and continuous process, essential for the smooth transmission of data across a network. This interaction begins at the uppermost layer of the model and moves down to the physical transmission of data, before traversing back up to the receiving end.

At the top of the OSI model, the **Application Layer** offers network services to end-user applications. When an application intends to send data, it communicates this to the **Presentation Layer**, which then translates this data into a format suitable for transmission over the network. This could involve encryption, data compression, or conversion between different data formats.

Once the data is formatted, it moves down to the **Session Layer**, where it's managed and coordinated into a communication session. This layer establishes, maintains, and terminates application connections, ensuring data flows smoothly between systems.

The formatted data is then passed to the **Transport Layer**, which is crucial for end-to-end communication. Data is segmented into smaller units, and necessary checks are implemented to ensure error-free transmission. This layer also controls the data flow to prevent congestion and ensures that segments are reassembled in the correct order at the destination.

Following this, the data reaches the **Network Layer**, where it is assigned logical addresses (like IP addresses). This layer determines the best physical path for the data to travel across the network, often across multiple nodes and networks.

Once the path is determined, the data moves to the **Data Link Layer**. The data is framed and assigned physical addresses (MAC addresses). This layer is responsible for node-to-node data transfer and error correction from the physical layer. This is where the data is prepared for physical transmission over the network.

Finally, the data reaches the **Physical Layer**. This layer transmits raw bits over a physical medium such as cables or radio waves. It converts the digital data into electrical, optical, or radio signals suitable for the transmission medium.

On the receiving end, this entire process happens in reverse. Data ascends from the Physical Layer up through the layers, each adding or extracting information, until it finally reaches the Application Layer in a form the receiving application can process and understand.

In essence, the layers of the OSI model work together in a highly coordinated way, ensuring that data is transmitted effectively and efficiently from one end of a network to another. Each layer plays its unique role, abstracting complexities for the layers above and relying on the functionalities below. This structured approach allows for more manageable network design and troubleshooting.

TCP/IP Model

While the OSI model provides a detailed and structured approach to understanding network layers, the TCP/IP model is a more simplified, practical framework used in actual network implementations. This model is based on a four-layer architecture, each corresponding to one or more layers of the OSI model.

Comparison with OSI Model

When comparing the TCP/IP model with the OSI model, several key differences become apparent, particularly in terms of simplicity, layer alignment, and practical application. The TCP/IP model, with its fewer layers, presents a less detailed and more streamlined approach than the OSI model, combining certain functionalities that the OSI model separates into distinct layers. This consolidation makes the TCP/IP model somewhat less granular but more straightforward for practical use.

In the OSI model, each layer has a specific function, such as the Physical Layer for physical transmission mediums and the Data Link Layer for node-to-node data transfer. However, in the TCP/IP model, these layers are merged. This merging is evident in how the TCP/IP model combines the functionalities of the OSI's Physical and Data Link layers, reflecting a more integrated approach to handling network protocols and data transmission.

One of the most significant aspects of the TCP/IP model is its practical application, particularly in how it aligns with the architecture of the Internet. The model was developed and refined based on the requirements of the early Internet, making it inherently suited to explaining and managing data transmission over Internet protocols. Its structure and design are closely tied to real-world Internet operation, from the basic transmission of data packets to the complex routing across diverse network infrastructures.

Overall, while the OSI model offers a more detailed and systematic framework for understanding network layers and their functions, the TCP/IP model provides a more pragmatic approach, especially useful for those working directly with internet-based technologies. Its less complex structure, combined with a focus on the practical aspects of network communication, makes the TCP/IP model a crucial framework for understanding how data is managed and transmitted in today's internet-centric world.

The Four-Layer Architecture

Link Layer (Network Interface Layer)

In the context of network models, the Link Layer, also known as the Network Interface Layer, plays a pivotal role in establishing and managing both physical and logical connections to the network. Corresponding closely with the Physical and Data Link layers of the OSI model, the Link Layer combines the functionalities of these two layers into a more integrated framework. It is responsible for various critical tasks, including framing of data, handling Media Access Control (MAC) addressing, and overseeing the physical transmission of data across the network.

The Link Layer's function is deeply intertwined with the actual hardware used in networking. It manages how data packets are formatted and addressed for transmission over physical media, such as copper wires, fiber optics, or wireless signals. The framing process involves the encapsulation of network layer packets, including the addition of headers and trailers that contain essential control information and error-checking data. This encapsulation ensures that the data can be correctly interpreted and processed by the receiving device.

Moreover, this layer deals with hardware addressing by using MAC addresses. These unique identifiers assigned to network interfaces play a crucial role in determining the destination of data packets within a local network segment. This hardware addressing is essential for delivering data to the correct device on a shared network medium.

In terms of its role in networking, the Link Layer encompasses various protocols that are fundamental to network communication, such as Ethernet for wired networks and PPP (Point-to-Point Protocol) for direct connections. Ethernet, in particular, is a widely used protocol in local area networks (LANs) and has been instrumental in standardizing the way data is transmitted over wired networks. These protocols define the rules and structures needed for transferring data reliably and efficiently over the network.

Internet Layer

The Internet Layer corresponds to the Network Layer of the OSI model and plays a crucial role in defining how data is logically addressed and routed across the network. This layer is where the Internet Protocol (IP), the backbone of the Internet, operates. The primary function of this layer is to handle the logical addressing of hosts, which is fundamental to ensuring that data packets reach their intended destinations correctly.

The Internet Protocol, or IP, provides unique identifiers known as IP addresses to each device on the network. These addresses are used to specify source and destination points for data packets as they travel across networks. The presence of an IP address on each packet ensures that the data can be correctly routed from its source to its destination, traversing multiple networks if necessary.

A key responsibility of this layer is routing, which involves determining the most efficient path for data to travel from one device to another. Routing decisions are made based on various factors such as network conditions, the quality of service requirements, and the destination IP address.

This process is vital in large-scale networks like the Internet, where data often needs to travel across multiple intermediary networks to reach its destination.

This layer is involved in handling various network protocols that determine how data is packaged, addressed, transmitted, routed, and received. These protocols ensure that despite the complexity of global networks, data can be sent and received reliably and efficiently.

Transport Layer

In the TCP/IP model, the Transport Layer, mirroring its counterpart in the OSI model, is tasked with ensuring efficient and error-free end-to-end communication. This layer is pivotal in managing how data is transmitted between systems across the network. It encompasses two fundamental protocols: TCP (Transmission Control Protocol) and UDP (User Datagram Protocol), each serving distinct communication needs.

TCP, renowned for its reliability, is designed to ensure that data is delivered accurately and in the correct order. It achieves this through error checking and confirmation of data delivery. If any segment of data fails to reach its destination, TCP mandates its retransmission. This protocol is ideal for applications where accuracy is critical, such as file transfers, web browsing, and email.

Conversely, UDP offers a quicker but less reliable communication method. It sends data without waiting for confirmation of receipt, thus sacrificing reliability for speed. This makes UDP suitable for applications where speed is more crucial than precision, like live video or audio streaming.

The role of the Transport Layer extends beyond simply choosing between TCP and UDP; it is instrumental in managing the data flow between network devices. This includes breaking down larger messages into smaller packets for transmission and ensuring they are correctly reassembled at the destination. The layer's ability to control the flow and sequencing of these packets prevents network congestion and ensures data integrity.

Furthermore, the Transport Layer handles crucial tasks like error detection and recovery. By checking for errors and ensuring data packets are received in the correct order, this layer maintains the integrity of communication. For instance, if a message is broken into multiple packets, the Transport Layer ensures these packets are reassembled in the correct sequence at the receiving end.

Application Layer

The Application Layer serves a comprehensive role by encompassing functionalities of three layers from the OSI model: the Session, Presentation, and Application Layers. This layer stands at the forefront of network communication, interfacing directly with end-user software applications to provide a wide range of network services.

The function of this layer is to enable those applications to access network resources. It utilizes various high-level protocols, each designed for specific network services. Protocols like HTTP (Hypertext Transfer Protocol) are used for web browsing, SMTP (Simple Mail Transfer Protocol) for email services, FTP (File Transfer Protocol) for file transfers, and DNS (Domain Name System) for resolving domain names to IP addresses. Each protocol defines rules and standards for how data should be transmitted and received across the network, making them fundamental to the operation of the Internet and other networks.

The Application Layer's role in networking extends beyond simply using these protocols; it also provides the crucial user interface for network communication. This layer translates the network services into a form that user applications can understand and interact with. For instance, when a user accesses a website, the Application Layer is responsible for initiating the HTTP request that fetches the webpage and then displaying it in a user-friendly format.

This layer acts as a bridge between the software applications and the lower-level network services provided by the layers below it. It abstracts the complexities of the network, allowing applications to send and receive data without needing to understand the underlying network technologies and protocols.

Interaction Between Layers

In the TCP/IP model, data transmission begins at the Application layer. It moves through the layers to the Link layer, then transmitted over a network. Each layer serves a specific function and prepares the data for the next layer. The receiving device processes this data from the Link to the Application layer.

Understanding the OSI and TCP/IP models is critical for networking professionals. The OSI model offers a detailed, theoretical framework for how networks operate, while the TCP/IP model provides a more practical, streamlined perspective that aligns closely with the protocols used in modern Internet-based networks.

Protocols and Ports

In networking, a protocol is a set of rules governing how data is transmitted over the network. Each protocol typically uses a specific port, which acts as a communication endpoint for different types of traffic. Understanding common protocols and their associated ports is crucial for network configuration and troubleshooting.

Common Protocols and Their Default Ports

HTTP (Hypertext Transfer Protocol)

Port: 80

Function: When you access a website through a web browser, HTTP is the underlying protocol that facilitates this interaction. Here's how it typically works: Your browser, acting as an HTTP client, sends an HTTP request to the server where the website is hosted. This request includes information about what the browser wants, such as retrieving a web page.

The server, upon receiving this HTTP request, processes it and sends back an HTTP response. This response contains the status of the request (like success or error codes) and any requested content. For instance, if you request a webpage, the server responds with the HTML, CSS, and JavaScript files necessary to render that page in your browser.

HTTP is a stateless protocol, meaning each request from a client to a server is independent; the server does not retain any session information between requests. This statelessness simplifies the server design because it doesn't need to keep track of the state of its interactions with each client.

Layer: Application Layer

HTTPS (HTTP Secure)

Port: 443

Function: HTTPS (Hypertext Transfer Protocol Secure) functions similarly to HTTP, with a critical addition: it incorporates security protocols such as SSL (Secure Sockets Layer) or TLS (Transport Layer Security) to encrypt communications. This secure version of HTTP is essential for safeguarding sensitive data exchanged during Internet transactions. When you engage in activities like online banking, shopping, or any service that requires the submission of personal information, HTTPS plays a crucial role in ensuring that the data exchanged between your browser and the server remains confidential and secure. By encrypting the data, HTTPS prevents unauthorized access, eavesdropping, and data tampering, making it a foundational technology for secure online communication and transactions.

Layer: Application Layer

FTP (File Transfer Protocol)

Port: 20 for data transfer, 21 for control (command) messages

Function: FTP is a key protocol for transferring files over a network or the internet. It allows for the upload and download of files between a client and a server. FTP is particularly useful for handling large files and for managing files on a server remotely. Users typically connect to an FTP server using a username and password, although anonymous FTP (without secure credentials) is also common. This protocol is essential in web development for uploading files to web servers, and in corporate networks, it facilitates file sharing and data backups.

Layer: Application Layer

SMTP (Simple Mail Transfer Protocol)

Port: 25

Function: SMTP is the cornerstone protocol for email transmission over the internet. It is specifically designed for sending and managing outgoing mail. When you send an email, your email client interacts with the SMTP server to handle the outgoing mail. The SMTP server then communicates with other SMTP servers to deliver the email to the correct inbox. Despite its simplicity, SMTP is incredibly efficient, supporting various types of mail servers and seamlessly integrating with other protocols for tasks like email routing and delivery.

Layer: Application Layer

DNS (Domain Name System)

Port: 53

Function: DNS functions as the internet's directory service, converting human-readable domain names into IP addresses that computers use to locate each other on the network. When you type a website address into your browser, DNS servers take that domain name and translate it into the numerical IP address of the website's server. This system is crucial for the functionality of the internet, as it allows users to access websites using easy-to-remember domain names instead of complex numeric IP addresses. DNS also plays a vital role in internet security and traffic routing.

Layer: Application Layer

DHCP (Dynamic Host Configuration Protocol)

Port: 67 for the server, 68 for the client

Function: DHCP is a network management protocol used for automatically assigning IP addresses and other communication parameters to devices on a network. By dynamically allocating IP addresses, DHCP eliminates the need for manual network configuration and helps prevent address conflicts. When a device connects to the network, DHCP assigns it a unique IP address and configures other network settings such as the subnet mask, default gateway, and DNS servers. This protocol is fundamental in large networks with numerous devices, ensuring seamless connectivity and network management.

Layer: Application Layer

SSH (Secure Shell)

Port: 22

Function: SSH is a cryptographic network protocol used for operating network services securely over an unsecured network. Predominantly, SSH is used for remote login and command execution, allowing users to securely access and manage servers over potentially insecure networks. It provides a secure channel over an unsecured network by encrypting the session, protecting the data from eavesdropping, connection hijacking, and other network-level attacks. SSH is a versatile tool used in many network operations, from system administration to file transfers with SFTP (SSH File Transfer Protocol).

Layer: Application Layer

Telnet

Port: 23

Function: Telnet, one of the earliest remote login protocols, is used to connect to remote devices or servers, primarily for running programs or accessing resources remotely. Unlike SSH, Telnet does not encrypt its data, which makes it vulnerable to interception and eavesdropping. This lack of security means Telnet is not recommended for use over the open internet or in any environment where security is a concern. Despite its security drawbacks, Telnet has historical significance and is still used in some closed, secure network environments for specific tasks that don't require secure data transmission.

Layer: Application Layer

IMAP (Internet Message Access Protocol)

Port: 143

Function: IMAP, renowned for its flexibility, is designed to manage emails directly on the email server. This protocol allows for multiple devices to access the same mailbox, making it ideal for today's mobile-centric world where users frequently switch between various devices like smartphones, tablets, and laptops. With IMAP, all changes made in the email client (like marking an email as read, deleting, or organizing into folders) are immediately reflected on the server. This real-time synchronization ensures that your email account presents a consistent state, regardless of which device is used to access it. Furthermore, IMAP supports complex operations like searching emails stored on the server and selectively downloading messages, thereby offering robust functionality for heavy email users and businesses that require efficient email management and accessibility.

Layer: Application Layer

POP3 (Post Office Protocol version 3)

Port: 110

Function: POP3, one of the oldest email retrieval protocols, operates on a download-and-delete model where emails are typically downloaded to a single device and then deleted from the server. This model suits users who prefer to store their emails locally and manage them from a single device. Once the emails are downloaded via POP3, they are accessible offline, and any subsequent email organization or management is confined to that device alone. While POP3 is simpler and less resource-intensive compared to IMAP, it lacks the ability to sync changes across multiple devices. As such, POP3 is a good choice for users with a straightforward email routine that involves accessing emails from a dedicated workstation or personal computer.

Layer: Application Layer

Importance of Protocols and Ports

Configuring firewalls based on port numbers and protocols is vital for effective network security and management. Protocols, each with its specific rules for data communication, dictate how information is transmitted across a network. Ports, serving as gateways for this data, are associated with specific protocols or services.

Knowledge of these default port assignments and protocol behaviors is essential for several reasons. It enables network professionals to configure firewalls to permit or block traffic, ensuring that only legitimate and necessary data is allowed. This selective filtering based on ports and protocols is key to preventing unauthorized access and maintaining network security.

Additionally, familiarity with protocol and port usage is critical in troubleshooting. Identifying whether the correct port is open and the appropriate protocol is being used can swiftly resolve connectivity issues. This knowledge assists in effective network monitoring, allowing professionals to spot unusual traffic patterns or potential security breaches quickly.

Routing and Switching

Routing and switching are fundamental aspects of network communication, playing crucial roles in directing data across a network. While routers manage traffic between different networks, switches manage traffic within a single network.

Role of Routers and Switches

Routers

Routers are pivotal in network communication, primarily functioning as devices that direct data packets between different networks. Their main task is to determine the optimal path for data to travel from its source to its intended destination, a process that is crucial for facilitating Internet connectivity. By analyzing the network conditions and available paths, routers ensure that data reaches its endpoint efficiently and reliably.

To accomplish this, routers employ routing tables and various routing protocols. These tools aid routers in deciding the most efficient path for data packet transmission across complex networks. Operating at the Network Layer (Layer 3) of the OSI model, routers handle logical addressing, such as IP addresses, which are essential for identifying the source and destination of data packets. This level of operation allows routers to interpret network addresses and route the data packets accordingly.

Beyond simply directing traffic, routers serve a key role in connecting different network segments. They manage the flow of traffic to prevent network congestion and ensure smooth data transmission. This includes performing packet filtering, where routers examine data packets and make decisions based on predefined rules, such as blocking certain types of traffic or prioritizing others. Additionally, routers can provide essential network security functions, offering a first line of defense against potential external threats. They can enforce security policies, filter traffic from suspicious sources, and protect the network from various cyberattacks.

Switches

Switches are fundamental networking devices that serve a critical role within single networks, such as Local Area Networks (LANs). Their primary function is to manage the flow of data across the network. This is achieved by receiving data packets and efficiently transmitting them to the intended device within the network. By doing so, switches facilitate smooth and organized communication among various networked devices.

Regarding their operational mechanics, switches function at the Data Link Layer (Layer 2) of the OSI model. This placement allows them to use MAC (Media Access Control) addresses and unique identifiers assigned to network interfaces. Switches utilize these MAC addresses to accurately forward data packets to the correct destination within the local network. This process is essential for ensuring that each device, whether it's a computer, printer, or server, receives the data intended for it without unnecessary data being sent to all devices on the network.

The key role of switches in networking extends to the very creation and maintenance of a network. They are instrumental in connecting multiple devices within a network segment, thus forming the backbone of a LAN. By linking these devices, switches enable them to communicate with each other effectively, share resources, and transfer data seamlessly. This connectivity is vital in various settings, from small home networks to large enterprise environments, where numerous devices must interact and exchange information reliably and efficiently.

Routing Algorithms

Routing algorithms play a pivotal role in the functionality of routers, enabling them to ascertain the most efficient route for data traversal across a network. These algorithms consider path length, available bandwidth, congestion levels, and network policies to optimize the data routing process. Understanding the common types of routing algorithms and their specific functionalities provides insight into how routers manage data traffic.

One such algorithm is the **Distance-Vector Routing Protocol, exemplified by RIP (Routing Information Protocol)**. This protocol type determines the best path based on the number of hops (or steps) and the direction to the destination. Distance-vector protocols are relatively simple and are best suited for smaller networks where frequent changes in network topology are less common. They periodically share updates between routers to ensure each router has a consistent network view.

In contrast, **Link-State Routing Protocols like OSPF (Open Shortest Path First)** offer a more dynamic approach. These protocols consider the state of the links, considering factors such as bandwidth and latency. They map the network's topology to determine the shortest or fastest path. Each router independently calculates the best path to every possible destination, leading to more efficient routing decisions in complex or constantly changing network environments.

For larger networks, particularly the Internet, **Path-Vector Protocols such as BGP (Border Gateway Protocol)** are used. These protocols are designed to consider not only the physical and technical aspects of the path but also the policy attributes. BGP is essential for exchanging routing information between different networks (autonomous systems), making it the backbone protocol of the internet. It enables routers to determine the best path based on extensive criteria, including network policies, which ensures efficient and stable data routing across diverse and vast networks.

Switching Techniques

Switching techniques are important for determining how data packets are managed and transmitted within a network infrastructure. These techniques vary depending on the desired balance between efficiency, speed, and accuracy in data transmission. Understanding these common switching methods provides insight into network performance and reliability.

Store-and-Forward Switching is one of the most traditional techniques. In this method, the switch stores the entire data packet in its buffers and performs an error check before forwarding it to the destination. While this method ensures that only error-free packets are forwarded, reducing the likelihood of transmission errors, it introduces a slight delay due to the time taken to process and check each packet. This delay can impact overall network speed but provides more data integrity.

Cut-Through Switching offers a faster approach. This technique involves the switch starting to forward the data packet as soon as it receives enough information to determine the destination address, typically just the packet's header. This leads to much faster transmission since the switch does not wait to receive and check the entire packet. However, this speed comes at the cost of potentially forwarding packets with errors, as no comprehensive error checking is performed.

Fragment-Free Switching presents a middle ground between store-and-forward and cut-through switching. It waits for the collision window (the first 64 bytes of the packet, which is the minimum packet size that can be collided) to pass before forwarding the packet. This method allows the switch to check for collisions and some errors in the initial part of the packet while still maintaining a faster transmission rate than store-and-forward switching. It offers a compromise between speed and reliability, reducing the chances of forwarding corrupted data compared to cut-through switching.

Understanding the roles of routers and switches, along with routing algorithms and switching techniques, is essential for effective network design, implementation, and troubleshooting. These components work together to ensure data is transmitted efficiently and accurately across local and wide area networks.

IP Addressing

IP addressing is a core element of network communication, crucial for identifying devices and facilitating data transmission. Understanding the differences between IPv4 and IPv6, along with concepts like subnetting, CIDR notation, and address assignment, is fundamental for network professionals.

IPv4 vs. IPv6

IPv4 (Internet Protocol version 4)

Structure: IPv4 is characterized by its 32-bit address system. These addresses are typically expressed in decimal format as four octets separated by periods, such as 192.168.1.1. This structure has been the backbone of internet addressing for several decades.

Address Space: IPv4 offers approximately 4.3 billion unique addresses. While this number initially seemed sufficient, the explosive growth of the internet and the proliferation of connected devices have led to the exhaustion of available IPv4 addresses, a significant challenge in network management.

Features: IPv4 includes several key features, such as subnetting, which allows the network to be partitioned into smaller segments, and address classes (Class A, B, C, D, E) for organizing the IP address space. To mitigate the issue of address exhaustion, IPv4 utilizes NAT (Network Address Translation), allowing multiple devices on a local network to share a single public IP address.

IPv6 (Internet Protocol version 6)

Structure: In contrast, IPv6 employs a 128-bit address system. These addresses are expressed in hexadecimal format and separated by colons, an example being

2001:0db8:85a3:0000:0000:8a2e:0370:7334. This expansion allows for a more complex and extensive addressing system.

Address Space: The shift to a 128-bit address system means that IPv6 provides an immensely larger pool of addresses. This effectively eliminates the problem of address exhaustion that plagues IPv4, future-proofing the protocol for the continuously expanding internet.

Features: IPv6 not only expands the address space but also introduces several enhancements. It simplifies address allocation and improves routing efficiency by reducing the size of routing tables. Additionally, IPv6 has integrated security features, notably IPSec (Internet Protocol Security), designed to provide end-to-end security at the IP layer by authenticating and encrypting each IP packet in a data stream.

Comparison:

The transition from IPv4 to IPv6 marks a significant evolution in internet technology. While IPv4's 32-bit addressing system has been foundational, its limited address space has become increasingly inadequate. IPv6 addresses this limitation with a vast address pool thanks to its 128-bit system, ensuring scalability for the foreseeable future. Additionally, IPv6 simplifies network configuration tasks and enhances security, which are critical aspects in modern networking. However, the widespread implementation of IPv6 has been gradual, with IPv4 still being widely used. This necessitates a dual-stack approach in many networks, where IPv4 and IPv6 are supported, ensuring seamless interoperability and transition between the two protocols.

Subnetting

Subnetting is a crucial technique in network management that involves dividing a larger network into multiple smaller networks, known as subnets. This process enhances network performance and security by segmenting a network into more manageable parts. One of the key benefits of subnetting is the more efficient use of IP addresses. By breaking down a large network into smaller subnets, IP addresses can be allocated in a way that reduces waste and maximizes utility. Additionally, subnetting helps in reducing network traffic congestion. By segregating networks, the volume of unnecessary traffic on each subnet is minimized, leading to improved overall network performance and reduced risk of network bottlenecks.

IPv4 Subnetting: In the realm of IPv4, subnetting is accomplished by manipulating the subnet mask. A subnet mask is a 32-bit number that masks an IP address and divides the IP address into network and host portions. By changing the subnet mask, network administrators can determine how many bits will be used for the network and how many for the host, effectively determining the network size. This allows precise control over network segmentation, addressing, and routing within the IPv4 space. It's a fundamental practice for optimizing network performance and ensuring efficient IP address usage, which is particularly important given the limited number of IPv4 addresses available.

IPv6 Subnetting: With IPv6, subnetting takes on a new dimension due to the protocol's significantly larger address space. The extensive size of IPv6 addresses offers more flexibility in subnetting practices. Typically, a /64 subnet is allocated for end-user networks. This allocation is standard practice and is recommended for most deployments, as it allows for a vast number of unique addresses within each subnet. The /64 subnetting ensures that each network segment has more than enough addresses for current and future needs without the risk of running out of addresses. This starkly contrasts with IPv4, where address conservation is often a primary concern. IPv6 subnetting simplifies network design and management, making it easier to implement hierarchical addressing and routing, which benefits large-scale networks.

CIDR Notation

Classless Inter-Domain Routing (CIDR) represents a significant advancement in the methodology for allocating IP addresses and routing IP packets. Developed to overcome the limitations of the older class-based IP addressing system, CIDR introduces a more flexible and efficient way of managing IP address spaces. This method is particularly crucial in the modern context, where the demand for IP addresses has exponentially increased due to the proliferation of internet-connected devices.

CIDR's format is distinctive and pragmatic. It is typically expressed as an IP address, followed by a slash, and then a number indicating the subnet mask length. For example, 192.168.1.0/24 represents an IP address (192.168.1.0) with a subnet mask length of 24 bits. This notation provides a concise way of representing a range of IP addresses grouped together, known as an IP block.

The purpose of CIDR is manifold, but one of its primary functions is to enable variable-length subnet masking (VLSM). This feature allows for more granular control over IP address allocation compared to the rigid boundaries set by the traditional class-based system. With VLSM, network administrators can divide an IP address space into subnets of varying sizes tailored to the specific needs of different network segments. This flexibility in subnet size allows for more precise and efficient use of IP address space, helping to delay IPv4 address exhaustion.

CIDR also simplifies routing. Aggregating routes into CIDR blocks reduces the size of routing tables in network routers, enhancing routing efficiency and performance. This consolidation of routes is particularly beneficial for the scalability of the internet's routing infrastructure.

Address Assignment Methodologies

In network configuration, various methodologies for IP address assignment are employed, each serving distinct scenarios and network scales. These methodologies range from manual interventions to fully automated configurations, balancing between control, efficiency, and ease of management.

Static IP Addressing is a traditional method where network administrators manually assign a specific, fixed IP address to each device on the network. This approach guarantees that a device always uses the same IP address, which can be crucial for servers, network printers, and other devices that need a consistent address for reliable access. However, in large networks, static IP addressing can become labor-intensive due to the need for manual configuration and management of every device's IP settings.

Dynamic IP Addressing, primarily facilitated by the Dynamic Host Configuration Protocol (DHCP), offers a more streamlined approach. DHCP servers automatically assign IP addresses to devices on the network. This dynamic assignment simplifies network management significantly, as IP addresses are allocated from a pool and assigned as devices connect to the network. DHCP is highly efficient in optimizing the available IP address pool, reducing manual workload, and minimizing the potential for address conflicts.

In scenarios where DHCP servers are unavailable, **APIPA (Automatic Private IP Addressing)** provides a fallback mechanism. Devices configured to use DHCP, upon failing to receive an IP address from a DHCP server, can automatically assign themselves an IP address from a designated range (169.254.0.1 to 169.254.255.254). While APIPA addresses enable basic network communication, they are limited to local network segments and do not provide internet connectivity.

For IPv6 networks, **SLAAC (Stateless Address Autoconfiguration)** is a prevalent method. SLAAC allows devices to autonomously configure their own IP addresses based on the network's prefix, which is advertised by routers, and their own hardware (MAC) address. This self-configuration capability, inherent to IPv6, eases network management and facilitates the seamless integration of devices into the network without requiring manual configuration or a DHCP server.

Each of these address assignment methodologies caters to different network requirements and scales, from the precise control of static IP addressing to the automated convenience of DHCP and SLAAC. The choice of methodology often depends on the specific needs of the network, such as the size of the network, the nature of the devices connected, and the desired level of administrative control.

Mastering IP addressing, including its different versions, subnetting practices, and address assignment methodologies, is vital for the design, deployment, and troubleshooting of modern networks.

Network Topologies

Physical Topologies
Physical topology in networking refers to the specific arrangement and physical layout of devices, cables, and other hardware components in a network. This layout significantly influences the network's performance, scalability, and fault tolerance. Different physical topologies offer distinct benefits and drawbacks, making them suitable for various network requirements.

Bus Topology: In a bus topology, all devices are connected to a single central cable, known as the bus. This setup is relatively simple and inexpensive to implement, requiring less cable length than other topologies. It's a straightforward design, suitable for small networks. However, bus topology has limitations in terms of size and scalability. A significant drawback is that a fault in the central cable can disrupt the entire network, making it less reliable for larger, more critical network implementations.

Star Topology: Star topology features a central hub or switch to which all network devices are connected. Each device has a dedicated cable to the hub, ensuring that if one cable or device fails, only that specific connection is affected, not the entire network. Star topology simplifies adding new devices and is generally easier to manage. The main disadvantage is the reliance on the central hub; if it fails, the entire network can be incapacitated. Additionally, this topology requires more cabling than a bus topology.

Ring Topology: In this setup, each network device is connected to exactly two other devices, forming a ring-like structure. One of the benefits of ring topology is the reliable data transfer it offers, even under heavy network load. However, the ring's integrity is crucial – a single failure in any cable or device can impact the entire network. Additionally, ring topology can be more challenging to troubleshoot and reconfigure than simpler topologies.

Mesh Topology: Mesh topology is characterized by a high level of interconnectivity among devices, with multiple redundant paths between any two nodes. This provides exceptional reliability and redundancy; if one connection fails, data can still be routed through alternative paths. However, the complexity and cost associated with mesh topology are significant, as it requires a substantial amount of cabling and network ports.

Tree Topology: Tree topology combines elements of both star and bus topologies. It structures multiple star-configured networks connected to a linear bus backbone. This hybrid approach offers scalability and ease of management. Networks can expand by adding more stars to the bus. However, the dependency on the backbone cable is a vulnerability – if it fails, it can disable an entire network branch.

Logical Topologies

Logical topology in networking is an abstract concept that focuses on how data is transmitted within a network, irrespective of the physical arrangement of the devices and cables. It's essential to network design, influencing data flow efficiency, network management, and overall communication effectiveness.

Bus Logical Topology: In this topology, data is broadcast to all nodes on the network but is only processed by the intended recipient, identified by its MAC (Media Access Control) address. This approach mirrors the physical bus topology, which connects devices to a single central cable. The primary benefit is its simplicity; however, the network can experience congestion as it grows, and a failure in the central communication line can disrupt the entire network.

Star Logical Topology: Data typically flows through a central hub or switch before reaching its destination. This centralization, characteristic of the physical star topology, allows the hub or switch to manage and direct data traffic effectively. One of the main advantages is the isolation of devices; if one connection fails, it doesn't impact the others. However, the central device becomes a critical point of the network – if it fails, the whole network can be affected.

Ring Logical Topology: In ring topology, data travels in a single direction from one device to the next and continues in a loop until it reaches its intended destination. This unidirectional flow, akin to its physical counterpart, ensures predictable data paths, which can be advantageous for troubleshooting. However, similar to the physical ring topology, the failure of a single device or connection can disrupt the entire network.

Point-to-Point: This topology involves a direct connection between two devices. It's a simple and reliable setup, often used for connecting a computer to a network peripheral or in WAN (Wide Area Network) scenarios for connecting two network nodes. While this topology is highly effective for small-scale or specific use cases, it lacks scalability and is impractical for larger networks due to the sheer number of required connections.

Logical topologies define the flow of data within a network and are crucial for understanding how network communication occurs. They help determine a network's efficiency and fault tolerance and play a significant role in network planning and troubleshooting. Each logical topology has unique advantages and constraints, influencing its use based on network requirements and objectives.

Each topology has unique characteristics that suit specific network environments and requirements. Understanding these differences is key to choosing the right topology for a given scenario.

Section 2: Network Types and Technologies

LAN/WAN/MAN

Understanding the differences between Local Area Networks (LANs), Wide Area Networks (WANs), and Metropolitan Area Networks (MANs) is crucial for grasping how different network types are optimized for various scales and use cases.

Local Area Network (LAN)

The scope and scale of a Local Area Network (LAN) are generally confined to a limited geographic area, such as an office building, educational institution, or a residential home. Typically, a LAN encompasses a small region, usually restricted to a single building or a group of closely situated buildings. This localized nature distinguishes it from wider networks, such as metropolitan area networks (MANs) or wide area networks (WANs), which cover larger geographic areas.

LANs are predominantly known for their high data transfer rates and relatively low latency. The proximity of devices within a LAN enables rapid data exchange, making it highly efficient for the network communication needs within its limited scope. Another defining characteristic of LANs is their ownership and management structure. They are usually owned, controlled, and managed by a single organization or individual, which allows for tailored network configuration, enhanced security, and streamlined management. This control contrasts larger networks, which might span multiple organizations and require more complex management and coordination.

The typical use cases for LANs revolve around connecting computers and various devices within a confined space to facilitate efficient and convenient internal communications. In a LAN setup, devices such as computers, printers, and servers are interconnected, allowing seamless file sharing, printer access, and local communications. For example, in an office environment, a LAN enables employees to connect to internal servers, share documents with colleagues, and access shared office resources like printers and scanners. In educational institutions, LANs allow students and faculty to access shared educational materials and institutional databases.

Furthermore, LANs often serve as the backbone of in-house communication systems, supporting various applications from simple office workflows to complex, data-intensive operations like video conferencing and collaborative software use. They also play a pivotal role in home networking, connecting personal devices and home appliances for shared internet access and multimedia streaming.

Wide Area Network (WAN)

Wide Area Networks (WANs) are expansive communication networks that cover a significantly larger geographical area than Local Area Networks (LANs), often extending across cities, states, or even spanning entire countries. The primary function of WANs is to interconnect multiple LANs, enabling them to communicate over vast distances. This broad scope makes WANs an essential component of global and regional communication infrastructures.

Unlike LANs, characterized by high data transfer rates and low latency due to their confined geographical spread, WANs typically experience slower data transfer rates and higher latency. This difference is primarily due to the greater distances data must travel and the more complex network infrastructure involved in WANs. Additionally, WANs usually operate over telecommunication circuits leased from service providers, as opposed to being owned and managed by a single organization. This reliance on external services for connectivity introduces unique challenges regarding network management, security, and reliability.

In terms of use cases, WANs are pivotal in connecting geographically dispersed entities. For instance, a multinational corporation might use a WAN to link its various offices around the globe. This interconnectivity allows for seamless resource sharing and communication, enabling remote branches to function cohesively as if they were locally connected. WANs facilitate not only internal communications within an organization but also external connectivity, such as connecting a business to the Internet or linking different institutions for collaborative projects.

WANs are instrumental in enabling large-scale business operations, educational collaborations, and government activities that require wide geographical coverage. They support various applications, from basic email communication and web browsing to complex cloud computing and real-time video conferencing across continents.

Metropolitan Area Network (MAN)

Metropolitan Area Networks (MANs) occupy a unique position in the network hierarchy, covering a geographical scope that is broader than Local Area Networks (LANs) but more confined than Wide Area Networks (WANs). Typically, MANs span across a city or a metropolitan area, bridging the gap between small-scale LANs and extensive WANs.

In terms of their characteristics, MANs often blend elements from both LANs and WANs. They frequently provide high-speed network connectivity, crucial for efficiently handling the diverse data and voice traffic typical in metropolitan settings. The ownership and operation of MANs can vary; in some cases, they might be managed by a single organization, while in others, they could be a collaborative effort involving multiple entities. This flexible approach to management allows MANs to be tailored to the specific needs of the area they serve.

Typical use cases of MANs reflect their intermediary scale. Local governments commonly employ them to interconnect public facilities, such as connecting various municipal offices, libraries, and emergency services, facilitating resource sharing and streamlined communication. Universities often use MANs for campus-wide connectivity, linking different buildings and facilities to enable seamless access to shared educational resources and internet connectivity. Additionally, Internet Service Providers (ISPs) utilize MANs to provide high-speed internet and network services within a city, offering robust connectivity to residential and commercial customers.

For example, a city might implement a MAN to integrate all its public libraries into a single network. This interconnection allows libraries to share digital resources, access centralized databases, and provide the public with consistent services across various locations. Similarly, universities use MANs to create interconnected campuses where students and faculty can access the same network resources, regardless of their specific location within the campus.

Understanding the distinct characteristics of each network type – LANs, MANs, and WANs – is crucial in network design and implementation. Each type is optimized for specific use cases, influenced by its geographic scale and scope. Recognizing these differences enables network designers and administrators to develop tailored solutions that meet the diverse requirements of different environments and applications, whether for small-scale local networks, citywide connectivity, or broader regional or global communication.

WLAN (Wireless Local Area Network)

Wireless Local Area Networks (WLANs) have become a cornerstone of modern networking, transforming how we connect to the internet and each other. Their rise to prominence is largely due to the flexibility and mobility they offer, a stark contrast to the constraints of traditional wired networks. The deployment and effective management of WLANs hinge on a comprehensive understanding of various wireless standards, security protocols, and configuration settings.

Wireless Standards (IEEE 802.11): The evolution of WLAN technology is marked by the development of several IEEE 802.11 standards, each building upon its predecessors to offer improved speed, range, and reliability.

- **802.11a:** This standard shifted WLAN technology by operating at 5 GHz, offering a maximum speed of 54 Mbps. The higher frequency allowed for less interference but at the cost of a shorter range compared to 2.4 GHz standards.
- **802.11b:** As one of the earliest widely-used WLAN standards, 802.11b operates at 2.4 GHz and provides speeds up to 11 Mbps. Its popularity stemmed from its wider range and compatibility with many devices, making it a standard choice for early home and office networks.
- **802.11g:** Building on the success of 802.11b, 802.11g maintained operation at 2.4 GHz but increased maximum speeds to 54 Mbps. This enhancement made it more suitable for applications requiring higher bandwidth while retaining backward compatibility with 802.11b devices.
- **802.11n (Wi-Fi 4):** A significant advancement came with 802.11n or Wi-Fi 4, which introduced MIMO (Multiple Input Multiple Output) technology. MIMO allowed for increased data throughput and range by using multiple antennas. Operating on both 2.4 GHz and 5 GHz bands, 802.11n offered speeds up to 600 Mbps, making it a versatile and powerful standard for home and business use.
- **802.11ac (Wi-Fi 5):** Focused on the 5 GHz band, 802.11ac, or Wi-Fi 5, brought potential speeds over 1 Gbps. It achieved this by utilizing wider channels, more spatial streams, and advanced modulation techniques. This standard significantly enhanced the capacity and speed of WLANs, catering to the increasing demand for high-bandwidth applications.
- **802.11ax (Wi-Fi 6):** The latest standard, 802.11ax, or Wi-Fi 6, is designed for increased efficiency, particularly in high-density areas. It offers improvements in speed and reduced latency, making it ideal for environments with many connected devices, such as smart homes, offices, and public hotspots.

In summary, as WLAN technology has evolved, each iteration of the IEEE 802.11 standards has brought significant advancements in speed, efficiency, and reliability. From the early days of 802.11b to the latest innovations in Wi-Fi 6, these standards have been pivotal in shaping the capabilities and applications of wireless networks. Understanding these standards is essential for anyone involved in the deployment and management of WLANs, as it directly impacts network design, performance optimization, and user experience.

Security Protocols

WEP (Wired Equivalent Privacy):

Description: An early encryption standard for wireless networks, now considered insecure and obsolete.

1. **WPA (Wi-Fi Protected Access)**:
    - **Description**: Improved upon WEP's weaknesses, providing better security through Temporal Key Integrity Protocol (TKIP).
2. **WPA2**:
    - **Description**: Introduced AES (Advanced Encryption Standard) for encryption, significantly enhancing security.
    - **Versions**: Includes WPA2-Personal (for home and small office use) and WPA2-Enterprise (for enterprise networks).
3. **WPA3**:
    - **Description**: The latest standard, providing stronger encryption and improved protection against brute-force attacks.

Configuration

Setting up a WLAN involves several key steps:

1. **Choosing the Right Hardware**: Selecting access points and routers that support desired speeds and standards (e.g., Wi-Fi 6 compatible devices).
2. **Placement and Range**: Optimally placing access points to ensure adequate coverage, considering obstacles that can interfere with the signal.
3. **Setting Up Security**: Configuring robust security settings, including selecting WPA3 for encryption, setting strong passwords, and enabling network firewalls.
4. **SSID Configuration**: Setting up and possibly hiding the Service Set Identifier (SSID) to identify the network while potentially making it less visible to unauthorized users.
5. **Channel and Bandwidth Selection**: Choosing the right channel and bandwidth to minimize interference and optimize performance, especially in areas with many overlapping networks.
6. **Guest Networks**: Configuring separate guest networks to provide visitors with internet access while keeping the main network secure.

Effective WLAN setup and management require a balance of performance, security, and usability, ensuring that the network meets the needs of its users while protecting against potential threats.

SAN (Storage Area Network) and PAN (Personal Area Network)

While SAN and PAN serve very different purposes, they are both essential components of modern networking, catering to specific needs in terms of data storage and personal device connectivity, respectively.

SAN (Storage Area Network)

A Storage Area Network (SAN) is a specialized, high-performance network designed explicitly for data storage. SANs play a crucial role in enterprise environments where the need for large-scale data storage, coupled with rapid access to this data, is paramount. The primary purpose of a SAN is to enable various storage devices, like disk arrays and tape libraries, to be connected to and accessible by multiple servers. This setup allows for a highly efficient storage management system, segregating storage traffic from the rest of the LAN.

Setup of a SAN:

- **Network Infrastructure:** SANs typically utilize a fiber channel fabric topology. This infrastructure choice is instrumental in providing high-speed data transfer rates and reliable connectivity, essential for handling large volumes of data and ensuring quick access.
- **Storage Devices:** In a SAN, multiple storage devices are often configured redundantly. This redundancy is key to ensuring data availability and effective disaster recovery. By having multiple copies of data, SANs protect against data loss and ensure continuity of operations.
- **SAN Switches:** To connect the storage devices with the servers, SANs employ specialized switches. These switches are designed to handle the high data throughput and are central to the SAN architecture, facilitating the communication between servers and storage devices.
- **Host Bus Adapters (HBAs):** Servers in a SAN environment are equipped with Host Bus Adapters. HBAs are critical for facilitating communication over the fiber channel, allowing servers to connect to the SAN's networked storage resources.
- **Management Software:** The operation of a SAN requires robust management software. This software is responsible for handling tasks like storage allocation, performance monitoring, and ensuring data integrity. It gives administrators the tools to manage the storage landscape efficiently, from provisioning to ensuring optimal performance.

Use Cases of SANs:

SANs are particularly suited for applications that demand high-speed data access and centralized management of large-scale storage. They are commonly used in settings with large databases, as rapid data retrieval and high storage capacity are essential for these applications. SANs also find extensive use in managing virtual machine file systems, where they provide the necessary performance and scalability. Additionally, in environments with high transaction processing demands, such as financial services or large e-commerce platforms, SANs offer the robustness and speed required for smooth operations.

In summary, SANs represent an advanced approach to network storage, offering distinct advantages in speed, scalability, and efficiency. Their role in enterprise environments is invaluable, especially when managing vast amounts of data quickly and reliably is critical. The architecture of a SAN, from its network infrastructure to its management software, is carefully designed to optimize storage performance and reliability, making it a key component in today's data-driven organizations.

PAN (Personal Area Network)

A Personal Area Network (PAN) is a network setup designed primarily for personal use and is typically effective within a small area, usually spanning only a few meters. The primary purpose of a PAN is to connect various personal devices - such as computers, smartphones, tablets, and wearable devices - allowing them to communicate and share data seamlessly within a close proximity. This type of network is particularly useful for individual users looking to integrate their electronic devices for increased convenience and functionality.

Setup of a PAN:

- **Connectivity:** PANs frequently employ wireless technologies for connectivity. The most common among these are Bluetooth and Wi-Fi Direct. These technologies are preferred for their ease of use and the ability to create ad-hoc networks without the need for additional networking hardware.
- **Device Pairing:** Establishing a PAN involves setting up connections between personal devices. For instance, when using Bluetooth, this process typically includes making the devices discoverable to each other and pairing them through a secure, simple pairing process. This pairing is crucial for establishing a secure communication link between the devices.
- **Network Configuration:** To facilitate proper communication within a PAN, network settings on each device need to be configured appropriately. This may involve enabling specific features like file sharing, network tethering, or synchronization settings that allow devices to interact and exchange data.
- **Security Measures:** Implementing security measures is vital in PANs to ensure data privacy and prevent unauthorized access. For example, when using Bluetooth connections, securing the network with PIN codes or secure pairing procedures can safeguard against potential security breaches.

Use Cases of PANs:

PANs are utilized in a variety of personal and business contexts. Common use cases include connecting a smartphone to a wireless headset for hands-free calling, sharing files between a laptop and a tablet for work or entertainment, or syncing data from a fitness tracker to a mobile app for health monitoring. These networks provide a convenient and efficient way for users to integrate their digital experiences across multiple devices.

While both SAN (Storage Area Network) and PAN (Personal Area Network) are integral to modern networking, they serve distinctly different purposes. SANs are designed to meet the demands of enterprise-level, high-capacity, and high-performance network storage solutions. In contrast, PANs focus on providing connectivity and interaction among personal devices within a small physical range, emphasizing ease of use, mobility, and personal data management. This distinction underscores the diverse spectrum of needs and applications in contemporary network environments.

Section 3: Cloud Concepts

Service Models: IaaS, PaaS, SaaS

In the dynamic world of cloud computing, distinguishing between the various service models – Infrastructure as a Service (IaaS), Platform as a Service (PaaS), and Software as a Service (SaaS) – is essential for selecting the appropriate cloud services to meet specific organizational needs. Each model offers unique features and benefits, catering to different aspects of IT infrastructure and application development.

IaaS (Infrastructure as a Service):

Infrastructure as a Service (IaaS) is a foundational model in cloud computing that delivers virtualized computing resources over the internet. This innovative service model is specifically designed to offer essential computing, storage, and networking resources on a flexible, on-demand basis. It caters to a wide range of computing needs, allowing users to scale up or down based on their specific requirements. The defining feature of IaaS is its operational flexibility, enabling users to tailor their IT solutions to their exact needs. This model operates on a pay-as-you-go pricing structure, which is a key factor in its cost-efficiency, making it an attractive option for many businesses and organizations.

The IaaS landscape is dominated by major providers such as Amazon Web Services (AWS), Microsoft Azure, and Google Cloud Platform (GCP). Each of these providers offers a broad spectrum of services and capabilities, ensuring that they can cater to a diverse range of IT needs. From advanced computing power and expansive storage options to sophisticated networking and security features, these providers equip users with the tools necessary for efficient and effective cloud computing.

IaaS is incredibly versatile and finds application in a multitude of scenarios. It is extensively used for hosting websites and web applications, providing a reliable and scalable environment for these digital platforms. The model is also ideal for storing, backing up, and recovering data efficiently, ensuring data integrity and availability. For businesses looking to support remote work or secure connections, hosting virtual desktops or VPNs through IaaS offers a practical solution. Additionally, the model is adept at handling big data analytics, providing the necessary computing power and storage capacity to analyze large datasets for patterns and insights.

The benefits of adopting an IaaS model are significant. Its high scalability allows businesses to adjust their resource usage in real-time, aligning with fluctuating demand and avoiding overprovisioning. This flexibility extends to the control over IT resources, where businesses can configure their network, storage, and computing resources as needed. This level of control and adaptability makes IaaS an excellent choice for businesses and organizations that require customizable IT solutions that can scale in tandem with their growth and evolving needs.

In summary, IaaS stands out as a powerful and flexible cloud computing model, offering scalable, customizable, and efficient virtualized computing resources. Its wide range of applications and benefits makes it a cornerstone in the cloud computing industry, particularly for businesses seeking a solution that combines cost-effectiveness with high adaptability and control.

PaaS (Platform as a Service):

Platform as a Service (PaaS) is a cloud computing model that significantly simplifies the process of developing, running, and managing applications. By providing customers with a ready-to-use platform, PaaS eliminates the complexities and resource-intensive overhead typically associated with building and maintaining the underlying infrastructure needed for application development and launch. This model allows developers to focus on the creative aspects of application development without worrying about hardware, software, and hosting.

Several notable providers dominate the PaaS market, including Microsoft Azure, Google App Engine, and AWS Elastic Beanstalk. Each of these platforms offers a unique set of tools and services designed to streamline the application development process. From specialized development tools, programming environments, to database management systems, these services are tailored to enhance productivity and simplify operations for developers.

PaaS proves to be exceptionally beneficial in scenarios involving the development, testing, and deployment of software applications. Its ability to streamline workflows becomes particularly advantageous in collaborative development environments where multiple developers are working on the same project. The platform facilitates easier coordination and integration of various development efforts, ensuring consistency and efficiency. Additionally, PaaS is incredibly useful for integrating web services and databases, providing a seamless process for developers to connect their applications with necessary data sources and services.

One of the most significant benefits of PaaS is its ability to simplify and expedite the development process. By reducing the time spent on coding and providing a rich array of development tools and libraries, PaaS enables developers to innovate and develop more efficiently. This not only speeds up the development cycle but also opens up opportunities for innovation, as developers can experiment and implement new features without the constraints of managing the underlying infrastructure.

In essence, PaaS stands out as a powerful solution in the cloud computing space, offering a comprehensive platform that addresses many challenges of application development. It provides the tools and environment necessary for developers to create and deploy applications more efficiently, fostering a more innovative and productive software development landscape.

SaaS (Software as a Service):

Software as a Service (SaaS) is a prevalent model in cloud computing that has fundamentally changed how software applications are delivered and used. This model provides software applications over the internet on a subscription basis, significantly simplifying access to and management of software. In the SaaS model, applications are centrally hosted and managed by the service provider, which means that users are freed from the complexities of installing, maintaining, and running these applications on their individual computers. This approach allows for ease of access to software applications, as they can be used directly from a web browser without any installation or hardware requirements.

The SaaS landscape is populated by a variety of prominent providers, each offering a range of applications designed to cater to different business functions and user needs. Some of the leading examples include Salesforce, known for its customer relationship management (CRM) solutions; Microsoft Office 365 and Google Workspace, which provide a suite of office tools and collaboration applications; and Dropbox, which offers cloud storage and file-sharing services. These providers have redefined software utility and accessibility, making sophisticated tools available to a broad audience.

The use cases for SaaS applications are incredibly diverse. They range from email services and office productivity tools to more specialized applications like CRM systems and software for human resources and payroll processing. This diversity makes SaaS suitable for a wide array of business operations, enabling organizations of all sizes to leverage advanced software solutions that were previously inaccessible due to high costs or technological barriers.

One of the most significant benefits of SaaS is its simplicity and convenience. By eliminating the need for installation and running applications on individual systems, SaaS simplifies both the deployment and maintenance of software. This not only reduces the burden on IT departments but also ensures that users always have access to the latest features and updates without manual intervention. Furthermore, the subscription-based model of SaaS allows for scalable and flexible software usage, catering to the changing needs of businesses and individuals.

In summary, SaaS stands out as a user-friendly, efficient, and versatile software delivery model. It offers a range of applications accessible via the internet, simplifying the way software is consumed and managed. This model has opened up new opportunities for businesses and individual users to leverage advanced software solutions with minimal investment and effort, significantly impacting the landscape of software usage and accessibility.

Understanding these cloud service models – IaaS, PaaS, and SaaS – is key to leveraging cloud computing's benefits. Each model offers distinct advantages and can be chosen based on specific requirements, such as infrastructure flexibility, ease of application development, or software accessibility and management. This understanding is crucial for businesses and organizations looking to optimize their IT operations and strategies in the cloud era.

Comparison

When comparing the three primary cloud service models – Infrastructure as a Service (IaaS), Platform as a Service (PaaS), and Software as a Service (SaaS) – several key factors such as control, flexibility, technical skill requirements, scalability, and cost-effectiveness come into play. Each model offers different levels of these elements, making them suitable for various use cases and organizational needs.

Control and Flexibility: IaaS provides the highest level of control and flexibility among the three models. Users have direct access to underlying infrastructure resources such as servers and storage, allowing them to configure and manage these resources according to their specific requirements. PaaS offers a moderate level of control; users can manage and customize their applications and data, but the provider manages the underlying infrastructure. SaaS offers the least control and flexibility as the service provider manages the entire application. This includes everything from the infrastructure and platform where the app runs to the app itself.

Technical Skill Requirements: IaaS requires a significant level of technical skill to manage effectively. Users are responsible for managing the infrastructure, which includes tasks like setting up virtual machines, configuring networks, and ensuring security. PaaS reduces the technical burden by managing the infrastructure and requiring users to focus on the deployment and management of their applications. SaaS is the most user-friendly, requiring minimal technical skills from the end-user, as the service provider manages all aspects of the application.

Scalability: All three models offer scalability to accommodate varying workload demands. However, IaaS provides more granular control over how resources are scaled. Users can scale specific resources up or down based on their exact requirements. In PaaS and SaaS, scalability is typically more automated and managed by the provider, offering less control but more convenience.

Cost-Effectiveness: The cost-effectiveness of these models varies based on the scale and complexity of the deployment. SaaS can be the most cost-effective solution for small-scale or short-term applications, as it eliminates the need for capital expenditure on infrastructure and reduces operational costs. For larger, more complex deployments, IaaS and PaaS can offer better cost savings. IaaS allows organizations to avoid the capital costs of purchasing hardware and provides the flexibility to pay only for the resources they use. PaaS can reduce the costs associated with application development and maintenance, making it a cost-effective solution for developing and deploying applications.

The choice between IaaS, PaaS, and SaaS depends on the specific needs of an organization, including the desired level of control, technical expertise available, scalability needs, and budget constraints. Understanding these differences is crucial for businesses to choose the most appropriate and cost-effective cloud service model for their operations.

Delivery Models: Public, Private, Hybrid, and Community Clouds

Cloud computing delivery models define how cloud services are set up and who has access to them. The four main models are public, private, hybrid, and community clouds, each with its unique architecture and use cases.

Public Cloud

Public clouds represent a widely adopted model in cloud computing, characterized by their ownership and operation by third-party cloud service providers. These providers offer computing resources such as servers, storage, and applications over the Internet, making them accessible to a wide range of users and organizations. Public clouds are known for their large-scale infrastructure and advanced technology, which are maintained and managed by the cloud providers.

One of the key characteristics of public clouds is that they operate on a multi-tenant model. This means that the same physical resources, such as servers and storage systems, are shared among multiple clients or tenants. This sharing of resources is efficiently managed to ensure that each client's data remains isolated and secure. The multi-tenant nature of public clouds enables providers to offer services at scale, resulting in cost efficiencies that are typically passed on to the users.

Prominent examples of public cloud providers include Amazon Web Services (AWS), Microsoft Azure, and Google Cloud Platform (GCP). These providers offer a wide range of services and capabilities, catering to various computing needs and applications. They continuously innovate and update their offerings, ensuring that they remain at the forefront of cloud technology.

Public clouds are particularly beneficial for small to medium-sized businesses. These organizations often require the flexibility and scalability of computing resources to grow and adapt to changing business needs, but may not have the capital or desire to invest in and maintain their own hardware and infrastructure. Public clouds allow these businesses to access state-of-the-art resources and capabilities without the associated costs of hardware, maintenance, and IT staffing.

The benefits of using public clouds are numerous. They offer a cost-effective solution for businesses by eliminating the need for significant upfront capital investments in hardware and ongoing maintenance costs. Additionally, public clouds provide scalability, allowing businesses to easily scale up or down their computing resources based on demand. This flexibility is invaluable for businesses experiencing fluctuating workloads or rapid growth. Furthermore, with less need for physical infrastructure and in-house IT staff, organizations can focus more on their core business activities rather than on managing IT resources.

In conclusion, public clouds offer a powerful, flexible, and cost-effective solution for businesses looking to leverage cloud computing. With the ability to scale resources as needed and access advanced technologies without significant investments, public clouds continue to be a popular choice for a wide range of business applications and needs.

Private Cloud

A private cloud represents a distinct category within cloud computing, tailored for exclusive use by a single organization. Unlike public clouds, which cater to multiple clients on shared infrastructure, a private cloud is dedicated entirely to the needs and requirements of one organization. This can be hosted and managed either internally within the organization's own data centers, or externally by a third-party provider, but in either case, it remains isolated for private use and is maintained on a private network.

The defining characteristics of a private cloud revolve around the heightened level of control and data security it offers. Since the infrastructure is not shared with other organizations, a private cloud allows for more stringent security measures and customized control over the computing environment. This degree of control extends to every aspect of the cloud, including storage, networking, and computing resources, allowing the organization to tailor the environment to their specific needs.

Private clouds are particularly well-suited for businesses and organizations that prioritize high levels of data security and privacy. This includes large enterprises that handle sensitive data, such as financial institutions, healthcare providers, and government agencies. The exclusive nature of the private cloud ensures that these organizations can maintain the integrity and confidentiality of their data, a critical requirement in sectors where data security is paramount.

The benefits of a private cloud are significant, especially in terms of enhanced security and privacy. By having a dedicated infrastructure, organizations can implement robust security protocols and compliance standards tailored to their specific operational needs. This results in a highly secure environment where the risk of external breaches is minimized. Additionally, having more control over resources and configurations enables organizations to optimize their cloud environment for specific workflows or applications, potentially leading to better overall performance. This level of customization also means that resources can be allocated and adjusted to meet the exact requirements of the organization, ensuring efficient use of the infrastructure.

In summary, private clouds offer a tailored solution for organizations seeking a dedicated, secure, and highly controllable cloud environment. They provide the benefits of cloud computing, such as scalability and flexibility, while also addressing the specific security, privacy, and performance needs of individual organizations. This makes private clouds an attractive option for entities that handle sensitive information or require a high degree of customization and control over their IT infrastructure.

Hybrid Cloud

Hybrid clouds represent a strategic blend of public and private cloud infrastructures, creating a versatile and dynamic computing environment. This model is designed to allow data and applications to move seamlessly between private and public clouds, providing businesses with more flexibility and greater control over their IT resources. Hybrid clouds are underpinned by technology that enables this interoperability, ensuring a cohesive and efficient cloud ecosystem.

The defining characteristic of a hybrid cloud is its ability to offer the best of both worlds: the scalability and extensive resources of the public cloud, and the enhanced security and control of the private cloud. This dual nature allows for a more flexible and nuanced approach to data deployment and application management. Businesses can choose where to place their resources based on specific requirements, such as compliance, performance, and security needs.

Hybrid clouds are particularly well-suited for businesses that require the expansive capabilities and elasticity of the public cloud but have certain data or applications that necessitate the heightened security and control of a private cloud. This need may arise from regulatory compliance, data sensitivity, or specific performance requirements. For example, a company might use the public cloud for high-volume, less sensitive data processing and storage, while keeping sensitive customer data or critical business applications on a private cloud.

The benefits of a hybrid cloud approach are multifaceted. It offers scalability, allowing businesses to expand their IT infrastructure quickly and efficiently in response to fluctuating demands. The hybrid model also enhances operational efficiency, enabling organizations to allocate resources more effectively and optimize their IT spend. Furthermore, it provides a balance between security and accessibility. Critical data can be stored in the private cloud, where it remains under the organization's direct control, while less sensitive resources can leverage the public cloud's robust infrastructure and computing power.

In summary, hybrid clouds offer a flexible and efficient solution for businesses navigating the complexities of modern IT demands. By combining the strengths of both public and private clouds, hybrid clouds provide a balanced approach to scalability, efficiency, and security. This adaptability makes them an increasingly popular choice for organizations looking to optimize their cloud strategy to suit a diverse range of operational needs and strategic goals.

Community Cloud

Community clouds represent a unique cloud computing model tailored to serve organizations or groups with shared goals, needs, or concerns. This type of cloud is specifically designed to be shared among multiple organizations, each participating as a tenant within the community cloud. Unlike public clouds that cater to a broad array of users with varied objectives, community clouds focus on a specific group of organizations that have common requirements in terms of resources, policy adherence, or security standards.

The defining characteristic of a community cloud is its multi-tenant environment, where each tenant is an organization that shares interests or objectives with the others. This shared environment fosters a sense of community among the users, as they all have similar needs and concerns regarding their cloud computing resources. This commonality often leads to optimized solutions tailored to the specific requirements of the group, making the community cloud a highly efficient and collaborative platform.

Community clouds are frequently utilized by governmental organizations, research groups, and businesses operating in similar industries. For example, government agencies with stringent data security and privacy requirements might collaborate on a community cloud to ensure compliance while benefiting from the shared infrastructure. Similarly, research institutions may leverage a community cloud to share large datasets and computational resources efficiently, facilitating collaborative research endeavors.

One of the primary benefits of a community cloud is cost-effectiveness. It can be more affordable than a private cloud, as the costs are distributed among the participating organizations. Additionally, it offers superior opportunities for collaboration and data sharing within the community. Organizations in the same industry or with similar goals can share insights, resources, and best practices more easily compared to operating in isolation or within a more generic public cloud environment.

Community clouds provide a tailored solution for groups of organizations with shared goals and requirements, offering a balance between the exclusivity of private clouds and the broad accessibility of public clouds. They enable better collaboration, efficient resource sharing, and cost savings, all while addressing the specific needs and concerns of the community. Each cloud delivery model – public, private, community, and hybrid – brings different levels of management, scalability, and security, making them suitable for various organizational needs and preferences. The choice of a cloud model depends on a careful assessment of these factors in alignment with an organization's specific requirements and strategic objectives

Virtualization

Virtualization in networking is a technology that allows the creation of multiple simulated environments or dedicated resources from a single, physical hardware system. It's a cornerstone of cloud computing and greatly enhances efficiency, flexibility, and resource utilization.

Virtual Machines (VMs)

A Virtual Machine (VM) is essentially a software-based simulation of a physical computer. It functions like a real computer, capable of running its own operating system and applications. This virtualization allows for a wide range of computing tasks to be carried out as if they were on an actual, physical machine.

One of the defining characteristics of VMs is their isolation from both the host computer and other virtual machines. This separation ensures that the activities or software within one VM do not affect or interfere with the host system or other VMs. This feature is particularly important for security; any problems, such as software malfunctions or security breaches within a VM, remain confined to that VM and do not impact the broader system. This containment is crucial in maintaining the integrity and stability of the host environment.

Virtual Machines are highly versatile and find use in numerous scenarios. They are frequently utilized for testing new applications or updates in a controlled, sandbox environment. This usage allows developers and IT professionals to safely test and validate software without risking the main operating system or other critical systems. VMs are also ideal for running applications that are designed for different operating systems, without the need to have multiple physical machines each running a separate OS. Furthermore, VMs are instrumental in server consolidation. By running multiple VMs on a single physical server, organizations can significantly reduce the need for multiple physical servers, leading to cost savings in terms of both hardware investment and ongoing maintenance.

In essence, Virtual Machines provide a flexible, secure, and cost-effective way of enhancing computing capabilities. They allow for the efficient use of physical hardware resources, reduce overhead costs, and offer a secure environment for testing and running diverse applications. Their ability to emulate separate, independent computers on a single physical machine has revolutionized various aspects of computing, from software development and testing to efficient resource management in large-scale IT environments.

Hypervisors

A hypervisor, commonly known as a virtual machine monitor (VMM), is a crucial piece of software in virtualization technology. Its primary function is to create and manage Virtual Machines (VMs). The hypervisor sits at the core of virtualization, enabling multiple VMs to share physical resources such as processors, memory, and storage, while functioning as if they were separate, independent machines.

There are two main types of hypervisors:

Type 1 Hypervisors: Also known as "bare-metal" hypervisors, these run directly on the host's hardware. They have direct access to hardware resources, controlling the hardware and managing the guest operating systems. This direct interaction with the physical hardware of the host machine allows Type 1 hypervisors to provide high efficiency and performance. Notable examples of Type 1 hypervisors include VMware ESXi, Microsoft Hyper-V for Windows Server, and Citrix XenServer.

Type 2 Hypervisors: These hypervisors run on a conventional operating system, much like any other computer program. They are installed on top of the host's operating system, making them easier to manage for users who might not have deep technical knowledge of the underlying hardware. However, this additional layer can potentially lead to reduced performance when compared to Type 1 hypervisors. Examples of Type 2 hypervisors include Oracle VirtualBox, VMware Workstation, and Parallels Desktop for Mac.

The hypervisor's role is to efficiently allocate physical resources from the host machine to each VM. It ensures that each virtual machine has access to the necessary resources, such as CPU time, memory space, and storage capacity, to function effectively. This allocation is done in a manner that maximizes resource use while maintaining isolation between each VM, ensuring that the activities in one VM do not adversely affect others.

Benefits of Virtualization in Networking

Virtualization in networking has brought about a transformative shift in how IT resources are managed and deployed, offering a range of significant benefits that enhance efficiency, reduce costs, and increase the agility of both local and cloud-based environments.

One of the primary benefits of virtualization is **Resource Efficiency**. By hosting multiple Virtual Machines (VMs) on a single physical server, virtualization maximizes the utilization of the server's resources. This efficient use of hardware resources means that more can be done with less, reducing the need for a large number of physical servers.

Another major advantage is **Cost Savings**. Virtualization significantly reduces the need for physical hardware, which in turn lowers hardware acquisition and maintenance costs. This reduction in physical infrastructure also leads to savings in related areas such as energy consumption and space requirements.

Flexibility and Scalability are also key benefits. Virtualization allows for the easy creation, modification, and deletion of VMs to align with changing business needs. This can be done rapidly and without the need for investing in new physical infrastructure, making it an ideal solution for businesses that experience fluctuating demand.

In terms of **Disaster Recovery and Business Continuity**, virtualization offers substantial advantages. VMs can be backed up and rapidly restored on other servers in the event of hardware failure, significantly reducing downtime and ensuring continuous business operations. This quick and efficient recovery capability is essential for maintaining service availability and data integrity.

For **Testing and Development**, virtualization provides an invaluable tool. It allows developers and IT professionals to create sandbox environments for testing applications, operating systems, and configurations without risking the stability of the physical network or systems. This isolated testing environment encourages experimentation and innovation without disrupting normal operations.

Additionally, virtualization aids in **Load Balancing and Performance**. By distributing workloads across multiple VMs, it optimizes network performance and efficiency. This distribution ensures that no single machine is overwhelmed, leading to better overall system responsiveness and user experience.

In summary, the advent of virtualization technology has revolutionized the IT landscape, providing a plethora of benefits that enhance operational efficiency, cost-effectiveness, and organizational agility. Its impact is evident in the way resources are now managed and deployed, marking a significant leap forward in both local and cloud-based network environments.

Section 4: Network Services

DHCP (Dynamic Host Configuration Protocol)

DHCP is a network management protocol used on IP networks whereby a DHCP server dynamically assigns an IP address and other network configuration parameters to each device on the network, so they can communicate with other IP networks.

DHCP Process

1. **Discovery**: The client device sends a broadcast message (DHCPDISCOVER) to identify any available DHCP servers.
2. **Offer**: DHCP servers respond to the discovery message with a DHCPOFFER, which includes an IP address offer and other DHCP options.
3. **Request**: The client responds to the offer with a DHCPREQUEST message, indicating its acceptance of the offered parameters.
4. **Acknowledgment**: The DHCP server sends a DHCPACK, confirming the allocated IP address and providing lease duration and other configuration information.

DHCP Scopes

A DHCP scope is defined as a specific range of IP addresses that are available for lease by a DHCP server to clients within a particular subnet. This concept is fundamental in network management, particularly in environments where devices frequently join and leave the network, such as in office settings or public Wi-Fi networks.

When configuring a DHCP scope on a server, various specific settings are defined to ensure efficient network management and connectivity. These settings typically include the range of IP addresses that can be assigned, often determined based on the network size and the number of devices expected to connect. Alongside the IP address range, the subnet mask is also specified, which helps in identifying the network and broadcast addresses within the subnet.

Additionally, configuration of a DHCP scope involves setting the default gateway address. This address is crucial as it facilitates communication between devices in the network and external networks, such as the internet. Another essential component of the DHCP scope configuration is the specification of DNS (Domain Name System) server addresses. These addresses are vital for resolving domain names to IP addresses, enabling users to access websites and other network services using familiar domain names rather than numerical IP addresses.

Lastly, the lease duration, which is the length of time an IP address is assigned to a device, is also configured in the DHCP scope. The lease duration can vary based on network requirements and the nature of the client devices. In a network with devices that connect for short durations, a shorter lease time might be preferable to ensure efficient reuse of IP addresses. Conversely, in more stable network environments, longer lease durations can be set to reduce the frequency of renewals.

In essence, the configuration of a DHCP scope is a critical aspect of network management, ensuring that IP addresses are efficiently allocated and managed, supporting seamless network connectivity and access to network resources.

DHCP Leases

A DHCP lease refers to the fixed period during which a client device is allowed to use an IP address that has been assigned to it by a DHCP server. This concept is central to the management of IP addresses in a network environment, particularly in DHCP (Dynamic Host Configuration Protocol), where IP addresses are dynamically assigned to client devices.

The duration of a DHCP lease can vary significantly, influenced by the specific policies and configurations set by network administrators. These configurations are typically based on the unique requirements of the network, such as the frequency of device turnover or the stability of the network environment. For instance, shorter lease durations might be preferred in a network with transient devices to ensure the efficient recycling of IP addresses.

As the lease nears its expiration, the client device is usually programmed to automatically request a new lease. This renewal process is often managed by the client's operating system, which negotiates with the DHCP server to extend the IP address assignment. This automatic renewal helps maintain uninterrupted network connectivity for the client device.

When the client device remains connected to the network as the lease approaches its expiration, it typically attempts to renew the lease to retain its current IP address. However, if the client device leaves the network or fails to renew the lease, the assigned IP address is returned to the pool of available addresses on the DHCP server. This address can then be reallocated to other devices on the network.

The mechanisms of lease duration, renewal, and expiration are fundamental to ensuring efficient and effective management of IP address allocation in DHCP networks. They balance maintaining stable network connections for client devices and optimizing the availability of IP addresses for new or returning devices on the network.

DHCP Relay Agents

DHCP relay agents come into play in networks where the DHCP server is situated on a different subnet from the client devices. Their primary purpose is to bridge the gap between clients and the DHCP server, enabling effective communication across different network segments.

The fundamental function of a DHCP relay agent is to forward DHCP requests made by clients to a DHCP server located on another subnet. In a typical network setup without a relay agent, a DHCP server can only serve clients within its own subnet. However, with the implementation of a DHCP relay agent, it becomes possible to have a centralized DHCP server managing IP addresses for multiple subnets. This centralization significantly streamlines the management of IP addresses and reduces the necessity for deploying multiple DHCP servers across an organization's network.

Configuring DHCP relay agents is usually done on network devices that connect various subnets, such as routers or switches. These devices are strategically positioned to intercept and relay DHCP messages between clients and the server. By enabling this relay function, these network devices facilitate the DHCP server in providing IP addresses and other network configuration details to clients on different subnets.

The use of DHCP in a network automates and dynamizes the allocation of IP addresses and other essential network settings. This automation simplifies network management tasks, ensuring that IP addresses are efficiently utilized and managed. By eliminating the need for manual IP address assignments, DHCP helps maintain a smoothly functioning network, reducing the likelihood of configuration errors and conflicts arising from manual setups. Overall, DHCP and its components, like relay agents, are integral to modern network infrastructures, enhancing their functionality and efficiency.

DNS (Domain Name System)

DNS is a decentralized and hierarchical naming system for computers, services, or any resource connected to the Internet or a private network. It translates human-readable domain names (like www.example.com) into numerical IP addresses for locating and identifying computer services and devices.

DNS Hierarchy

1. **Root Level**: At the top of the DNS hierarchy are the root servers. There are 13 sets of these globally distributed servers, identified by letters A through M.
2. **Top-Level Domains (TLDs)**: Below the root servers are TLDs, which include generic top-level domains (gTLDs) like .com, .net, .org, and country-code top-level domains (ccTLDs) like .uk, .us, .ca.
3. **Second-Level Domains**: These are the names directly below a TLD (e.g., example in example.com).
4. **Subdomains**: Further subdivisions of domains (e.g., www or mail in www.example.com or mail.example.com).

DNS Record Types

A Record (Address Record): This is one of the most fundamental types of DNS records. An A Record maps a domain name to its corresponding IPv4 address, the numerical label assigned to each device participating in a computer network that uses the Internet Protocol for communication. For example, an A Record would link a domain like "example.com" to its respective IPv4 address, such as "192.0.2.1". This mapping is crucial for allowing users to access websites using domain names instead of remembering complex numerical IP addresses.

AAAA Record (Quad-A Record): Similar to the A Record, the AAAA Record maps a domain name to an IPv6 address, the most recent version of Internet Protocol addresses. IPv6 addresses are longer than IPv4 to accommodate a larger number of unique IP addresses, an essential upgrade due to the expansive growth of the internet. An AAAA Record ensures that a domain name correctly points to its corresponding IPv6 address, facilitating access to websites and services in networks that use the IPv6 protocol.

CNAME Record (Canonical Name Record): A CNAME Record is used to alias one domain name to another. This is particularly useful for directing multiple domain names to a single domain. For instance, a CNAME Record can redirect traffic from "www.example.com" to the primary domain "example.com." This type of record is essential for websites that need to be accessible through various domain aliases.

MX Record (Mail Exchange Record): An MX Record is specifically used for email purposes. It specifies the mail server responsible for accepting email messages on behalf of a domain. This record is crucial for directing email to the correct server, ensuring that emails sent to an address at the domain (like "user@example.com") are routed to the specified mail server.

NS Record (Name Server Record): The NS Record indicates the authoritative name servers for a domain. This record points to servers with complete, authoritative knowledge of the domain's DNS records. It is essential for directing traffic to the right location where DNS information is stored and managed for the domain.

PTR Record (Pointer Record): The PTR Record maps an IP address back to a host name, essentially functioning as the reverse of an A or AAAA record. It's primarily used in reverse DNS lookups, where you start with an IP address and want to find the corresponding hostname. This type of record is crucial for network troubleshooting and for services that rely on reverse DNS lookups for validation or logging purposes.

TXT Record (Text Record): A TXT Record holds text information for external sources outside the domain. This versatile record type can serve various purposes but is often used for verifying domain ownership or implementing email security measures, such as Sender Policy Framework (SPF) and DomainKeys Identified Mail (DKIM). These applications are vital for enhancing the security and integrity of domains, particularly in preventing email spoofing and ensuring that the domain is recognized as a legitimate sender of emails.

Each DNS record type plays a specific and important role in the overall functionality and management of domain names and their associated services, ensuring smooth and secure internet navigation and communication.

DNS Query Process

1. **Recursive Query**: When a user types a domain name into a web browser, the client device makes a recursive query to the DNS resolver (usually provided by the ISP).
2. **Resolver to Root Server**: The resolver forwards the query to a root server, which responds with the address of the TLD server for the domain.
3. **Resolver to TLD Server**: The resolver then queries the TLD server, which replies with the address of the domain's authoritative name server.
4. **Final Query to Authoritative Server**: Finally, the resolver queries the authoritative server, which provides the IP address of the domain. This IP address is then sent back to the client, allowing the browser to connect to the web server hosting the domain.

The DNS system enables user-friendly navigation of the web and routing email and other network services.

NTP (Network Time Protocol)

NTP, or Network Time Protocol, plays a significant role in network services, particularly in maintaining accurate time synchronization across computer systems. This precise timekeeping serves several important functions in computing and network operations.

Importance of Time Synchronization:

Security: Time synchronization is important in security protocols. For instance, mechanisms like Kerberos authentication rely on synchronized time stamps. If the time is not consistent across systems, it can result in authentication errors or even security vulnerabilities.

Log Management: Maintaining accurate time stamps is also vital for log management. When analyzing log files from multiple systems, synchronized time stamps enable effective correlation of events. This synchronization is particularly valuable for troubleshooting issues and conducting security audits.

Transaction Ordering: In systems where transactions are a frequent occurrence, such as financial systems, the sequence of these transactions often relies heavily on time stamps. Ensuring that these time stamps are synchronized is important for maintaining the correct order of operations.

Scheduled Operations: In network environments, many automated tasks are dependent on synchronized time settings. Tasks like data backups, batch processing, and system updates are scheduled based on the system time, making accurate timekeeping important for their proper execution.

Database Management: In the realm of database management, operations like transactions and replication processes often need synchronized timestamps. This synchronization is necessary to ensure data integrity and consistency across databases.

How NTP Servers Maintain Time Synchronization

NTP Servers and Strata: At the foundation of this hierarchy are Stratum 0 devices. These are high-precision timekeeping devices, typically not directly connected to the network, such as atomic clocks and GPS clocks, which are known for their extremely accurate timekeeping capabilities. Stratum 1 servers are directly connected to these Stratum 0 devices. Being at the top of the network hierarchy, Stratum 1 servers obtain their time directly from the precise Stratum 0 devices and are considered primary time sources. As you move up to higher stratum levels (Stratum 2, Stratum 3, and so on), the servers are further down the hierarchy. These servers receive their time from a server at one stratum level lower and are considered secondary time sources. The higher the stratum level, the greater the number of network hops and potential delay from the primary time source.

Time Synchronization Process: The process of time synchronization in NTP involves several key steps:

- **Client-Server Model:** In this model, an NTP client initiates a communication transaction with an NTP server to request current time data. The server responds to this request by sending a time-stamped message back to the client.
- **Round-Trip Delay and Offset Calculation:** One of the critical functions of NTP is to estimate the time delay (round-trip delay) between the client and the server. It also calculates the offset, or the difference, between the client's clock and the server's clock. NTP uses these calculations to make precise adjustments to the client's clock to bring it in line with the server's time.
- **Polling:** To maintain accurate timekeeping, NTP clients periodically poll one or more NTP servers. This regular polling is essential to adjust for any changes in delay or offset that might occur over time, ensuring that the client's clock remains as accurate and synchronized as possible.

Synchronization Networks: NTP operates within a well-structured network of servers to ensure reliable and accurate time synchronization across various clients. In practical scenarios, clients are configured to query not just one but multiple NTP servers. This approach is key to maintaining redundancy and enhancing the overall accuracy of time synchronization. By querying multiple servers, clients can compare the results and choose the most reliable time source, or even average the time from different sources to achieve greater accuracy. This redundancy is crucial in scenarios where one or more servers might be temporarily unavailable or experiencing issues. The network of NTP servers, often spread across different geographical locations, ensures that time synchronization is not only accurate but also resilient against individual server failures or network issues.

Algorithms: NTP utilizes a set of sophisticated algorithms designed to accurately account for variable network delays and jitter. Network delay, the time taken for a packet to travel from a client to a server and back, can vary due to numerous factors such as network congestion or route changes. Jitter, which refers to the variation in packet delay, can also impact the accuracy of time synchronization. NTP's algorithms effectively analyze these delays and fluctuations, making necessary adjustments to keep the client's time synchronized within milliseconds of the universal coordinated time (UTC). This high level of accuracy is achieved by calculating the best estimate of the time offset and round-trip delay, continuously adjusting as network conditions change. This precision is crucial for ensuring that all networked systems and devices operate in unison and in accordance with the global time standard.

Through the effective implementation of NTP, networked systems and devices across various organizations and industries can maintain essential time synchronization. This synchronization is not just a matter of convenience; it is vital for the operational integrity of these systems. Accurate timekeeping is foundational in ensuring that processes and transactions are conducted and recorded correctly. In the realm of security, synchronized time stamps are critical for tracking and responding to events, as well as for maintaining accurate logs for auditing and compliance purposes. Additionally, in network environments where efficiency and coordination are paramount, such as in data centers or financial trading platforms, NTP provides the necessary time accuracy to ensure smooth and synchronized operations.

IPAM (IP Address Management)

IP Address Management (IPAM) is a methodology and suite of tools for planning, tracking, and managing the IP address space used in a network. Effective IPAM strategies are crucial for the efficient operation of large-scale networks, particularly in avoiding conflicts and ensuring that network resources are optimally utilized.

IPAM Strategies

Centralized Management: Centralized management involves maintaining a single, comprehensive repository for all IP address-related information. This centralized approach ensures consistency across the network, significantly reducing the likelihood of IP address conflicts and duplication. It allows network administrators to have a unified view of the entire IP address space, making it easier to manage and make informed decisions about allocations, reassignments, or expansions. Centralized management is particularly beneficial in large and complex networks where keeping track of IP addresses can be challenging.

Hierarchical Address Allocation: Organizing the IP address space hierarchically, often in a way that mirrors the physical or logical layout of the network, simplifies both management and troubleshooting. This method involves structuring IP addresses in a tiered manner, where each level of the hierarchy represents a specific segment or area of the network. Hierarchical allocation makes it easier to identify where in the network a particular IP address is used and aids in efficient routing and network organization.

Subnet Management: Efficient subnetting is a key component of IPAM. It involves dividing the network into smaller, manageable subnets to optimize performance and manageability. Effective subnet management includes planning for future growth and accommodating networks of different sizes and requirements. It allows for better control of traffic flow, enhances security by segregating different parts of the network, and improves address efficiency by reducing address wastage.

Tracking and Documentation: Meticulous documentation of IP addresses, subnets, assignments, and reservations is crucial in maintaining a clear and updated overview of the network's IP landscape. Proper documentation helps in quick troubleshooting, planning for expansions, and understanding the usage patterns. This record-keeping is essential for maintaining operational continuity and for training new staff.

Dynamic vs. Static Addressing: Balancing the use of dynamic (DHCP) and static IP addressing involves choosing the most appropriate method based on the specific needs of each network segment or device type. Dynamic addressing is suitable for devices that require temporary network access or where devices frequently join and leave the network. Static addressing, on the other hand, is ideal for servers, network printers, and other critical network devices that require permanent, consistent IP addresses.

Audit and Compliance: Regular audits of the IP address space are vital for detecting irregularities, unauthorized changes, or instances of policy non-compliance. Auditing ensures that the IPAM practices are adhering to the set standards and policies and helps in identifying potential security risks or network inefficiencies.

IPAM Tools

Commercial IPAM Solutions: In the realm of IP Address Management (IPAM), commercial solutions like Infoblox, BlueCat, and SolarWinds stand out by offering a comprehensive range of IPAM functionalities. These solutions are designed to seamlessly integrate with DNS (Domain Name System) and DHCP (Dynamic Host Configuration Protocol) services, creating a unified management platform for network addresses. One of the key strengths of these commercial solutions is their advanced feature sets, which typically include robust reporting and alerting capabilities. They also often provide API (Application Programming Interface) access, which is crucial for automating various network management tasks, thus enhancing efficiency and reducing the potential for human error. These features make commercial IPAM solutions ideal for larger organizations or those with complex network infrastructures that require detailed tracking, management, and analysis of their IP address space.

Open-Source Tools: For smaller organizations or those operating with budget constraints, open-source IPAM solutions offer a viable alternative. Tools like phpIPAM and NetBox provide the basic functionalities needed for effective IPAM. While they might not have all the advanced features of their commercial counterparts, these open-source tools are often quite capable of meeting the essential needs of IP address management. They are particularly suitable for smaller networks where the complexity and scale of management are relatively manageable.

Integrated DHCP/DNS/IPAM (DDI) Solutions: Some organizations opt for integrated DDI solutions, which offer a comprehensive approach to managing DHCP, DNS, and IPAM under a single unified system. These integrated solutions provide centralized control and visibility across the three critical areas of network management. The holistic approach of DDI solutions simplifies the management process, making it easier to maintain consistency, enforce policies, and ensure the overall health and efficiency of the network.

Spreadsheet-Based Management: In smaller networks or in scenarios where dedicated IPAM tools are not in use, managing IP addresses using spreadsheets is a common practice. This method involves manually tracking and updating IP allocations using spreadsheet software. While this approach can be sufficient for very small networks, it is generally not recommended for larger or more dynamic environments. Spreadsheet-based IPAM can lead to issues with scalability, accuracy, and data integrity, and it lacks the automation and integration capabilities of specialized IPAM tools.

Effective IPAM is critical in avoiding IP conflicts, conserving IP space, and ensuring efficient network operation. It's especially important in environments with rapid growth or those transitioning to IPv6, where the complexity of IP address management significantly increases.

QoS (Quality of Service)

Quality of Service (QoS) refers to a broad set of networking technologies and techniques designed to ensure that the network provides the desired performance levels for specific applications and services. QoS is particularly important in networks where bandwidth is limited and must be allocated according to priorities.

QoS Concepts

Bandwidth Management: One of the primary functions of QoS is bandwidth management, which involves the allocation and control of network resources to ensure that there is always sufficient bandwidth available for critical applications. This is particularly important in scenarios where the network faces congestion. Effective bandwidth management ensures that essential applications, such as those required for business operations, are not starved of the resources they need due to other less critical traffic on the network. Techniques like rate limiting or bandwidth reservation are often used to control how much bandwidth is available to different types of traffic.

Latency and Jitter Control: For real-time applications such as VoIP (Voice over IP) and video conferencing, minimizing latency (the time it takes for data to travel from source to destination) and jitter (variations in the delay of received packets) is crucial. High latency or jitter can severely degrade the quality of these applications, resulting in poor audio or video quality. QoS mechanisms work to reduce these delays and variations, often by prioritizing real-time traffic over less time-sensitive types of data.

Loss Sensitivity: Another aspect of QoS is managing packet loss to maintain the quality of applications that are sensitive to packet drops. In network environments where packet loss is a concern, QoS techniques are employed to identify and prioritize traffic for which packet loss could be detrimental. For example, while some data applications can tolerate a degree of packet loss without a noticeable impact on performance, the same level of loss might be unacceptable for a video stream or a VoIP call.

Priority Levels: QoS often involves assigning different priority levels to various types of network traffic. By doing so, network administrators can ensure that the most critical applications always have the bandwidth they need, even when the network is under heavy load. This prioritization might involve ensuring that business-critical traffic, like enterprise resource planning (ERP) system data, is prioritized over less critical traffic, such as web browsing.

QoS Mechanisms

Quality of Service (QoS) mechanisms are a set of techniques used to manage network resources effectively and ensure optimal performance of various types of network traffic. These mechanisms are essential in controlling how data packets are treated within the network, particularly in ensuring that critical services maintain high performance and reliability. Here's an expanded overview of some fundamental QoS mechanisms:

Classification and Marking: This mechanism involves identifying and categorizing packets based on specific criteria such as service type, source, destination, or other parameters. Once classified, packets are then marked accordingly, which aids in their subsequent handling as they traverse the network. By classifying and marking packets, network devices can differentiate between various types of traffic and apply appropriate policies. For example, video conference traffic might be marked as high priority, while standard web browsing traffic is marked as lower priority.

Traffic Shaping and Policing: These techniques are employed to control the rate of network traffic, which is crucial in preventing congestion that can degrade network performance. Traffic shaping involves delaying packets to spread out their transmission over time, ensuring that the data flow does not exceed the capacity of the network. On the other hand, traffic policing monitors the rate of traffic and either drops or marks packets that exceed the specified rate limit. While shaping tries to conform traffic to a certain profile through buffering, policing is more about enforcing hard limits on the traffic rate.

Congestion Management (Queuing): During periods of network congestion, managing how packets are queued and transmitted becomes essential. Various queueing strategies are implemented for this purpose. FIFO (First-In-First-Out) is a simple method where packets are processed in the order they arrive. Priority Queuing allows packets with higher priority to be processed first, which is crucial for time-sensitive data. Weighted Fair Queuing is more sophisticated, providing fair bandwidth allocation to different traffic flows based on weights or priorities.

Congestion Avoidance: Congestion avoidance mechanisms, such as RED (Random Early Detection), are proactive approaches to prevent network congestion before it becomes problematic. RED works by randomly dropping packets early when it detects the onset of congestion, which signals to the sending devices to reduce their transmission rate. This early intervention helps to stabilize the network and prevent congestion from escalating to a point where it significantly impacts network performance.

Configuration Example

VoIP Optimization: For Voice over IP (VoIP) applications, ensuring high call quality is paramount. This can be achieved by configuring QoS to prioritize VoIP traffic. The process typically involves classifying VoIP packets and assigning them a higher priority in the network queue. By doing so, these packets receive preferential treatment, resulting in reduced latency and jitter, which are critical factors for maintaining clear and uninterrupted voice communication. This prioritization ensures that VoIP calls remain stable and clear, even when the network is under significant load from other types of traffic.

Bandwidth Allocation for Critical Applications: An organization might need to ensure that certain critical applications, such as a Customer Relationship Management (CRM) system, have sufficient bandwidth to function smoothly, especially during peak business hours. To achieve this, QoS can be configured to allocate a higher percentage of available bandwidth to such applications. This allocation guarantees that even during periods of high network traffic, critical applications maintain high performance and accessibility, thereby supporting core business operations without interruption.

Traffic Shaping for Non-Critical Traffic: Conversely, QoS can also be used to limit the bandwidth available to non-critical services. For example, bandwidth for activities like file downloads or video streaming can be restricted during peak hours. This traffic shaping prevents these less critical services from consuming excessive bandwidth, ensuring that more important network traffic is not adversely affected.

QoS in Different Networks

Wired Networks: Implementing QoS in wired networks typically involves configuring settings on network routers and switches. This might include setting up traffic prioritization rules, bandwidth limits, and queue management strategies to ensure optimal distribution of network resources according to the defined QoS policies.

Wireless Networks: Wireless networks require special considerations for QoS due to their shared and less predictable nature. The wireless medium's inherent variability makes it essential to prioritize certain types of traffic, such as multimedia streaming, to ensure quality delivery over wireless LANs. Techniques might involve prioritizing traffic types that are sensitive to delay and packet loss, ensuring that even in a fluctuating wireless environment, critical applications maintain their performance standards.

QoS configuration and implementation can vary widely depending on the specific equipment and network architecture. Properly implemented, QoS helps in maintaining network efficiency and ensuring critical business applications function effectively even under heavy network load.

Load Balancing

Load balancing is a technique used to distribute network or application traffic across multiple servers. This distribution improves response times, maximizes throughput, prevents any single server from becoming a bottleneck, and enhances redundancy.

Types of Load Balancers

Hardware Load Balancers: These are dedicated appliances specifically designed for load balancing tasks. Hardware load balancers are generally considered more powerful due to their specialized hardware optimized for data processing and distribution. They are often employed in large-scale and high-traffic environments where performance and reliability are paramount. However, this performance comes at a higher cost, both in terms of initial investment and maintenance.

Software Load Balancers: In contrast, software load balancers are applications that run on standard server hardware. They offer a more flexible and cost-effective solution, especially for smaller or more dynamic environments. Software load balancers can be easily updated or modified to adapt to changing network demands. While they might not offer the raw performance capabilities of hardware solutions, their versatility and lower cost make them a popular choice for many organizations.

Load Balancing Algorithms:

Load balancers utilize various algorithms to determine how to distribute traffic among servers:

Round Robin: This is one of the simplest load balancing methods. It distributes client requests sequentially among the servers in a pool, moving to the next server with each new request. While easy to implement, Round Robin does not consider the current load or capacity of each server, which can lead to uneven distribution if servers have different capabilities or current loads.

Least Connections: This algorithm directs incoming traffic to the server with the fewest active connections. It is particularly effective in environments where session lengths are highly variable, as it helps prevent any single server from becoming overloaded with long-lasting connections.

IP Hash: This method uses a hash of the client's IP address to determine which server will handle the request, ensuring that a particular client consistently connects to the same server. This can be useful for maintaining user session consistency.

Weighted Algorithms: These are variations of the Round Robin or Least Connections algorithms that assign a weight to each server based on its capacity, performance, or other criteria. This approach allows for more nuanced traffic distribution, taking into account the varying capabilities of each server in the pool.

Health Checks: Regular health checks are conducted on servers to ensure they are functioning correctly and can handle incoming requests. If a server fails a health check, it is temporarily removed from the pool until it is back online and functioning properly. This mechanism helps maintain the overall efficiency and reliability of the service.

Effective load balancing is more than just evenly distributing traffic; it requires careful planning and configuration to align with the network's specific needs and architecture. Choosing the right type of load balancer and the appropriate algorithm is crucial in creating a network environment that is both resilient and efficient, capable of handling varying traffic loads while maintaining high levels of performance and availability.

As we conclude our exploration of key network services, our journey in understanding the intricacies of networking continues. In the next chapter, we will delve into the world of **Infrastructure and Cabling**, examining the foundational elements that underpin network connectivity. This includes a detailed look at cabling types, network devices, advanced networking hardware, and the vital role of virtual networking components in modern network architecture. Stay tuned for a comprehensive guide to the physical and virtual elements that make up the backbone of any network.

Chapter 2: Infrastructure

Section 1: Cabling, Devices, and Storage

Cable Types

In network infrastructure, the choice of cabling is critical for determining network speed, capacity, distance, and overall performance. The two primary types of network cables are copper and fiber-optic, each with its categories and specific use cases.

Copper Cables

Categories:

Cat 5e: Supports speeds up to 1 Gbps at 100 MHz. Commonly used in residential and business networks.

Cat 6: Offers higher performance, with speeds up to 10 Gbps at 250 MHz for up to 55 meters. Better suited for business environments where higher bandwidth is required.

Cat 6a: Extends Cat 6 capabilities to 10 Gbps speeds over 100 meters.

Cat 7: Provides speeds up to 10 Gbps with a much higher frequency of 600 MHz. It's shielded, reducing interference.

Cat 8: Designed for data centers and enterprise environments, offering 25-40 Gbps speeds over short distances (up to 30 meters).

Copper cables are typically used for shorter distances, such as within a building or campus. They are widely utilized for Ethernet connections, office networks, and home internet connections.

Fiber-Optic Cables

Types:

Single-Mode Fiber: Offers higher bandwidth over longer distances using a single ray of light. Ideal for long-distance, high-bandwidth applications.

Multi-Mode Fiber: Uses multiple rays of light, suitable for shorter distances with high bandwidth.

Use Cases:

Fiber-optic cables are used for long-haul network connections, in data centers, and in areas where high data transfer rates are needed over long distances. They are immune to electromagnetic interference, making them suitable for environments with heavy electrical equipment.

When comparing Fiber Optic Cables and Copper Cables, several key factors come into play that can influence the choice between the two in different network environments.

Distance: One of the primary advantages of fiber-optic cables is their ability to carry signals over much longer distances than copper cables without experiencing signal degradation. This makes fiber-optic cables an ideal choice for network setups that require data transmission over long distances, such as between buildings in a campus setting or for wide area network (WAN) applications.

Bandwidth: In terms of bandwidth, fiber generally surpasses copper. Fiber-optic cables offer significantly higher bandwidth capacities, making them well-suited for applications that demand high data transfer rates. This includes networks that handle large volumes of data or high-definition video streaming.

Interference: A notable difference between the two types of cables is their susceptibility to electromagnetic interference (EMI). Copper cables can be affected by EMI, which can degrade signal quality and lead to transmission errors. In contrast, fiber-optic cables are immune to EMI, as they use light to transmit data. This characteristic makes fiber-optic cables more reliable in environments with high electromagnetic activity, such as industrial settings or areas with heavy electrical equipment.

Cost: When it comes to cost, copper cabling generally presents a more budget-friendly option. It is less expensive and easier to install compared to fiber-optic cabling. However, the trade-off might be in performance, especially over long distances or in scenarios that require handling high-bandwidth applications. The decision to opt for copper cabling should consider these potential limitations.

The choice between fiber-optic and copper cabling depends on the specific requirements of the network, including factors like transmission distance, bandwidth needs, susceptibility to interference, and budget constraints. While fiber-optic cables offer superior performance in terms of distance and bandwidth, and are immune to EMI, they come at a higher cost. Copper cables, while more affordable and easier to install, may not deliver the same level of performance in certain situations. Understanding these differences is key to making an informed decision that aligns with the network's needs and goals.

Networking Devices

Understanding traditional networking devices, including their functions and roles, is fundamental to grasping how networks are built and operated. Devices like Network Interface Cards (NICs), repeaters, and hubs form the basic building blocks of network infrastructure.

Network Interface Cards (NICs)

A Network Interface Card (NIC), commonly referred to as a network adapter, plays a pivotal role in connecting a computer or server to a network. This hardware component is crucial for facilitating communication between a computer and its network environment. The primary function of a NIC is to convert data from the computer into a format that can be transmitted over the network and to convert incoming network data into a format that the computer can process. In essence, it acts as a translator, enabling two-way communication between the computer and the network.

NICs come in various types, catering to different networking needs and environments. The most common types are wired NICs, often known as Ethernet NICs, and wireless NICs, typically referred to as Wi-Fi NICs. Ethernet NICs are used for wired network connections and are a standard feature in most desktop computers, servers, and many laptops. They provide a stable and fast connection, making them ideal for environments where high-speed data transmission and security are paramount. On the other hand, Wi-Fi NICs facilitate wireless network connections, offering the convenience and flexibility of connecting to the network without physical cables. They are particularly useful in mobile devices and in environments where running physical cabling is impractical.

The role of NICs extends beyond just data conversion. They provide the physical interface between a computer and the network cabling. For copper cable networks, NICs translate the data into electrical signals that travel through the cables. In networks that use fiber-optic cables, NICs convert the data into light signals, which are then transmitted through the fiber-optic cables. This versatility makes NICs an integral component in a wide range of network setups, from traditional wired office networks to modern wireless configurations.

In summary, Network Interface Cards are essential hardware components that enable computers and servers to connect to and communicate with a network. Whether it's for a wired Ethernet connection or a wireless Wi-Fi network, NICs serve as the critical bridge that translates and transmits data between a computer and the network infrastructure, ensuring seamless network connectivity and communication.

Repeaters

Repeaters are relatively straightforward yet essential devices in network hardware, primarily used to regenerate or amplify signals. Their primary function is to extend the transmission distance of network signals, ensuring that the data can travel longer distances without degradation. This capability is particularly important in maintaining the integrity and reliability of network communications over extended areas.

In the context of a wired network, one of the challenges is signal degradation over distance, a phenomenon known as attenuation. As signals travel along a cable, they gradually lose strength, which can lead to data loss or transmission errors. Repeaters play a pivotal role in addressing this issue. They are strategically placed along the cable run to boost the signal strength. By regenerating and amplifying the signals, repeaters ensure that they can cover longer distances while maintaining their integrity. This makes them invaluable in situations where cabling needs to span large areas.

A typical use case for repeaters is in large building complexes or scenarios where network cabling needs to connect separate buildings. In such environments, the distance between network endpoints can be significant, often exceeding the standard transmission capabilities of regular network cabling. Repeaters are deployed at specific intervals to regenerate the signal, thereby facilitating effective network communication across these larger distances. They ensure that the network remains functional and efficient, even when covering extensive areas.

In summary, repeaters are crucial for extending the reach of network signals in wired networks. They are especially useful in large-scale network environments, where they mitigate the effects of signal attenuation over long cable runs. By amplifying and regenerating weakened signals, repeaters maintain the overall health and performance of the network, ensuring consistent and reliable data transmission across extended distances.

Hubs

A hub is a foundational networking device, designed to connect multiple Ethernet devices together, essentially forming a single network segment. This device is fundamental in creating basic local area networks (LANs) and plays a significant role in how data is transmitted within these networks.

Regarding the types of hubs, there are two main categories: active hubs and passive hubs. Active hubs are equipped with the capability to amplify the electrical signal before transmitting it to other network segments. This amplification can be crucial in maintaining signal strength across longer distances or more extensive network setups. On the other hand, passive hubs do not amplify the signal. They simply act as a conduit, passing the incoming signal to the other ports without any enhancement. The choice between an active or passive hub generally depends on the specific requirements of the network, such as the size of the network and the distance the signal needs to travel.

The primary role of a hub in a network is to facilitate communication among connected devices. When a data packet arrives at one port on the hub, the hub duplicates this packet and sends it out through all other ports. This means that all segments of the LAN connected to the hub can receive the packet, ensuring that the data reaches its intended destination on the network.

However, this method of operation introduces certain limitations. Hubs operate on the principle of broadcast, where every packet sent by one connected device is distributed to all other connected devices. While this ensures broad data dissemination, it can lead to network inefficiencies. For instance, network congestion can occur when multiple data packets are broadcast simultaneously. Additionally, there are security concerns, as all devices on the network can see all data packets, potentially leading to data privacy issues. In a hub-based network, there is no differentiation between intended recipients, meaning sensitive information could be accessible to all devices connected to the hub.

In summary, hubs are basic yet essential devices in the construction of simple networks, particularly useful for small-scale, basic network setups. Their ability to connect multiple devices and facilitate data transmission across a single network segment makes them a key component in LANs. However, their broadcast-based operation and lack of signal discrimination mean they are better suited for smaller, less complex network environments where security and efficiency are not primary concerns.

These basic networking devices play essential roles in creating and maintaining a network. While some, like hubs, have largely been replaced by more advanced technology (like switches), understanding their functionality provides foundational knowledge of network operation and design.

Section 2: Networking Devices

Switches

Switches are integral devices in a network, connecting multiple devices and managing the flow of data between them. They come in different types, each with specialized functions and features.

Layer 2 Switches

Layer 2 switches are specialized networking devices that operate at the Data Link layer of the OSI (Open Systems Interconnection) model. Their primary function revolves around the use of MAC (Media Access Control) addresses to accurately forward data to the appropriate destination within a local area network (LAN). This capability is essential for managing and directing network traffic efficiently within a network segment.

The role of Layer 2 switches is primarily focused on switching data packets between devices that are part of the same network segment or VLAN (Virtual Local Area Network). By managing data traffic at the MAC address level, these switches can ensure that packets are sent only to their intended destinations within the LAN. This not only streamlines data flow but also enhances network security and efficiency, as data is not unnecessarily broadcast to all network devices.

Layer 2 switches also come equipped with a variety of advanced features that further enhance their functionality in a network. One key feature is VLAN support, which allows for the creation of distinct network segments within a LAN. VLANs can segregate network traffic, improving both security and performance by limiting broadcast domains. Additionally, Layer 2 switches often include Quality of Service (QoS) controls. These controls enable network administrators to prioritize certain types of network traffic, ensuring that critical applications like VoIP (Voice over IP) and video conferencing receive the bandwidth and low latency they require to function effectively. Another important feature is link aggregation, which allows multiple network connections to be combined for higher throughput and increased redundancy, enhancing both the speed and reliability of the network connection.

Multilayer Switches

Multilayer switches, commonly known as Layer 3 switches, are advanced network devices that function across both the Data Link and Network layers (Layer 2 and Layer 3) of the OSI model. These switches combine the capabilities of standard Layer 2 switches with additional features typically found in routers. This dual functionality makes them highly versatile and valuable in complex network environments.

The primary role of a multilayer switch is to facilitate standard switching functions at the Data Link layer while also possessing the ability to perform routing functions. This routing capability enables them to direct data across different subnets or VLANs (Virtual Local Area Networks), similar to how a traditional router operates. This means that in addition to handling switching tasks within the same network segment, multilayer switches can also intelligently route traffic between different segments or subnets. This is particularly useful in large and complex network setups where data needs to be efficiently managed and routed across various parts of the network.

In terms of features, multilayer switches come equipped with a range of functionalities that extend beyond those of typical Layer 2 switches. They support various routing protocols, which are essential for determining the best paths for data to travel across the network. Additionally, they handle IP addressing and subnetting, allowing for sophisticated management of network address spaces. This includes dividing a larger network into smaller, more manageable sub-networks (subnets), enhancing overall network performance and organization. Alongside these Layer 3 features, multilayer switches also retain all the functionalities of Layer 2 switches, such as VLAN support, Quality of Service (QoS) controls, and link aggregation.

VLANs (Virtual Local Area Networks)

Virtual Local Area Networks (VLANs) play a crucial role in modern network management by segmenting a physical network into multiple logical networks. This segmentation allows groups of devices to communicate effectively as though they were on the same physical network, regardless of their actual physical locations. The primary purpose of using VLANs is to create distinct, isolated network segments within a larger network infrastructure. This approach enables devices within the same VLAN to interact as if they were part of a standalone network, enhancing the overall organization and efficiency of the network.

The benefits of implementing VLANs are manifold. One significant advantage is the enhancement of network security. By segregating different parts of a network into VLANs, sensitive information can be contained within a specific segment, reducing the risk of unauthorized access. Additionally, VLANs effectively reduce network congestion. They achieve this by isolating broadcast domains – when a device broadcasts a message, it is confined to its own VLAN, preventing unnecessary data traffic on other parts of the network. This isolation not only improves network performance but also ensures smoother operation by limiting the spread of broadcast traffic.

In terms of implementation, VLANs are typically configured through software on network switches. This software-based management allows for flexible and dynamic control over network resources and segmentation. Administrators can easily create, modify, or delete VLANs to adapt to changing network requirements. This flexibility is a key advantage of VLANs, as it allows for efficient management and allocation of network resources based on the evolving needs of the organization. By using VLANs, networks can be made more secure, efficient, and adaptable, making them an essential component in contemporary network design and management.

STP (Spanning Tree Protocol)

The Spanning Tree Protocol (STP) serves a vital purpose in network management, especially in larger and more complex networks where redundant paths are common. The primary objective of STP is to prevent network loops, which can occur when there are multiple paths between any two nodes in a network. Network loops can lead to serious problems, including broadcast storms, where multiple copies of the same data flood the network, causing significant disruptions.

STP functions by identifying and deactivating these redundant paths within the network. By doing so, it ensures that at any given time, there is only one active path between any two network nodes. This selective activation and deactivation of network paths help in creating a loop-free network topology, which is crucial for the smooth functioning of the network.

The importance of STP in maintaining network stability cannot be overstated. Network loops are not just a minor inconvenience; they can severely impact the performance and reliability of a network. In the absence of STP, loops can lead to excessive data replication, overwhelming network resources, and causing major downtimes. Thus, implementing STP is critical in ensuring that networks remain stable, efficient, and free from disruptive loop-related issues. This makes STP an indispensable tool in the network administrator's toolkit, particularly in environments with complex network topologies and multiple redundant paths.

Switches, particularly in complex network environments, are pivotal in maintaining efficient, stable, and secure data flow. Understanding the differences between Layer 2 and multilayer switches, along with concepts like VLANs and STP, is crucial for network design, implementation, and management.

Routers

Routers are fundamental networking devices that manage traffic between different network segments, typically between LANs and WANs. They operate at the network layer (Layer 3) of the OSI model and use IP addresses to determine the best path for forwarding data packets.

Static and Dynamic Routing

Static Routing:

Static routing is a method in network management where network routes are manually established and entered into the routing table by a network administrator. This approach contrasts with dynamic routing, where routes are determined and adjusted automatically by algorithms based on the current network conditions. In static routing, each route to a specific network or subnet is explicitly defined and remains constant unless manually changed or updated by the administrator.

The use cases for static routing are particularly well-suited to small networks, where network traffic patterns are predictable and the network topology does not change frequently. In such environments, the simplicity and stability of static routing can be very efficient. Since the routes do not change unless manually altered, network behavior is predictable and consistent, which can be advantageous in controlled environments where changes are infrequent and can be planned and implemented carefully.

One of the main advantages of static routing is the level of control it provides. Network administrators have complete oversight over the path that data takes across the network, which can be crucial for ensuring security or meeting specific network performance criteria. This control allows for a consistent and dependable routing environment.

However, static routing also has its limitations, particularly in terms of scalability and adaptability. In large networks with complex topologies and frequent changes, the manual configuration of routes can become cumbersome and impractical. Static routing also lacks the ability to automatically adjust to dynamic network changes, such as link failures or changes in network topology. This lack of flexibility means that in the event of network changes or disruptions, manual intervention is required to update the routing tables, which can lead to increased downtime and a higher potential for errors.

While static routing offers control and consistency, making it suitable for smaller, more stable networks, its limitations in terms of scalability and adaptability render it less practical for larger, more dynamic network environments. This underscores the importance of carefully considering the specific needs and characteristics of the network when choosing between static and dynamic routing approaches.

Dynamic Routing:

Dynamic routing is a sophisticated approach to network route management, utilizing routing protocols to automatically adjust the paths that data takes, based on the current conditions of the network. This method is a contrast to static routing, where routes are manually set and remain constant unless changed by an administrator. In dynamic routing, algorithms within the routing protocols continually analyze the network and make adjustments to the routes as needed, ensuring optimal data flow and network efficiency.

Dynamic routing is particularly well-suited for larger and more complex networks that experience changing traffic patterns and network conditions. These environments benefit from the flexibility and adaptability that dynamic routing offers. As the network topology changes – whether due to link failures, congestion, or new routes being added – dynamic routing protocols can quickly respond, recalculating and updating routes to maintain smooth network operations. This responsiveness is crucial in maintaining network performance and reliability, especially in large-scale and enterprise-level networks.

One of the key advantages of dynamic routing is its ability to automatically adapt to changes in the network, significantly reducing the administrative burden. Unlike static routing, which requires manual intervention to adjust routes, dynamic routing protocols handle these adjustments automatically, saving time and reducing the potential for human error. This automation is particularly valuable in complex networks where frequent manual updates would be impractical and error-prone.

Dynamic routing encompasses various types of routing protocols, each designed to suit different network requirements and scenarios. Among these are distance-vector routing protocols, such as RIP (Routing Information Protocol), which determine the best path based on the distance to the destination. Another category is link-state routing protocols, like OSPF (Open Shortest Path First) and IS-IS (Intermediate System to Intermediate System), which build a comprehensive map of the network's topology to determine the best routes. Each type of routing protocol has its unique mechanisms and characteristics, making them suitable for different network architectures and performance needs.

Dynamic routing offers a flexible and efficient way to manage routes in complex network environments. Its ability to automatically adjust to network changes and reduce administrative overhead, coupled with the diversity of routing protocols available, makes it an essential strategy for modern, large-scale networks that require robust and adaptable network management.

Routing Protocols

OSPF (Open Shortest Path First) is classified as a link-state routing protocol, known for its efficiency and speed in calculating the shortest path for routing data across a network. It utilizes the Dijkstra algorithm, a well-established method for finding the shortest path between nodes in a graph, which in this case, are the various elements in a network. This capability allows OSPF to quickly determine the most efficient route for data, an essential feature for maintaining high performance in dynamic network environments.

One of the key features of OSPF is its scalability. It can be implemented in a wide range of network sizes, from small local networks to large enterprise networks. Additionally, OSPF supports Variable Length Subnet Masking (VLSM), which enables more efficient and flexible subnetting within the network. Due to these features, OSPF is a popular choice in large enterprise networks where robustness and flexibility are crucial requirements for effective network management.

BGP (Border Gateway Protocol) stands as a path-vector protocol, primarily used for routing between autonomous systems on the internet. It plays a fundamental role in the global internet routing system, directing data across different networks, often encompassing vast geographical distances. BGP is known for its complexity, mainly because it involves intricate policies for path selection and route advertising. These policies are essential for managing how data routes through the various interconnected networks on the internet.

BGP's complexity arises from its need to handle the enormous scale and diversity of the internet's infrastructure. The protocol allows for a high degree of control over routing, enabling the definition of specific policies that dictate how and where data should traverse. This level of control is necessary to handle the intricacies of global internet routing, where decisions need to be made about which paths data should take based on factors like network policies, reliability, and speed.

Both OSPF and BGP are critical routing protocols used in modern network infrastructures, each suited for different aspects of network routing. OSPF, with its quick path calculation and support for large, complex networks, is ideal for enterprise-level internal routing. In contrast, BGP's ability to handle routing on a global scale and its policy-based control make it indispensable for the internet's overall routing architecture. Together, these protocols facilitate efficient and reliable data movement across both internal networks and the vast reaches of the internet.

Routers and routing protocols are central to efficiently managing network traffic, ensuring data packets are delivered through optimal paths, and maintaining connectivity across different network segments and the broader internet.

Firewalls

Firewalls are critical security devices that monitor and control incoming and outgoing network traffic based on predetermined security rules. They establish a barrier between trusted internal networks and untrusted external networks, such as the internet, to prevent unauthorized access and potential security breaches.

Packet Filtering

Packet filtering is a fundamental network security process that involves controlling data access to a network by either allowing or blocking packets based on predetermined criteria. This is typically done at a network interface and is based on the packet's source and destination addresses, ports, or the protocols being used. The core function of packet filtering is carried out by a firewall, which inspects each packet's header as it arrives at the network interface. The firewall then makes a decision to either forward the packet to its destination or drop it, depending on a set of established rules. These rules are defined by the network administrator and dictate the criteria for how incoming and outgoing traffic should be handled.

While packet filtering is an effective method of firewall protection, it does have its limitations. One of the primary limitations is that packet filtering only examines the header of the packet, not the payload or the actual data contained within the packet. As a result, while packet filtering can prevent unauthorized access based on IP addresses or ports, it cannot detect if the contents of the packet are malicious. This means that as long as a packet's header conforms to the rules set in the firewall, it will be allowed through, regardless of whether the payload is harmful. Therefore, packet filtering is considered a basic form of firewall protection, providing a first line of defense against unwanted network traffic but requiring additional layers of security to protect against more sophisticated threats.

Stateful Inspection

Stateful inspection, often referred to as dynamic packet filtering, represents a more advanced approach to network security compared to basic packet filtering. Unlike simple packet filtering, which only examines packet headers, stateful inspection goes a step further by not only inspecting each packet but also keeping track of active connections. This method involves examining both the header and the state of the packet, considering the context of the entire traffic stream.

The primary function of stateful inspection is to analyze the ongoing state of each network connection and make decisions about allowing or blocking traffic based on this state. By monitoring the state of active connections, a stateful firewall can understand the context of network traffic, such as whether a packet is part of an established and trusted connection or if it's an unsolicited attempt to access the network. This context-aware approach allows the firewall to make more informed and precise decisions about network traffic.

One of the key advantages of stateful inspection over simple packet filtering is its enhanced security capabilities. Since stateful inspection monitors the state of active connections, it is more adept at identifying and blocking potentially harmful traffic. It can detect unusual or malicious patterns in network traffic that may not be apparent from packet headers alone. For example, it can identify and block unauthorized attempts to access the network, even if the packets appear legitimate based on their headers. As a result, stateful inspection provides a more robust and effective security mechanism for protecting networks from a wide range of threats.

Next-Generation Firewalls (NGFW)

Next-Generation Firewalls (NGFWs) represent an advanced evolution in network security technology, offering a suite of capabilities that extend far beyond those of traditional firewalls. Traditional firewalls typically focus on basic functions like packet filtering and stateful inspection, but NGFWs incorporate additional features to provide a more comprehensive and in-depth approach to network security.

One of the key features of NGFWs is Deep Packet Inspection (DPI). Unlike traditional methods that inspect only the packet header, DPI delves into both the header and the payload of each packet. This thorough examination allows for a more detailed analysis of the transmitted data, enabling the firewall to identify and block not just based on source and destination addresses but also on the actual content of the packets.

Another critical feature of NGFWs is the integration of Intrusion Prevention Systems (IPS). IPS capabilities allow NGFWs to detect potential threats and attacks and take immediate action to mitigate them in real-time. This proactive stance is crucial in defending against the rapidly evolving landscape of cyber threats.

NGFWs also possess application awareness, which means they can control and manage traffic based on application-specific policies. This feature enables more granular control over network traffic, allowing for the enforcement of policies tailored to the unique characteristics and requirements of different applications.

Additionally, NGFWs are equipped with advanced threat protection mechanisms. These mechanisms are designed to identify and protect against modern, sophisticated threats and vulnerabilities that might evade traditional security measures. This includes protection against advanced malware, ransomware, and network-based attacks.

In their role, NGFWs are particularly well-suited for complex, modern network environments where security needs are more intricate and demanding. They are designed to offer comprehensive protection against a wide range of attacks, addressing the multifaceted nature of current network security challenges. The advanced capabilities of NGFWs, such as DPI, IPS, application awareness, and advanced threat protection, make them essential in safeguarding networks against the diverse array of threats in today's digital landscape.

Firewalls, especially NGFWs, protect network security by monitoring and controlling traffic flow based on a comprehensive understanding of the network, its applications, and potential threats.

Modems

Modems (short for modulator-demodulator) are devices that play a crucial role in connecting networks to the Internet, particularly in residential and small business settings. They convert digital data from a computer or network into analog signals suitable for sending over telephone lines, cable systems, or other standard physical media.

Modulation/Demodulation

Modulation: This process involves converting digital data from a computer into an analog signal that can be transmitted over traditional phone lines, cable networks, or other analog mediums. Modulation enables the transfer of digital information over analog communication lines.

Demodulation: Conversely, demodulation is the process of converting these analog signals back into digital data that a computer can understand. This occurs when the modem receives data from the internet.

DSL Modems

DSL (Digital Subscriber Line) technology capitalizes on existing copper telephone line infrastructure to deliver high-speed internet access. This approach allows for the widespread availability of internet services, leveraging the already extensive telephone network.

The primary functionality of DSL modems lies in their ability to modulate digital data into high-frequency signals that are suitable for transmission over telephone lines. These modems are designed to efficiently handle both internet data and voice signals simultaneously. This dual-functionality is a significant advantage of DSL technology, as it enables users to access the internet without interrupting standard telephone services. Users can browse the internet and use their telephone line for voice calls at the same time, a feature that's particularly beneficial in residential and small business settings.

DSL technology encompasses various types, each catering to different needs and use cases. Among the common types are ADSL (Asymmetric DSL) and SDSL (Symmetric DSL). ADSL is known for offering different speeds for upstream (sending data) and downstream (receiving data) data transmission. Typically, ADSL provides higher speeds for downstream data, which aligns well with common internet usage patterns like streaming videos and downloading files. On the other hand, SDSL offers equal speeds for both upstream and downstream data. This symmetry makes SDSL an appealing choice for applications that require significant data upload capabilities, such as hosting servers or frequent large file uploads.

Cable Modems

Cable modems play a crucial role in providing high-speed internet access by utilizing coaxial cable lines, which were originally designed for cable television. In terms of functionality, they resemble DSL modems as they both modulate and demodulate digital data to and from analog signals over their respective networks. However, cable modems often have an edge over DSL regarding bandwidth. This is because coaxial cables, the medium for cable modems, have a significantly greater capacity for data transmission. Despite this advantage, it's important to note that cable internet is typically a shared service. This means the bandwidth is distributed among users within the same geographical area. As a result, users might experience variations in internet speed, especially during peak usage times when multiple users are accessing the service simultaneously.

Both DSL and cable modems are fundamental in providing internet access to homes and businesses, leveraging existing infrastructure to bridge the gap between digital network data and the analog transmission capabilities of telephone and cable lines.

Section 3: Advanced Networking Devices

Multilayer Switches

Multilayer switches, or Layer 3 switches, represent an evolution in networking hardware, combining the functionalities of routers and switches. These devices can operate at multiple layers of the OSI model, primarily the Data Link layer (Layer 2) and the Network layer (Layer 3).

Combining Routing and Switching

Switching (Layer 2):

At the Data Link layer, multilayer switches perform typical switching functions. They use MAC addresses to forward data and frames within a local network segment or VLAN.

They efficiently handle high amounts of internal network traffic with low latency.

Routing (Layer 3):

In addition to switching, these devices are capable of performing routing functions. They use IP addresses to route data between subnets or VLANs, functioning similarly to traditional routers.

They can execute routing protocols, perform subnet traffic management, and handle inter-VLAN routing.

Advantages of Multilayer Switches

Multilayer switches bring a host of advantages to network infrastructures, primarily enhancing performance, simplifying network architecture, offering flexibility, and supporting scalability. One of the key benefits lies in their performance capabilities. By integrating routing functionalities directly within the switch, multilayer switches can route traffic at significantly higher speeds than traditional routers. This integration not only accelerates data flow across the network but also reduces latency, making these switches ideal for high-speed data environments.

In terms of simplicity and efficiency, multilayer switches streamline network management considerably. By consolidating the roles of traditional routers and switches into a single device, they reduce the need for multiple devices in a network. This consolidation simplifies the network architecture, making it easier to manage and maintain. Fewer devices also mean a reduction in the space and power requirements, contributing to cost savings and a lower total cost of ownership.

Flexibility is another crucial advantage of multilayer switches. They offer the versatility of configuring specific ports to operate at either Layer 2 (data link layer) or Layer 3 (network layer). This capability allows network administrators to tailor the switch's operation to meet varying network requirements, adapting easily to different deployment scenarios. Such flexibility is particularly beneficial in complex networks where both layer 2 switching and layer 3 routing are required.

Lastly, scalability is a significant feature of multilayer switches. As networks grow and evolve, the need to handle increasing traffic and more complex network topologies becomes critical. Multilayer switches are designed to accommodate this growth seamlessly. They can handle an expanding number of network nodes and more diverse network architectures. This ability to scale is essential for businesses and organizations that anticipate growth and need their network infrastructure to be both reliable and adaptable to changing demands.

Use Cases

In the context of large enterprise networks, such as those found in major corporations or data centers, the need for both high-speed switching and routing is paramount. These environments typically handle a vast amount of data traffic, necessitating robust network infrastructure capable of high-speed data transfer and efficient routing. The complexity and scale of these networks demand not only the rapid transmission of data but also the smart routing of traffic to ensure seamless communication across various departments, servers, and external connections. The integration of high-performance switching and routing in such settings is crucial to maintain network efficiency, minimize latency, and ensure the reliable delivery of services.

Similarly, campus networks, which are commonly found in educational institutions or large organizational campuses, benefit greatly from advanced networking solutions. These environments usually consist of multiple buildings, each potentially operating on different subnets. Efficient traffic management and routing between these subnets are essential to maintain seamless network connectivity across the entire campus. The challenge lies in effectively handling the inter-building data traffic, providing reliable internet access, and supporting various campus services like online learning platforms, administrative operations, and security systems. The ability to manage and route traffic efficiently in such a diverse and widespread network is key to ensuring that all segments of the campus are well-connected and that network resources are optimally utilized.

Multilayer switches are a testament to the advancements in networking technology, offering robust, high-performance solutions that combine the best routing and switching in a single device. Their deployment can significantly enhance the capability and efficiency of a network infrastructure.

Load Balancers

Load balancers are critical in managing the distribution of network or application traffic across multiple servers. They ensure optimal resource utilization, maximize throughput, reduce response time, and increase the reliability of applications. Advanced load balancers, often called Application Delivery Controllers (ADCs), go beyond simple traffic distribution.

Application Delivery Controllers (ADCs)

Application Delivery Controllers (ADCs) are an advanced form of load balancers, offering a suite of services that extend well beyond basic load balancing. Their functionality encompasses not only the efficient distribution of client requests or network load across multiple servers but also includes aspects such as application acceleration, security, and SSL offloading. This multi-faceted role makes ADCs crucial in enhancing the reliability and availability of applications in network environments.

A key role of ADCs is traffic distribution, where they intelligently distribute client requests or network load across several servers. This distribution ensures that no single server is overwhelmed, thereby enhancing the reliability and high availability of network services. In addition to load balancing, ADCs significantly improve application performance through application acceleration. This is achieved using compression, caching, and SSL acceleration, which collectively speed up the application response time and improve the end-user experience.

Security is another vital component of ADCs' functionality. They offer application-specific security capabilities, such as Web Application Firewall (WAF) functionalities. These capabilities are crucial in protecting against application-layer attacks and ensuring the integrity and security of critical applications. By integrating these diverse functions – load balancing, application acceleration, and security – ADCs play an essential role in optimizing, securing, and managing application traffic in modern network environments, making them an invaluable asset for any organization reliant on continuous and secure application delivery.

Content Switching

Content switching represents a sophisticated feature within advanced load balancers, where routing decisions are made based on various elements of the incoming request, such as content type, URL, headers, or cookies. This approach to traffic management significantly enhances the efficiency and effectiveness of how network resources are utilized. By analyzing the specifics of each request, content switching directs user requests to the server most suitable for handling that particular type of content or request attribute. This intelligent traffic management is especially beneficial in environments where servers are optimized for different types of content, ensuring that the most appropriate server processes each request.

Moreover, content switching plays a crucial role in enhancing the user experience. It ensures that user requests are not just randomly distributed across servers but are rather directed to the server that is best equipped to handle them efficiently and effectively. This targeted approach to request handling can lead to faster response times and more efficient processing, contributing to a smoother and more satisfactory user experience. By optimizing how requests are allocated to servers, content switching helps maximize the performance and responsiveness of web applications and services, making it a valuable tool in network management and optimization.

Use Cases of Load Balancers

Load balancers find their applications in various domains, notably in enhancing the performance and reliability of web applications, e-commerce platforms, and enterprise applications. In the context of web applications, load balancers play a pivotal role in distributing incoming traffic across multiple servers. This distribution is particularly crucial during periods of peak traffic, ensuring that the website or web application maintains consistent performance and does not succumb to the strain of increased load. The importance of load balancing becomes even more pronounced in e-commerce platforms, especially during high-traffic events such as sales or promotions. By balancing the load between servers, load balancers prevent potential downtime, a critical factor in maintaining a smooth and uninterrupted customer experience, which is essential for the success of e-commerce operations.

In the realm of corporate networks, load balancers are indispensable in ensuring the continuous availability and balanced performance of enterprise applications. These applications are often critical to business operations, and any disruption can lead to significant operational inefficiencies and financial losses. Load balancers effectively distribute network and application traffic across multiple servers, thereby not only preventing any single server from becoming a bottleneck but also ensuring that applications remain available and perform optimally, even under varying load conditions. This capability is vital for maintaining the robustness and reliability of business-critical applications in enterprise environments.

Load balancers, particularly ADCs and content switches, are essential in modern network architectures. They not only distribute network traffic to optimize resource utilization but also enhance application performance and security, playing a pivotal role in the overall user experience and system efficiency.

Proxy Servers

Proxy servers act as intermediaries between end users and the internet, providing various functions like caching, filtering, and access control. They play a significant role in enhancing network performance, security, and management.

Caching

Caching, primarily implemented through proxy servers, serves a crucial function in the efficient management and delivery of web content. These proxy servers are designed to store copies of frequently accessed web pages or files. When a user requests a specific page or file, the proxy server first checks its own cache to determine if the requested content is already stored. If the content is available in the cache, the server serves it directly to the user. This process of caching offers significant benefits in terms of both bandwidth usage and access speed. Since requests can often be served from the local cache, there is a substantial reduction in the need to fetch data from the internet. This not only conserves bandwidth but also significantly speeds up the access time for users, as retrieving content from a local cache is generally much faster than downloading it from a remote server. As a result, caching enhances the overall user experience by providing quicker access to web content and reducing the load on network resources.

Filtering

Filtering, a key function often associated with proxy servers, plays an important role in managing and securing internet access in various network environments. Web filtering, one aspect of this function, involves the use of proxy servers to block access to certain websites. This blocking is typically based on specific criteria such as content, URL, or other parameters. Commonly implemented in business and educational networks, web filtering is a crucial tool for restricting access to websites that are considered inappropriate or unrelated to work or educational purposes. By controlling the websites that users can access, organizations can maintain a focused and productive environment and reduce the risk of exposure to harmful content.

In addition to web filtering, proxy servers are also capable of content filtering. This involves inspecting the actual content being requested and blocking specific types of data. Content filtering is particularly useful for security purposes. For instance, it can be employed to prevent access to websites or content that are malicious or pose a security threat. By scrutinizing the content, proxy servers can identify and block access to sites known for distributing malware, phishing attempts, or other harmful materials. This level of filtering is essential in safeguarding network integrity and protecting users from various cyber threats. Overall, the filtering capabilities of proxy servers, encompassing both web and content filtering, are instrumental in enhancing network security and managing internet usage effectively.

Access Control

Proxy servers offer the functionality of user authentication, a critical aspect in managing and securing network access. They can be configured to require users to authenticate themselves before they are granted access to internet resources. This process of authentication not only enhances network security but also aids in monitoring and controlling user activity on the network. By verifying the identity of users, organizations can keep track of who is accessing what resources, thereby maintaining a secure and controlled network environment.

Additionally, proxy servers play a pivotal role in policy implementation within network infrastructures. They enable network administrators to implement and enforce specific policies related to internet usage. For instance, administrators can set up rules to limit access to the internet during certain hours, or they can track internet usage for billing or auditing purposes.

This capability is particularly useful in organizational settings where managing and regulating internet access is essential for maintaining productivity and ensuring compliance with organizational policies. Through these functionalities, proxy servers not only provide a secure gateway to the internet but also serve as a powerful tool for network administration, allowing for a tailored and controlled internet experience within the network.

Additional Roles

Proxy servers offer significant benefits in terms of privacy and anonymity as well as load balancing, enhancing both security and performance in network environments. When it comes to privacy and anonymity, proxy servers play a crucial role by masking the user's IP address and other identifying information. This feature is particularly valuable for users who wish to browse the internet without revealing their identity or location. By routing requests through the proxy server, which then communicates with internet resources on behalf of the user, the proxy effectively hides the user's actual IP address. This anonymity can protect users from being tracked by websites, advertisers, and potentially malicious actors, thereby enhancing their privacy and security online.

In addition to privacy features, some proxy servers are equipped with load balancing capabilities. This functionality involves the distribution of incoming network and internet requests across multiple servers. By balancing the load in this manner, proxy servers can prevent any single server from becoming overwhelmed, thereby improving the overall performance and reliability of the network. This is especially beneficial in environments with high traffic, where load balancing ensures that requests are handled efficiently and downtime is minimized. By distributing the load, proxy servers not only enhance the user experience through reduced latency and faster processing but also contribute to the robustness of the network infrastructure.

Proxy servers are versatile tools in network infrastructure, providing critical services in terms of performance optimization, security enhancement, and administrative control. They are especially valuable in organizational environments where internet access needs to be monitored, controlled, and optimized.

Virtual Switches/Routers

Virtual switches and routers are software-based applications that emulate the functionality of their physical counterparts within a virtualized environment. They are key components in managing network traffic and functionality in virtual networks.

Virtual Switches

Virtual switches play a pivotal role in virtualized environments, functioning similarly to physical switches but within a virtual context. Their primary functionality is to connect virtual machines (VMs), either within the same host or across different hosts. By directing traffic between VMs on the same virtual network, virtual switches manage communication in a way that is analogous to how physical switches handle hardware devices. This includes routing traffic and handling data packets among the VMs, ensuring efficient and orderly network communication.

In terms of implementation, virtual switches are typically integrated into hypervisor software, which includes platforms like VMware ESXi, Microsoft Hyper-V, or KVM. This integration allows VMs hosted on the same server to communicate with each other efficiently and effectively. This is crucial for maintaining a high-performance virtualized environment where multiple VMs might need to interact or share resources.

The benefits of virtual switches extend beyond mere connectivity. They are instrumental in enabling network segmentation, efficient traffic management, and the implementation of security policies within a virtualized environment. Network segmentation allows for the division of a network into distinct segments, each of which can be independently managed and secured. This enhances not only the security but also the performance of the network, as traffic can be more effectively controlled and routed. Furthermore, virtual switches provide administrators with the flexibility and control needed to manage virtual network traffic effectively. This includes the ability to apply various network policies and oversee the flow of traffic within the virtual network, thus ensuring that the network operates securely and efficiently. In summary, virtual switches are a key component in virtualized environments, offering the essential capabilities required for advanced network management and security in a virtual context.

Virtual Routers

Virtual routers are an essential component in virtualized environments, mirroring the functionality of their physical counterparts but within a virtual context. Their core role involves routing traffic not only between different virtual networks but also between virtual and physical networks. This capability is crucial for maintaining efficient network communication and connectivity in complex network architectures that involve a mix of virtual and physical elements.

In terms of their implementation, virtual routers are typically deployed as part of network virtualization platforms. One of the key advantages of virtual routers is that they can be configured and managed in a manner similar to physical routers, but without the limitations and constraints imposed by physical hardware. This flexibility allows for easier modification, scaling, and deployment, which is particularly beneficial in rapidly changing network environments.

Virtual routers are commonly utilized in cloud environments and data centers, where the need for dynamic routing and network isolation is paramount. In such settings, they enable the creation of isolated virtual networks, each with its own routing logic and policies. This isolation is essential for security, performance, and compliance reasons, as it allows different network segments to operate independently and securely. Additionally, the dynamic routing capabilities of virtual routers make them ideal for environments where network paths and priorities need to be adjusted frequently to optimize traffic flow and resource utilization. Overall, virtual routers offer the flexibility, scalability, and functionality required to manage and maintain efficient network operations in increasingly virtualized and cloud-based environments.

Key Advantages

The key advantages of virtual switches and routers lie in their flexibility, scalability, cost-effectiveness, and seamless integration with virtual environments. These virtual networking components can be easily configured, scaled up or down, or reconfigured to meet evolving network needs, all without the necessity for physical hardware adjustments. This flexibility and scalability are particularly beneficial in dynamic network environments where demands and configurations can change rapidly.

From a financial perspective, virtual switches and routers significantly reduce the need for physical hardware. This reduction translates into lower costs associated with purchasing, maintaining, and powering network devices. The move away from physical infrastructure not only cuts down on direct hardware expenses but also on the indirect costs of space, energy, and cooling requirements typically associated with running physical network devices.

Virtual switches and routers are seamlessly integrated into virtual environments. This integration allows for the implementation of advanced networking features within virtualized infrastructures. For instance, they enable features like VM mobility, which is crucial for the efficient management of virtual machines, and the creation of isolated tenant networks, which are essential in cloud deployments. These capabilities ensure that virtualized infrastructures can support complex, multi-tenant environments while maintaining high levels of performance, security, and efficiency. In summary, the flexibility, cost savings, and advanced networking capabilities offered by virtual switches and routers make them indispensable tools in modern virtualized and cloud-based infrastructures.

In summary, virtual switches and routers are foundational elements in virtual networking, providing the necessary tools to manage network traffic, security, and policies within virtualized environments, mirroring the functionalities of physical networking in a more flexible and cost-effective manner.

Chapter 3: Network Operations

Best Practices in Network Documentation

Network documentation is a critical aspect of network management, providing a detailed and organized record of the network's structure, configurations, processes, and changes. Effective documentation is essential for efficient network operation, troubleshooting, and long-term maintenance.

Importance of Network Documentation

The importance of comprehensive network documentation in the management and maintenance of network infrastructures cannot be overstated, as it plays a critical role in various aspects of network operations. Firstly, when it comes to troubleshooting and problem resolution, having detailed documentation is invaluable. It allows network professionals to quickly identify and resolve network issues by providing clear insights into the network's configurations and any historical changes that have been made. This clarity can significantly speed up the troubleshooting process and ensure more effective problem resolution.

In the context of network planning and scaling, accurate and up-to-date documentation is equally crucial. It assists network planners in understanding the current capabilities and limitations of the network, which is essential for making informed decisions about network growth and expansion. By having a comprehensive view of the network's existing infrastructure, planners can more accurately forecast future needs and design a network that can accommodate growth without sacrificing performance or reliability.

From a compliance and security standpoint, keeping detailed records of the network is often a mandatory requirement for adhering to various standards and regulations. Good documentation practices aid in security auditing by providing a clear record of the network's configuration and changes over time. This can be instrumental in pinpointing vulnerabilities or deviations from established security policies, thereby enhancing the overall security posture of the network.

Change management is another area where network documentation proves indispensable. By meticulously documenting changes made to the network, organizations can better manage these modifications and understand their impact over time. This understanding is crucial for maintaining the stability and efficiency of the network, as well as for planning future changes in a manner that minimizes disruption and maximizes benefits.

In terms of knowledge transfer, detailed network documentation is invaluable. It plays a key role in the onboarding process of new team members, ensuring that they can quickly come up to speed on the network's configuration and history. Additionally, thorough documentation ensures that critical knowledge is not lost when staff changes occur, thereby preserving the continuity and stability of network operations. Comprehensive network documentation is a cornerstone of effective network management, underpinning every aspect, from daily operations to long-term strategic planning.

Elements of Effective Network Documentation

Effective network documentation is a multifaceted undertaking encompassing several key elements, each contributing to a comprehensive understanding and management of the network infrastructure. One of the primary elements is the creation of network diagrams. These diagrams are visual representations that include topology maps, wiring schematics, and both physical and logical layouts of the network. These visual aids provide a clear and immediate understanding of how the network is structured and how different components are interconnected, making them indispensable for planning and troubleshooting.

Another critical component is maintaining detailed hardware and software inventories. This involves keeping updated records of all network equipment, including specific models, software versions, licenses, and configurations. Such inventories are essential not only for managing assets and ensuring compliance with licensing agreements but also for planning upgrades and responding effectively to security vulnerabilities or hardware failures.

The backup of configuration files and settings for network devices constitutes another essential element. Network administrators can quickly restore network operations in case of a device failure or other issues that necessitate reverting to a previous configuration by having a reliable backup of all critical configuration files. This practice is crucial for minimizing downtime and ensuring the quick recovery of network services.

Documentation should also include comprehensive policy and procedure manuals. These documents describe network policies, operational procedures, and best practice guidelines. They are vital for maintaining consistent and efficient network operations. They are particularly useful for training new staff and ensuring all team members align with the organization's standards and practices.

Lastly, the compilation of logs and historical data is essential. Keeping records of system logs, incident reports, and historical data enables network administrators to analyze trends and investigate past network issues. This historical perspective is invaluable for understanding and improving network performance and security over time, as it provides insights into recurrent problems, performance bottlenecks, and security breaches.

Best Practices for Network Documentation

Adhering to best practices for network documentation is crucial for ensuring that it remains effective and useful. One of the key best practices is maintaining consistency across all documentation. This means using a uniform format and having a standardized process for updates. Consistency makes it easier for anyone referencing the documentation to find and understand the necessary information without confusion or misinterpretation.

Accessibility is another important aspect. Documentation should be easily accessible to all authorized personnel. However, it's equally important to keep this information secure, as network documentation can be sensitive. Striking the right balance between accessibility and security ensures that the right people have access to the necessary information while protecting the network from potential security breaches.

Regular updates are essential to keep the documentation reflective of the current state of the network. This involves conducting regular reviews and updating the documentation following any network change, whether minor or major. Keeping the documentation up-to-date ensures that it remains a reliable resource for network management and troubleshooting.

Being detail-oriented is crucial in network documentation. The documentation should include as much detail as necessary to provide a clear and comprehensive understanding of the network.

However, it's important to avoid unnecessary complexity, as overly complicated documentation can be difficult to use and may lead to misunderstandings or errors.

Finally, leveraging automated tools for documentation can significantly enhance accuracy and efficiency. Documentation tools and software can help in maintaining up-to-date records, generating network diagrams, and managing inventories more effectively than manual methods. Automated tools can also reduce the likelihood of human error and ensure that the documentation process is as streamlined and efficient as possible.

In conclusion, effective network documentation is not just about maintaining records; it's a fundamental practice for the operational health and sustainability of the network infrastructure. It provides a foundation for making informed decisions, ensuring continuity, and achieving operational excellence.

Symbols in Network Diagrams

In network diagrams, symbols are standardized icons representing various network elements like devices, connections, and services. Using universally recognized symbols ensures that network diagrams are easily understandable by anyone familiar with networking.

Standard Symbols

Router: Typically depicted as a box with arrows in a circular arrangement, symbolizing the routing functionality between different networks.

Switch: Represented by a rectangle with multiple lines (representing ports) on one side. A Layer 3 switch may have an additional layering to indicate its routing capability.

Wireless Router/Access Point: A symbol similar to the router but with concentric curved lines on one side, indicating wireless capabilities.

Firewall: Illustrated as a wall or barrier, signifying its role in network security.

Server: Represented by a rectangle with a small square on top, symbolizing the server's role in storing and managing data.

Client Computers: Depicted as desktop or laptop icons, indicating end-user devices.

Cloud: The cloud symbol represents external networks or services, commonly the Internet, but can also depict cloud services.

Modem: A smaller rectangle, sometimes with wavy lines indicating its role in signal modulation and demodulation.

Cable Connections: Straight lines, often with a plug symbol at each end, indicating wired connections.

Fiber Optic Cable: A line with a light symbol or waves to denote fiber optic transmission.

Virtualized Devices: Often represented with a dashed border or a special overlay symbol to differentiate from physical hardware.

Usage in Network Diagrams

Clarity: Using these standard symbols helps make the network diagrams clear and easily understood.

Detailing: Labels and brief descriptions are often added next to the symbols for additional clarity, especially when representing specific models or configurations.

Layout: The arrangement of symbols in a network diagram provides a visual representation of the network's physical and logical topology.

Importance

Standard symbols in network diagrams are crucial in network design, troubleshooting, and documentation. They provide a clear and concise way to represent the components and architecture of a network, facilitating effective communication and understanding among network professionals and stakeholders.

The use of standardized symbols is a key aspect of network documentation, ensuring that diagrams are not only informative but also universally interpretable, laying the groundwork for effective network management and communication.

Types of Network Diagrams: Physical vs. Logical

Network diagrams are vital for understanding, documenting, and managing network infrastructures. They typically fall into two main categories: physical and logical diagrams. Each type serves different purposes and offers unique insights into the network's structure and operation.

Physical Network Diagrams

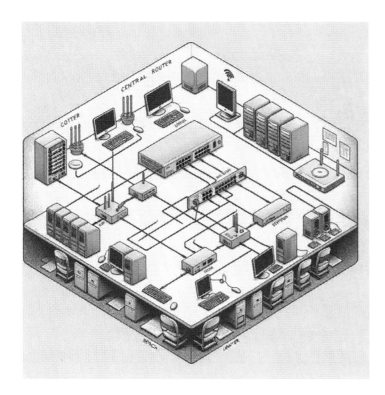

Physical network diagrams depict the actual physical layout of the network. They show the physical connections between devices and the location of network components.

It includes routers, switches, hubs, firewalls, devices like servers and computers, and wiring types and pathways.

They are useful for network installation and troubleshooting physical connections. They help identify the exact placement of hardware and how they are interconnected.

When to Use:

When setting up or modifying the network infrastructure.

For maintenance tasks or when troubleshooting physical connectivity issues.

In planning for hardware upgrades or physical expansions of the network.

Logical Network Diagrams

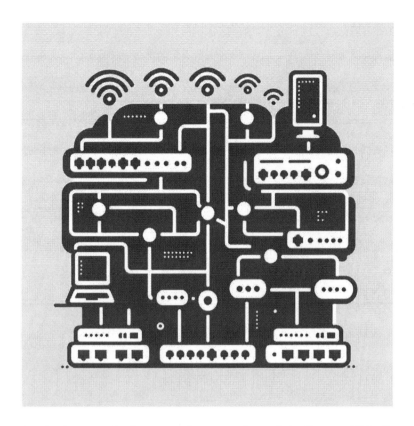

Logical network diagrams focus on how data flows within the network, regardless of its physical connections. They illustrate the architecture of the network and how different components communicate.

Components: Includes subnets, network devices, segments, and routing protocols, but represented in a way that shows their roles and relationships rather than physical connections.

Purpose: Aids understanding and managing network operations, policies, and data flow. Useful for network planning, performance analysis, and security auditing.

When to Use:

For network planning, understand how data moves through the network.

When configuring or troubleshooting network operations, security, and protocols.

In discussions with stakeholders who need to understand network operation but not necessarily the physical layout.

Importance of Both Diagrams

Comprehensive Understanding: Using physical and logical network diagrams provides a complete overview of the network's structure and functionality.

Different Audiences: Physical diagrams are more relevant for technical staff involved in the physical setup and maintenance, while logical diagrams are crucial for network administrators and those focusing on operational aspects.

Physical and logical network diagrams are essential components of network documentation, each serving distinct purposes. Understanding when and how to use each type is key to effective network management, planning, and troubleshooting.

Section 2: Business Continuity and Disaster Recovery

Backup and Recovery

In business continuity and disaster recovery, backup and recovery strategies are essential to ensure that data and systems can be quickly restored following a disruption. This area encompasses various technologies, methodologies, and testing practices to safeguard critical business data and maintain operational resilience.

Data Backup Approaches:

In data backup, several approaches are utilized, each with advantages and considerations. **Full Backup** involves copying all data to the backup storage. This method is comprehensive but time-consuming and requires significant storage space, making it a thorough but resource-intensive option. On the other hand, **Incremental Backup** takes a more selective approach by only copying the data that has changed since the last backup, whether a full or another incremental backup. This method is faster and conserves storage space, but it can complicate the restoration process, as it requires a sequence of backups for a complete restore.

Another strategy is the **Differential Backup**, which captures data that has changed since the last full backup. This method is easier to restore than incremental backups, as it only needs the last full backup and the latest differential backup. However, it requires more storage space than incremental backups. The decision on **Backup Frequency** is a critical aspect of a backup strategy. It involves a balance between the risk of data loss and resource utilization. For instance, critical systems may necessitate daily or real-time backups, while weekly backups might adequately serve less critical data.

In addition to these methods, an effective backup strategy also considers the location of backups. Combining **Offsite and Onsite Backups** ensures a robust approach. Onsite backups offer quick access and swift recovery capabilities, vital in many scenarios. In contrast, offsite backups, including cloud storage solutions, safeguard against local disasters. This dual approach ensures that data is protected not only against technical failures but also against physical events that could impact the primary storage location.

Recovery Solutions:

In the landscape of data backup and recovery, various solutions are employed, each catering to different needs and scenarios. **Traditional Backup Solutions** such as tape drives, external hard drives, and Network Attached Storage (NAS) devices have been long-standing staples in data backup strategies. These physical devices are reliable and useful for onsite data storage and backups, offering a tangible and immediate access point for data recovery.

On the other hand, **Cloud-based Backup Solutions** have gained immense popularity and utility in the modern digital age. Services like AWS S3, Azure Storage, or specialized cloud backup providers offer flexible, scalable, and often cost-effective backup storage solutions. The cloud-based approach provides offsite data storage, enhancing data safety in case of local disasters, but also offers the convenience of remote accessibility and often includes advanced features like automation and integration with various applications.

Another critical aspect of modern backup strategies is **Disaster Recovery as a Service (DRaaS)**. These are cloud-based disaster recovery solutions that provide businesses with rapid recovery times in case of major incidents. DRaaS typically includes not just data backup but also comprehensive plans for quick restoration of services, minimizing downtime in case of significant disruptions.

Furthermore, the role of **Virtualization in Recovery** is increasingly prominent. By utilizing virtualized environments, organizations can quickly spin up affected systems and applications in the event of hardware failure or a disaster. This approach significantly reduces recovery time, as virtual machines can be activated much faster than restoring physical systems. Virtualization also provides flexibility regarding recovery locations, as virtual systems can be hosted in various environments, including cloud platforms, further enhancing the robustness of disaster recovery plans.

Backup and Recovery Testing

Importance of Regular Testing: Regular testing of backup and recovery procedures ensures that they work as intended and identifies areas for improvement.

In ensuring the effectiveness of backup and recovery strategies, various **Testing Approaches** play a crucial role. One such approach is conducting **Mock Drills**, which involve simulating a disaster scenario to rigorously test the recovery process and response times. These drills provide a realistic assessment of how well an organization can execute its disaster recovery plan under pressure, highlighting areas of strength and pinpointing areas needing improvement.

Another key testing method is **Recovery Time Objective (RTO) Testing**. This type of testing is centered around ensuring that systems and applications can be restored and brought back online within the desired timeframe set by the organization's recovery objectives. RTO testing is critical to ensure minimal downtime and the impact on business operations is manageable during a disruption.

Similarly, **Recovery Point Objective (RPO) Testing** is essential in verifying that data can be recovered to a point that aligns with business continuity requirements. RPO testing ensures that data loss is within acceptable limits as defined by the organization. This type of testing is particularly important for data-intensive businesses where data loss can have significant implications.

Best Practices

Automation: Automating backup processes to ensure consistency and reduce the likelihood of human error.

Regular Updates: Keeping backup and recovery plans up to date with changes in the IT environment.

Documentation: Meticulously documenting backup and recovery procedures, including clear recovery steps and contacts.

Backup and recovery are cornerstones of business continuity and disaster recovery planning, providing a safety net against data loss and ensuring operational resilience. A well-structured approach, encompassing robust strategies, advanced technologies, and regular testing, is essential for safeguarding business assets and maintaining continuity in the face of disruptions.

Business Continuity Planning (BCP)

Business Continuity Planning (BCP) is a proactive process to ensure that a business can continue operating during and after a disaster or major disruption. A comprehensive BCP minimizes the impact on business operations and helps in the quick restoration of services.

Steps to Create a Comprehensive BCP

Risk Assessment and Business Impact Analysis (BIA):

Identify potential threats and the impact they could have on business operations, including financial, legal, and reputational impacts. Determine critical business functions and processes and the resources required to support them.

Define Objectives:

Establish clear Recovery Time Objectives (RTO) and Recovery Point Objectives (RPO) for different business processes. RTO determines the maximum tolerable downtime, while RPO defines the maximum period data might be lost.

Develop Recovery Strategies:

Identify and evaluate various recovery strategies for restoring business operations after a disruption. This may include using alternate sites, outsourcing certain functions, or implementing redundant systems.

Plan Development:

Document the BCP, detailing the response and recovery procedures for various disaster scenarios. Include contact lists, resources, and procedures for emergency response, crisis communications, and recovery activities.

Plan Testing and Maintenance:

Regularly test and update the plan to ensure its effectiveness. This could include tabletop exercises, simulation drills, or actual recovery testing. Revise the plan based on changes in the business environment, new potential threats, and outcomes from testing activities.

Training and Awareness:

Conduct training sessions to ensure staff know the plan and their respective roles and responsibilities in a disaster scenario. Foster a culture of business continuity awareness across the organization.

Communication Plan:

Develop a communication plan that includes internal communication with employees and external communication with customers, suppliers, and other stakeholders. Ensure clear and effective communication during and after a disaster to maintain trust and confidence.

Integration with Other Plans:

Ensure that the BCP aligns with other organizational plans, such as disaster recovery plans, emergency response plans, and operational procedures.

A comprehensive Business Continuity Plan ensures an organization's resilience and capability to withstand and quickly recover from disruptive events. It encompasses many considerations, from understanding potential risks to developing and regularly testing and updating response and recovery procedures.

Section 3: Scanning, Monitoring, and Patching Processes

Tools and Methodologies

Effective network management requires continuous scanning, monitoring, and updating of network systems. Various tools and methodologies, including Simple Network Management Protocol (SNMP), syslog, and network management systems, play crucial roles in this ongoing process.

Simple Network Management Protocol (SNMP)

The Simple Network Management Protocol (SNMP) serves a vital purpose in network management, particularly for devices on IP networks. Its primary role is to monitor network-attached devices for conditions that require administrative attention. SNMP's functionality hinges on agents installed on these network devices. These agents are responsible for collecting data and reporting to a central SNMP manager. The data gathered includes metrics on performance, utilization, errors, and other critical operational statistics, providing a comprehensive view of the network's health and efficiency.

SNMP has evolved over time, with different versions offering varying features and capabilities. The earlier versions, SNMPv1 and SNMPv2, provide basic features essential for network management. However, SNMPv3 brings significant advancements, particularly in the realm of security. SNMPv3 offers enhanced security features, including robust authentication and encryption. This is crucial in ensuring that the management and monitoring of network devices are done securely, protecting sensitive data and network operations from unauthorized access or breaches. The evolution from SNMPv1 and SNMPv2 to SNMPv3 reflects the growing need for secure network management practices in increasingly complex network environments.

Syslog

Syslog plays a crucial role in the monitoring of networks and systems, functioning as a standard protocol designed to send system log or event messages to a specific server, known as a syslog server. Its widespread use in network and system monitoring stems from its efficiency in handling log data, a key component in maintaining the health and security of network infrastructures. The syslog servers are tasked with collecting and storing this log data, which encompasses a broad range of information regarding system operations, events, and errors. Beyond mere collection and storage, these servers also offer capabilities for analysis and reporting. This functionality is indispensable for various critical tasks such as troubleshooting issues, maintaining network security, and fulfilling compliance reporting requirements.

In addition to its primary roles, syslog can be integrated with a variety of other tools to create comprehensive monitoring and alerting solutions. This integration enhances the overall network management system, enabling more sophisticated monitoring and quicker response to potential issues. By leveraging syslog in conjunction with other monitoring tools, network administrators can achieve a more holistic view of their network's performance and security status, ensuring that they are well-equipped to handle the complexities of modern network environments.

Network Management Systems (NMS)

Network Management Systems (NMS) are sophisticated platforms that offer a unified and comprehensive view of a network's state. They employ a range of tools and protocols, such as SNMP (Simple Network Management Protocol) and syslog, to effectively monitor and manage network resources. These systems are designed to handle a broad spectrum of network-related tasks. This includes monitoring network traffic and performance, which is critical for maintaining optimal network operation. Additionally, NMS are capable of automating routine network management tasks, thereby enhancing efficiency and reducing the potential for human error.

Beyond these functionalities, NMS platforms are equipped to provide various forms of support to network administrators. They offer alerts for immediate notification of network issues, dashboards for a real-time overview of network status, and reports for in-depth analysis and review of network performance. These features are essential for proactive network management, allowing administrators to swiftly identify and address issues, plan for network upgrades, and ensure consistent network performance.

Examples of popular Network Management Systems include SolarWinds Network Performance Monitor, Nagios, and Zabbix. These systems are renowned for their robust capabilities and are widely used in diverse IT environments. These NMS platforms bring unique features and strengths, catering to different network management needs and preferences. Their widespread adoption underscores the critical role of NMS in modern network environments, where they serve as indispensable tools for efficient and effective network management.

Best Practices in Utilizing These Tools

A key practice involves **Regular Updates and Configurations**. Keeping these tools updated and correctly configured is crucial, as this ensures accurate monitoring and reporting. An up-to-date system is more secure and more efficient in tracking network activities and identifying potential issues.

Another important aspect is **Comprehensive Coverage**. When setting up SNMP and syslog monitoring, ensuring coverage of all critical network components is vital. Comprehensive monitoring allows for a complete view of the network's health, enabling administrators to make informed decisions and quickly pinpoint areas of concern.

Alerting and Thresholds are also crucial in network management. Configuring alerts for abnormal activities or performance issues is key to maintaining network integrity. These alerts immediately notify of potential problems, enabling quick response and mitigation efforts to prevent further issues or downtimes.

Lastly, **Data Analysis and Review** play a significant role in network management. Regularly analyzing the data collected by SNMP and syslog can reveal trends and insights, leading to potential improvements in network performance and security. This proactive approach to reviewing and understanding network data helps optimize operations and plan future enhancements or expansions.

Utilizing SNMP, syslog, and network management systems provides a robust framework for continuous scanning, monitoring, and managing networks efficiently. These tools and methodologies are essential for maintaining network health, performance, and security, ensuring quick response to operational issues.

Remote Access Methods

Remote access methods are essential for managing and troubleshooting network devices and servers from different locations. Key remote access methodologies include remote desktop protocols, Secure Shell (SSH), and console access.

Remote Desktop

Remote desktop protocols provide a vital functionality by allowing users to control a computer or server remotely, offering a graphical interface to interact with the system from another location. This capability is essential for various tasks that require direct interaction with the remote system's graphical user interface, such as software installations or configurations within a GUI environment. Among the common protocols used for this purpose are Microsoft's Remote Desktop Protocol (RDP) and VNC (Virtual Network Computing), each enabling remote control of computers over a network. Additionally, tools like TeamViewer or AnyDesk further facilitate remote desktop access, providing intuitive and user-friendly platforms for connecting to and managing remote systems. These tools and protocols are ideal for a wide range of use cases, particularly where tasks necessitate a full graphical interface rather than command-line interactions.

Secure Shell (SSH)

SSH, or Secure Shell, serves as a cryptographic network protocol with a fundamental purpose of operating network services securely over an unsecured network. This protocol is pivotal in ensuring the security and integrity of network communications, particularly in environments where sensitive data is transmitted. The core functionality of SSH lies in its ability to provide secure command-line access to a remote device. By establishing a secure channel, SSH offers strong user authentication and ensures that data communications are encrypted and protected from unauthorized access or interception.

The use cases for SSH are varied and integral to many aspects of network management and cybersecurity. It is commonly used for secure file transfers, utilizing protocols such as SFTP (SSH File Transfer Protocol) or SCP (Secure Copy Protocol). Additionally, SSH is a go-to solution for remote server maintenance, allowing administrators to securely access and manage servers from remote locations. Another common application is running command-line programs on remote machines, where secure and reliable access is necessary.

One of the key advantages of SSH is its robust encryption and security features, which have established it as a standard for secure network services. The protocol's ability to shield data from potential eavesdropping or hijacking makes it an essential tool in today's security-conscious digital environment. SSH's encryption ensures that the content remains unreadable to unauthorized parties even if network traffic is intercepted. This level of security is critical for maintaining the confidentiality and integrity of sensitive data and communications, making SSH a trusted and widely used tool in various network and IT operations.

Console Access

Console access is a fundamental concept in network management, referring to connecting directly to a network device's console port, such as a router, switch, or server. This connection method typically involves using a console cable that links to the device's console port, coupled with terminal emulation software on a computer or terminal. This setup enables direct interaction with the device, bypassing network-based connections.

The use cases for console access are critical and varied. It is particularly essential for initial device setups, where configuring the device for the first time requires a direct connection. Additionally, console access is a vital tool for recovering lost credentials, allowing administrators to regain control over devices when standard network-based access is compromised or unavailable. Moreover, in situations where remote network access is not possible, either due to network failures or when the device is not reachable over the network, console access provides an indispensable alternative for troubleshooting and configuring devices.

One of the significant advantages of console access is its level of directness and security. Unlike network connections that rely on various network protocols and configurations, console access directly links the device. This direct connection is independent of the network's state or configuration, making it reliable for accessing devices even in complex network scenarios or during outages. Furthermore, because console access is not routed through the network, it is inherently secure from network-based threats, ensuring a safe and controlled environment for device configuration and troubleshooting. This makes console access a crucial component in the toolkit of network administrators, particularly in maintaining, securing, and troubleshooting network infrastructures.

Best Practices in Remote Access

In the realm of remote access, **Security** is a paramount concern. It's essential to secure all remote access methods with strong authentication methods. Where feasible, implementing multi-factor authentication (MFA) adds an additional layer of security, significantly reducing the risk of unauthorized access. MFA requires users to provide two or more verification factors to access a resource, making it much harder for potential intruders to breach network defenses simply by stealing a user's credentials.

Monitoring and Logging are also critical components of a robust remote access strategy. Maintaining logs of all remote access sessions is crucial for tracking who accesses the network and when. These logs provide valuable insights and are essential for forensic analysis during a security incident. Regular monitoring of these logs is equally important, as it helps in the early detection of any unauthorized access attempts or suspicious activities. By actively monitoring and analyzing log data, organizations can quickly respond to potential security breaches, minimizing the risk and impact of such events.

For remote access, particularly when accessing network devices over the internet, a **VPN (Virtual Private Network)** is strongly recommended. A VPN encrypts the traffic between the remote user and the network, ensuring that any data transmitted during the session is protected from eavesdropping or interception. This encryption is vital for maintaining the integrity and confidentiality of sensitive information accessed or transmitted remotely. Using a VPN is a fundamental practice for securing remote network access, providing a secure tunnel for data to traverse the often insecure expanse of the internet.

Remote access methods are integral for effective network management, particularly troubleshooting, maintenance, and configuration tasks. They offer the flexibility to manage network resources from various locations securely and efficiently, an essential capability in modern network operations.

VPNs (Virtual Private Networks)

VPNs are crucial in modern network infrastructures, providing secure access to network resources over public networks like the Internet. They are used to encrypt and tunnel network traffic, ensuring confidentiality and data integrity.

Types of VPNs

SSL VPN (Secure Sockets Layer VPN):

SSL VPN, or Secure Sockets Layer Virtual Private Network, is a type of VPN that enables users to securely access a network from a remote location using a standard web browser. Unlike other types of VPNs, SSL VPNs do not require installing specialized client software, making them a convenient option for users. This functionality is particularly advantageous for remote workers or users who need access to their organization's network from external locations. SSL VPNs are ideally suited for providing remote access to web applications, client/server applications, and internal network resources. This makes them a versatile solution for various remote access needs, from accessing email and corporate websites to more complex tasks like accessing internal databases and network drives.

In terms of security, SSL VPNs offer robust encryption and secure access to a network, ensuring that the data transmitted is protected from eavesdropping or interception. However, it is generally considered that SSL VPNs provide a less comprehensive approach to network access control compared to IPSec VPNs. While they excel in providing secure access to specific applications or services, they may not offer the same level of control over the entire network. Despite this, SSL VPNs remain a popular choice due to their ease of use, compatibility with standard web browsers, and sufficient security for many common use cases in remote access scenarios.

IPSec VPN (Internet Protocol Security VPN):

IPSec VPN, for Internet Protocol Security Virtual Private Network, is a widely used technology designed to establish secure network connections. Its primary functionality is creating a protected communication link between remote devices or networks and a main network. Unlike

SSL VPNs, IPSec VPN typically requires installing VPN client software on the user's device, making it a more integrated but less browser-dependent solution.

The use cases for IPSec VPN are particularly common in scenarios requiring site-to-site connections. For example, it is often used to connect branch offices to a central corporate network, ensuring secure and reliable communication across different geographical locations. This makes IPSec VPN an essential component in the networking infrastructure of organizations that operate multiple sites or require secure, site-to-site data transfer.

Regarding security, IPSec VPN is known for providing robust encryption, ensuring that the data transmitted over the network is protected against unauthorized access or interception. Additionally, it can be configured to support strong user authentication methods, further enhancing the security of the connections. One of the key strengths of IPSec VPN is its extensive network access control. This capability allows network administrators to control the network resources and services accessible to users connected via the VPN. This comprehensive approach to network access and security makes IPSec VPN a reliable choice for organizations that require a high degree of protection and control over their network communications, particularly in scenarios involving multiple network sites or complex networking requirements.

VPN Setup

Setting up a Virtual Private Network (VPN) involves several crucial steps to ensure secure and efficient operation. The first step is the **VPN Server Configuration**. This involves setting up a VPN server that will handle incoming VPN connections. The server can either be a dedicated hardware device specifically designed for this purpose or a software solution that runs on an existing server. The choice between a dedicated device or a software solution often depends on the specific needs, scale, and existing infrastructure of the organization.

The next important step is **Client Configuration**. To access the VPN, VPN client software must be installed and configured on their devices. This process involves setting up the necessary software with the correct settings to connect to the VPN server. In the case of SSL VPNs, client configuration might simply involve using a web browser for web-based access, which typically requires less setup on the user's device.

Network Configuration is another critical aspect of VPN setup. This step involves configuring the network settings to ensure that VPN traffic is routed correctly and securely through the network. It also includes firewalls and routers to support and secure VPN connections. Proper network configuration is essential to ensure not only the functionality of the VPN but also the overall security and integrity.

Finally, an **Authentication Setup** is necessary to ensure that only authorized users can access the VPN. This involves implementing strong authentication methods, such as digital certificates, security tokens, or multi-factor authentication mechanisms. Strong authentication is crucial in preventing unauthorized access and protecting sensitive data and resources that the VPN provides access to. By carefully configuring each component - the VPN server, client, network, and authentication - organizations can establish a secure, efficient, and reliable VPN setup that meets their specific networking requirements and security standards.

Security Considerations

In the realm of VPN security and efficiency, adhering to certain standards and practices is crucial. A fundamental aspect is the use of **Strong Encryption Standards** such as AES (Advanced Encryption Standard). AES is widely recognized for protecting data transmitted over VPN connections, ensuring that sensitive information remains confidential and secure from potential interceptions or breaches.

Alongside encryption, the **Use of Secure Protocols** is essential in establishing and maintaining a robust VPN. Protocols like OpenVPN, L2TP/IPSec, or IKEv2 are known for security and reliability. These protocols provide a secure foundation for VPN connections, safeguarding data integrity and privacy across the network.

Another critical aspect is **Access Control**. This involves defining and enforcing policies regarding who can access the network via the VPN and what resources they can access. Effective access control ensures that only authorized users can connect to the network and that they can only access resources necessary for their roles, thereby enhancing the security and efficiency of the network.

Keeping VPN software and hardware updated with **Regular Updates and Patches** is also vital. This practice protects against emerging vulnerabilities and threats, ensuring the VPN infrastructure remains secure against the latest known security issues.

Lastly, **Monitoring and Auditing** of VPN traffic and systems play a key role in network security. Regular monitoring allows for detecting any unusual or unauthorized activities, while auditing helps maintain an overview of the system's usage and security. This ongoing vigilance is crucial for quickly identifying and responding to potential security breaches or anomalies, ensuring the continuous security and integrity of the VPN connection.

Together, these practices form a comprehensive approach to VPN management, ensuring that the VPN not only provides secure and efficient connectivity but also aligns with the highest standards of network security and management.

VPNs are an essential tool for ensuring secure remote access and connectivity in network operations. They balance accessibility and security, enabling remote workers and branch offices to safely access central network resources while protecting data integrity and confidentiality over public networks.

RADIUS and TACACS

RADIUS (Remote Authentication Dial-In User Service) and TACACS (Terminal Access Controller Access-Control System) are authentication protocols used in network security. They play crucial roles in managing access to network resources, ensuring that only authenticated users can access these services.

RADIUS

RADIUS, which stands for Remote Authentication Dial-In User Service, is a client/server protocol that plays a pivotal role in network management. It provides centralized Authentication, Authorization, and Accounting (AAA) management for users who connect to and utilize a network service. This functionality is crucial in managing network access, ensuring that only authorized users can gain entry and that their activities are properly recorded and accounted for. RADIUS is extensively used for network access control, with its applications being especially prevalent in Internet Service Provider (ISP) environments and for managing VPN access.

A key characteristic of RADIUS is its approach to combining authentication and authorization into a single process, streamlining the steps required for a user to gain access to network resources. However, when it comes to security, while RADIUS encrypts the password in the access-request packet, it leaves the remainder of the packet, including the username, unencrypted. This aspect of RADIUS underlines the importance of using it within a secure network environment to mitigate potential security risks. Despite this, RADIUS remains a widely adopted protocol due to its effectiveness in centralized user management and compatibility with various network types and configurations.

TACACS+

TACACS+, an advanced evolution of the original Terminal Access Controller Access-Control System (TACACS), is a client/server protocol primarily used for Authentication, Authorization, and Accounting (AAA). This protocol is commonly employed in larger businesses or enterprises, where robust and secure management of network access is crucial. TACACS+ is particularly valuable for device administration, controlling access to routers, switches, and other critical network devices. A distinctive characteristic of TACACS+ is its approach to separating the authentication, authorization, and accounting processes, as opposed to combining them. This separation offers more flexibility in how each function is handled and configured, allowing for a more tailored access control environment.

One of the major advantages of TACACS+ over protocols like RADIUS is its enhanced security. TACACS+ encrypts the entire packet contents, not just the authentication portion. This comprehensive encryption ensures that sensitive information, including user credentials and authorization data, is protected throughout the transmission process. This level of security is particularly important in environments where the confidentiality and integrity of user data and access control communications are of utmost importance. As a result, TACACS+ has become a preferred choice for organizations seeking a more secure and flexible approach to managing network access and device administration.

Differences Between RADIUS and TACACS+

When comparing **Encryption** capabilities, TACACS+ offers a more comprehensive solution than RADIUS. While RADIUS encrypts only the password portion of the authentication packet, TACACS+ secures the entire packet content. This difference marks TACACS+ as a more secure option, especially in environments where safeguarding the integrity and confidentiality of the entire authentication and authorization process is crucial.

In terms of **Protocol Operation**, the two protocols exhibit key differences. TACACS+ is designed to separate authentication, authorization, and accounting processes, which provides more flexibility in managing these functions independently. On the other hand, RADIUS combines authentication and authorization into a single process, which can simplify configuration but may offer less flexibility than TACACS+.

For **Network Device Administration**, TACACS+ is often the preferred choice. Its ability to offer granular control and enhanced security features make it suitable for administering routers, switches, and other network devices. The protocol's detailed logging capabilities and the separation of authentication, authorization, and accounting functions allow for more precise control and monitoring of user activities on these devices.

Regarding **Interoperability**, RADIUS tends to be more commonly supported, especially for general network access services. This is largely due to its broader interoperability with various network equipment and simpler implementation. RADIUS's widespread adoption and ease of integration make it a go-to option for many organizations seeking a reliable and straightforward solution for network access control.

Understanding RADIUS and TACACS+ and their applications in network operations is essential for securing remote access and maintaining control over network resources.

Moving into the next chapter, we will delve deeper into **Network Security**, exploring the various strategies, technologies, and protocols that protect networks from threats and unauthorized access. This exploration will include advanced security measures, threat mitigation techniques, and the role of policies and compliance in network security.

Chapter 4: Network Security

Section 1: Physical Security Devices

Surveillance in Network Security

In network security, physical surveillance plays a crucial role in safeguarding network infrastructure against unauthorized physical access, tampering, and theft. Key elements of a physical surveillance system include cameras, motion detectors, and logging mechanisms.

Surveillance Cameras

Surveillance cameras have become an integral component in the security and monitoring of physical spaces where network devices are located. These cameras are strategically placed in critical areas such as data centers, server rooms, and locations housing important IT equipment. Their primary function is to continuously monitor these areas, providing a visual record of activities and helping to detect any unauthorized access or unusual events. The types of surveillance cameras used in such setups vary, including fixed cameras, which offer a constant view of a specific area; pan-tilt-zoom (PTZ) cameras, which can be controlled to cover a larger area and focus on specific points of interest; and infrared cameras, which are particularly useful in low-light conditions.

In the context of modern network security, the integration of surveillance systems with network management systems is increasingly common. This integration allows for enhanced monitoring capabilities. Network administrators can remotely access camera feeds, ensuring that they can keep an eye on critical infrastructure from anywhere. This remote monitoring capability is often complemented by alert systems that notify administrators of any suspicious activities the cameras detect. Such integration not only enhances the physical security of important network components but also forms a part of a comprehensive security strategy, encompassing both digital and physical aspects of network security. This holistic approach is crucial in safeguarding against a wide array of potential threats and ensuring the ongoing integrity and reliability of network infrastructures.

Motion Detectors

Motion detectors play a vital role in enhancing security, particularly in areas where sensitive network equipment is stored, or critical operations occur. Their primary purpose is to augment security measures by triggering alerts or activating cameras when movement is detected in secured areas. This function is crucial for early detection of unauthorized access or unusual activity, providing a proactive security measure.

There are several motion detectors, each employing different technologies to detect movement. Passive infrared sensors are among the most common; they detect changes in heat, such as when a person enters a room. Ultrasonic detectors use sound waves to sense movement, while microwave detectors emit microwave pulses and measure the reflection of moving objects. Each type has advantages and ideal use cases, depending on the environment and specific security requirements.

The strategic placement of motion detectors is key to their effectiveness. They are particularly valuable in areas that are not constantly monitored by personnel. By placing these detectors in critical zones, such as near server rooms, data centers, or other vital network infrastructure, they can provide an early warning system against intrusions. This early detection is crucial in mitigating potential risks, allowing security personnel to respond promptly to secure the area. In essence, motion detectors are an indispensable part of a comprehensive security strategy, offering an additional layer of protection to safeguard against unauthorized access and potential security breaches.

Logging

Effective surveillance systems are underscored by robust logging mechanisms, which play a crucial role in security management. These logging mechanisms are designed to meticulously record all detected events, providing a comprehensive record of activities within the monitored area. This includes recording video footage, which offers visual evidence of events, logging access times to track when individuals enter and leave secured areas, and capturing motion detection events to note any unexpected or unauthorized movement.

The importance of these logs cannot be overstated, particularly regarding post-incident analysis. In security breaches or physical intrusions, logs serve as a vital source of evidence, helping to identify what occurred and potentially who was involved. This information is crucial not only for understanding how the incident happened and who may be responsible but also for taking steps to prevent future occurrences.

In managing these logs, verifying that they are securely stored and protected from unauthorized access or tampering is essential. This involves not only employing robust security measures to safeguard the data but also implementing reliable backup systems to prevent data loss. Protecting the integrity and confidentiality of surveillance logs is paramount, as they often contain sensitive information. Effective data storage and protection strategies are, therefore, integral to maintaining the reliability and effectiveness of surveillance systems, ensuring that they continue to serve as an essential tool in security management and incident response.

Best Practices

Regular Testing and Maintenance of surveillance equipment is crucial to ensure it functions correctly and effectively. This involves routinely checking cameras, motion detectors, and other components of the surveillance system to confirm they are operational and properly recording or detecting as intended. Regular maintenance helps in promptly identifying and rectifying any issues, thereby maintaining the continuous efficacy of the surveillance system.

Ensuring **Coverage and Visibility** is another important aspect. It's essential to ensure that surveillance cameras and motion detectors adequately cover all critical and sensitive areas within the premises. This comprehensive coverage ensures no blind spots where unauthorized activities could occur undetected. Proper placement and calibration of surveillance equipment are key to achieving maximum visibility and effectiveness.

Adherence to **Compliance with Legal Requirements** is a must when implementing surveillance systems. This includes respecting privacy laws and adhering to data protection regulations. Ensuring legal compliance not only protects against potential legal repercussions but also respects the privacy rights of individuals, balancing security needs with ethical considerations.

Finally, the effectiveness of a surveillance system can be significantly enhanced by **Integration with Other Security Measures**. This includes combining physical surveillance with systems such as access control and environmental monitoring. Such integration creates a multi-layered security infrastructure, providing a more comprehensive approach to securing premises and sensitive areas. By leveraging the strengths of various security systems, organizations can establish a more robust and resilient security posture.

Surveillance systems are vital to physical security in network environments, providing a means to monitor, detect, and respond to physical threats to network infrastructure.

Access Controls

Access control systems are fundamental to network security, ensuring only authorized personnel access critical network infrastructure like data centers, server rooms, and communication closets. These systems can include card readers, biometrics, and mantraps, each offering different levels of security.

Card Readers

Card readers are essential devices in access control, used for authenticating access using security cards. These cards can either be swiped or tapped against the reader, depending on the technology in use. There are several card readers and cards, including magnetic stripe cards, proximity cards, and smart cards. Each type has its own security features and data capacities, catering to different security needs. Magnetic stripe cards are traditional and common, while smart cards offer more advanced security features and higher data capacity. In implementation, card readers are often integrated with an access control system that logs entries and exits. This integration provides an invaluable audit trail detailing who accessed specific areas and when which is crucial for security monitoring and investigation.

Biometric Systems

Biometric systems represent another facet of access control, utilizing unique physical characteristics for identification and authentication. These systems can include various methods such as fingerprint scanning, facial recognition, iris scans, or hand geometry. The primary advantage of biometric systems is the higher level of security they provide compared to card systems. This is because biometrics are unique to each individual and much harder to forge or transfer, making them ideal for high-security areas or controlling access to sensitive network equipment. However, when implementing biometric systems, it's important to consider and balance security with privacy concerns. Ensuring that biometrics comply with relevant privacy laws and regulations is essential, as these systems handle highly sensitive personal information. Proper implementation and management of biometric systems are crucial to maintaining security while respecting individual privacy.

Mantraps

A mantrap is a specialized physical security system comprising two or more interlocking doors, designed such that only one door can be opened at a time. This design temporarily traps individuals between the doors until they complete the necessary authentication process. The primary purpose of a mantrap is to prevent tailgating, a security breach that occurs when an unauthorized person follows an authorized person into a secured area. By controlling individual access through these interlocking doors, mantraps significantly mitigate the risk of such unauthorized access.

In terms of design, mantraps can be equipped with various security measures to authenticate individuals. These may include biometric scanners, card readers, or even security guards. The authentication method choice depends on the security level required for the protected area. Biometric scanners offer a high level of security by using unique physical characteristics for identification, while card readers are a more common and less intrusive method. Security guards may sometimes be employed for manual verification and authentication. Mantraps are particularly useful in sensitive areas where strict access control is necessary, acting as an effective physical barrier and a checkpoint to ensure that only authorized individuals gain entry. This added layer of security is essential in protecting critical areas against potential security breaches.

Integrated Security Approach

An integrated security approach is vital for comprehensively protecting sensitive network areas. Implementing a **Layered Security** strategy is key to this approach. Organizations can significantly enhance their defensive capabilities by combining various security measures like card readers, biometrics, and mantraps. Each layer adds an additional barrier, making unauthorized access increasingly difficult. For instance, while card readers provide a basic level of security, adding biometrics introduces a personal identification factor, and mantraps offer a physical barrier to control individual movement into secure areas.

The efficacy of this integrated approach depends on **Regular Updates and Audits**. Security landscapes and organizational needs are constantly evolving, as should access control measures. Regular assessments and updates help adapt to new security threats and organizational changes. This could involve updating security protocols, upgrading technology, or revising access policies to address new vulnerabilities or operational requirements.

Another crucial aspect is **Training and Awareness** among staff. Employees should be regularly trained on the importance of access control protocols and the critical role these protocols play in overall network security. This training helps foster a security-conscious culture where every organization member understands their responsibilities in maintaining security and is vigilant about following access control procedures. Educating staff about potential security threats and the correct usage of security systems ensures that these measures are effectively utilized and supports the overall security strategy of the organization.

Access control systems are critical in securing physical network infrastructure, providing the necessary barriers to prevent unauthorized access and ensuring that sensitive network resources are protected from physical intrusion and tampering.

Detection Systems: IDS and IPS

Intrusion Detection Systems (IDS) and Intrusion Prevention Systems (IPS) are critical components of a comprehensive network security strategy. They provide essential capabilities for detecting and, in the case of IPS, taking action against malicious activities and threats within a network.

Intrusion Detection Systems (IDS)

An Intrusion Detection System (IDS) is designed to monitor network traffic, vigilantly scanning for any suspicious activities or potential threats. Its primary functionality is to analyze the flow of traffic across the network, identifying patterns or anomalies that may indicate a network or system attack. There are two main types of IDS: Network-Based IDS (NIDS) and Host-Based IDS (HIDS). NIDS is set up to monitor the traffic for all devices on a network, providing a comprehensive overview of network activity and potential threats. In contrast, HIDS is installed on individual devices, focusing on monitoring both the inbound and outbound traffic specific to that device, offering a more localized perspective.

When an IDS detects potential threats, it is programmed to generate alerts for network administrators. These alerts are crucial as they inform administrators of possible security incidents, allowing them to take necessary actions. However, it's important to note that an IDS itself does not take direct action to stop an attack. Its role is purely diagnostic and alerting in nature, making it an essential tool in the broader context of network security management, where it complements other security measures that actively prevent or mitigate attacks.

Intrusion Prevention Systems (IPS)

Intrusion Prevention Systems (IPS) are often regarded as an advanced extension of Intrusion Detection Systems (IDS), with enhanced capabilities not just to detect threats but also to take proactive steps to block or prevent them. The core functionality of an IPS lies in its ability to not only monitor network traffic for potential threats but also to actively intervene, stopping threats before they impact the network. In terms of operation, an IPS is strategically positioned within the network's data flow, commonly placed directly behind the firewall. This positioning allows the IPS to actively analyze and take automated actions on all network traffic flows, providing a crucial line of defense against malicious activities.

There are two primary types of IPS: Network-Based IPS (NIPS) and Host-Based IPS (HIPS). NIPS is designed to protect the entire network. It analyzes and responds to threats in real time, ensuring that any malicious activity is quickly identified and mitigated, thereby safeguarding the network's integrity. On the other hand, HIPS resides on individual devices, offering a more focused form of protection. It defends against both network-based threats and system-level attacks, providing comprehensive security coverage for each device. By combining both NIPS and HIPS, organizations can achieve a robust security posture, effectively protecting their networks and devices from a wide array of cybersecurity threats.

Key Differences and Use Cases

The key differences between Intrusion Detection Systems (IDS) and Intrusion Prevention Systems (IPS) lie primarily in their approaches to handling network threats, which also influences their use cases. IDS focuses on detection and alerting, designed to monitor network traffic and identify potential threats. When an IDS detects suspicious activity, it alerts network administrators, allowing them to take necessary actions. This makes IDS particularly suitable for environments where it's crucial to closely monitor network traffic for any signs of security breaches or anomalies, without actively modifying or interfering with the traffic itself.

In contrast, IPS involves not only the detection of threats but also their active prevention and mitigation. An IPS is deployed with the capability to block or prevent identified threats in real-time, actively intervening to protect the network. This level of active protection is essential in environments where immediate response to security threats is necessary. In such settings, IPS serves as a critical defense mechanism, automatically responding to and mitigating attacks as they occur, thereby ensuring the security and integrity of the network without the need for manual intervention. The choice between IDS and IPS depends on the specific security needs of the network environment, balancing the need for monitoring with the requirement for active threat prevention.

Best Practices

Regular Updates are crucial. It is important to keep both the IDS/IPS software and their threat databases consistently updated. This ensures that the systems are equipped to protect against new vulnerabilities and evolving attack methods. Regular updates help in safeguarding the network against the latest threats, keeping the security measures current and effective.

Configuration and Tuning of the IDS/IPS systems are equally vital. These systems must be properly configured and regularly tuned to minimize occurrences of false positives and false negatives. Effective tuning ensures that the systems accurately identify legitimate threats, thereby enhancing the effectiveness of threat detection. It also prevents overwhelming administrators with irrelevant alerts, allowing them to focus on genuine threats. Regular tuning and configuration adjustments are key to maintaining the balance between sensitivity and accuracy in threat detection.

Integrating IDS/IPS with other security systems forms another important aspect of a robust security strategy. **Integration with Other Security Systems**, such as firewalls and SIEM (Security Information and Event Management) systems, creates a more comprehensive security posture. This integration allows for a coordinated response to security incidents, leveraging the strengths of each system for more effective threat detection, prevention, and response. By combining IDS/IPS with other layers of security, organizations can create a more resilient and multi-faceted defense against cyber threats.

IDS and IPS are essential for identifying and responding to threats in a network environment. They provide layers of defense, from passive monitoring to active prevention, playing a critical role in maintaining the integrity and security of network infrastructure.

Section 2: Authentication and Access Controls

AAA Framework: Authentication, Authorization, and Accounting

The AAA (Authentication, Authorization, and Accounting) framework is a cornerstone of network security and access control, ensuring that only authenticated users can access network resources, that they have the right permissions, and that their activities are tracked for security and management purposes.

Authentication

Authentication plays a crucial role in network security by verifying the identity of a user or device attempting to access the network. This process can involve various methods, each designed to confirm the identity of the entity requesting access. These methods include something the user knows, such as passwords or PINs; something the user has, like smart cards or security tokens; and something the user is, exemplified by biometric verification (like fingerprints or facial recognition). Often, for enhanced security, a combination of these methods is used, known as multi-factor authentication, which significantly increases the security level. The authentication process typically involves the presentation of credentials, such as usernames and passwords, which are then verified against a database or an authentication server. If the credentials match what's stored in the database, access is granted; if not, access is denied. This system is fundamental in ensuring that only authorized users and devices are able to access the network, thereby protecting sensitive data and resources from unauthorized access.

Authorization

After successful authentication, the next critical step in network security is authorization, which determines what an individual or device is permitted to do on the network. A common model used in this context is Role-Based Access Control (RBAC). In RBAC, users are assigned specific roles within the organization, and each of these roles comes with a predefined set of access rights and privileges. This approach simplifies the management of user permissions, as rights and privileges are controlled at the role level rather than for each individual user.

The implementation of authorization is typically managed through a set of policies and rules that define the access levels and restrictions for various network resources. These resources could include files, directories, services, and more. By establishing clear policies and rules, organizations can effectively control who has access to what resources and to what extent. This not only ensures that users have the access they need to perform their duties but also prevents unauthorized access to sensitive areas of the network, thereby enhancing overall network security and integrity.

Accounting

Accounting in the context of network management serves the purpose of meticulously keeping track of user activities on the network. This includes recording when users log in and out, the duration of their sessions, and the specific actions they perform during these sessions. Such detailed tracking is essential for several reasons, primarily for monitoring and reporting purposes related to security, auditing, and, in some cases, billing.

The usage of accounting data is manifold. In terms of security, it allows for the identification of unusual or suspicious behavior patterns, which could indicate potential security violations. For auditing purposes, this data provides a transparent and traceable record of user activities, ensuring compliance with various regulatory standards and internal policies. In scenarios where billing for network resources is based on usage, accounting data can be used to accurately calculate charges.

To effectively manage this accounting data, various tools are employed. These tools are designed for logging and analyzing the data, offering insights that can be used for trend analysis and capacity planning. By analyzing usage patterns and network load, organizations can make informed decisions regarding network management and capacity expansion. Additionally, the analysis of accounting data plays a crucial role in identifying potential security violations, aiding in the prompt response to and resolution of security incidents. This makes accounting a critical component in the overall management and security strategy of network infrastructures.

AAA Protocols

RADIUS and TACACS+: Common protocols that provide AAA services. RADIUS is widely used for network access, while TACACS+ is often used for device administration.

Integration: AAA services are integrated into network devices and servers, ensuring a consistent and unified approach to security and access control across the network.

Best Practices

Consistency in Policies is crucial. It's important to ensure that authentication and authorization policies are consistently applied and enforced across all network systems. This uniformity helps in maintaining a secure and controlled access environment, reducing the risk of security breaches due to inconsistent policy application. A consistent approach also simplifies the management and monitoring of these policies, as the same standards are applied throughout the network.

Implementing **Strong Authentication Mechanisms** is another vital practice, especially for protecting sensitive systems and data. Strong authentication methods, such as multi-factor authentication, provide an additional layer of security, making it more difficult for unauthorized users to gain access. This is particularly important in areas where sensitive or critical information is processed or stored, as it significantly reduces the risk of data breaches and unauthorized access.

Furthermore, conducting **Regular Review and Audits** of access controls and user activities is essential to ensure ongoing compliance with established security policies. Regular audits help in identifying any irregularities or deviations from the policies, allowing for timely corrective actions. These reviews also provide insights into user behavior and system usage, facilitating continuous improvement of security measures and strategies. By consistently applying these best practices, organizations can strengthen their network security, ensuring robust protection against various cyber threats.

The AAA framework is integral to managing and securing network access. By effectively implementing authentication, authorization, and accounting, organizations can safeguard their networks against unauthorized access and misuse, while maintaining comprehensive records of user activities for auditing and compliance purposes.

Multifactor Authentication (MFA)

Multifactor Authentication (MFA) enhances security by requiring users to provide two or more verification factors to gain access to a resource such as a network, application, or online account. MFA is an effective defense against many common types of cybersecurity threats, particularly credential theft and phishing.

Different Factors of MFA

Knowledge Factors involve something the user knows. This could be a password, a Personal Identification Number (PIN), or answers to specific security questions. These factors rely on information that is supposed to be known only to the user, making them a common first line of defense in authentication processes.

Possession Factors are based on something the user has in their possession. This can include various items like a security token, a smart card, a smartphone app, or a key fob that generates a time-sensitive code. These devices provide an additional layer of security, requiring the user to have a specific physical item to gain access.

Inherence Factors are related to biometrics, which are unique physical characteristics of the user. These include fingerprints, facial recognition, iris scans, and voice recognition. Because these traits are unique to each individual, they offer a high level of security and are increasingly being used in various secure authentication processes.

Location Factors add another dimension to MFA by considering the user's location. This is typically determined through network addresses or GPS signals. It ensures that access attempts are being made from a location that is expected or usual for the user, adding an extra layer of security.

Finally, **Behavioral Factors** involve patterns of behavior that are unique to the user, such as typing rhythm, mouse movements, or even walking patterns. These subtle and often subconscious behaviors can be difficult to replicate, providing a sophisticated and unobtrusive way to verify a user's identity.

Technologies and Methods

SMS and Email-Based Verification involves sending a code to the user's phone or email, which they then enter with their password. This method is widely appreciated for its simplicity and ease of use. **Authentication Applications**, like Google Authenticator or Microsoft Authenticator, offer a more sophisticated approach by generating time-limited codes that users must input during the authentication process.

Hardware Tokens represent a more tangible method: physical devices that generate a code at the push of a button, used alongside a password. Biometric Scanners are employed in the biometric domain to scan unique physical traits such as fingerprints, retinas, or faces for identity verification. Additionally, **Smart Cards and USB Keys** are physical devices that must be inserted into a computer or scanned to grant access, providing a physical layer of security.

When implementing these technologies, there are important **Security Considerations** to remember. Balancing **Strength vs. Convenience** is crucial; while more factors generally increase security, they can also lead to user frustration or resistance due to added complexity. **Backup Methods** are essential to ensure continued access in case the primary method fails, such as losing a phone used for SMS verification.

Moreover, **Privacy Concerns** are particularly pertinent to biometric data. Using biometric information requires careful handling and robust personal data protection to maintain user privacy and comply with data protection regulations. The choice and implementation of these authentication technologies and methods must, therefore, consider the security they provide and their impact on user experience and privacy.

Best Practices

Regular Review and Update: Regularly update MFA settings and policies to align with emerging threats and new technologies.

User Education and Training: Educate users on the importance of MFA and train them on how to use various authentication methods effectively.

Integration with Identity Management: Integrating MFA with existing identity and access management systems for streamlined user authentication across various services.

Multifactor Authentication is a critical component in a layered security approach, significantly enhancing the protection of sensitive data and systems by adding additional barriers to unauthorized access. Its implementation is increasingly becoming a standard security practice for organizations of all sizes.

Access Control Models

Access control models are frameworks that define how users and systems can access resources in a computing environment. The most common models are Discretionary Access Control (DAC), Mandatory Access Control (MAC), and Role-Based Access Control (RBAC). Each model offers different methodologies for managing permissions and access rights.

Discretionary Access Control (DAC)

Discretionary Access Control (DAC) is a model where the control of access to resources is assigned to the owners of those resources. In this system, the owners have the discretion to decide who can access their resources and at what level. This model is commonly implemented in most operating systems, where users have the capability to set permissions on their own files and folders. For example, when a user creates a document, they can define who else has the authority to read or edit that document. This level of control allows users to manage access to their resources based on their individual needs or preferences.

While DAC offers flexibility, it also comes with certain considerations. One of the main challenges is that its security efficacy heavily relies on the users to set their own access controls appropriately. This reliance on users means that the overall security of the system can be compromised if users do not manage their permissions correctly or understand the implications of their settings. Therefore, while DAC allows for a high degree of user control, it can potentially be less secure than other access control models, especially in environments where users might not be well-versed in security best practices.

Mandatory Access Control (MAC)

Mandatory Access Control (MAC) represents a more rigid and structured approach to access control, where access to resource objects is determined based on the information clearance level of the users and the classification of the objects themselves. This model is particularly prevalent in environments that demand a high level of security, such as military or government institutions. In such settings, the MAC system ensures that sensitive information is only accessible to individuals who possess the appropriate level of security clearance.

For instance, a classified document in a MAC environment can only be accessed by individuals who have been granted the specific security clearance that matches the classification level of that document. This ensures that sensitive information is tightly controlled and protected from unauthorized access.

While MAC provides a higher degree of security compared to Discretionary Access Control (DAC), it also comes with its own set of considerations. MAC systems are generally less flexible and more complex to manage. The rigidity of MAC, while beneficial for security, means that the system might not be as adaptable to changing needs or as user-friendly as DAC systems. Moreover, the complexity involved in managing MAC systems, particularly in terms of setting and maintaining the classifications and clearances, can be a significant administrative burden. This makes MAC most suitable for environments where the need for stringent security outweighs the need for flexibility and ease of management.

Role-Based Access Control (RBAC)

Description: In RBAC, access is based on the roles of individual users within an organization. Permissions to perform certain operations are assigned to specific roles, and users are assigned roles.

Implementation: Widely used in commercial and enterprise environments for its flexibility and ease of management.

Example: An employee in the HR department having access to personnel files, while an employee in the engineering department does not.

Considerations: RBAC is effective for managing user permissions in large organizations but requires careful planning and role definition.

Best Practices

- **Policy-Driven Approach**: Implement access controls in alignment with organizational policies and compliance requirements.
- **Principle of Least Privilege**: Users should be given the minimum levels of access—or permissions—needed to perform their job functions.
- **Regular Audits and Updates**: Regularly review and update access controls to ensure they are effective and reflect current organizational needs and structures.

Access control models are fundamental to network security, determining how resources are protected and accessed within an organization. Choosing the right model depends on the organization's specific security requirements, operational needs, and the sensitivity of the data being protected.

Section 3: Network Attacks and Mitigation

Types of Network Attacks

Network attacks are unauthorized actions on digital devices and networks aimed at stealing, altering, destroying, or denying access to data. Understanding various types of attacks is crucial for implementing effective security measures and mitigations.

Distributed Denial of Service (DDoS)

1. **Description**: DDoS attacks involve overwhelming a network or server with a flood of internet traffic, typically sourced from many different devices.
2. **Impact**: The sheer volume of traffic can overload the system, making it unavailable to legitimate users.
3. **Mitigation**: Strategies include network redundancy, traffic filtering, and anti-DDoS solutions from ISPs or cloud-based services.

Phishing

1. **Description**: Phishing attacks use fraudulent communication, usually email, that appears to come from a reputable source, with the goal of tricking individuals into revealing sensitive information.
2. **Impact**: Can lead to unauthorized access to personal and corporate data, financial loss, and identity theft.
3. **Mitigation**: User education, email filtering systems, and regularly updating security protocols are key defenses.

Man-in-the-Middle (MitM)

1. **Description**: In MitM attacks, the attacker secretly intercepts and possibly alters the communication between two parties who believe they are directly communicating with each other.
2. **Impact**: Can result in data breaches, eavesdropping, session hijacking, and credential theft.
3. **Mitigation**: Use of encryption (like HTTPS), secure Wi-Fi networks, VPNs, and avoiding untrusted network connections.

Other Common Attacks

1. **SQL Injection**: Occurs when an attacker manipulates a standard SQL query in a database-driven website.

2. **Cross-Site Scripting (XSS)**: Involves injecting malicious scripts into benign and trusted websites.
3. **Ransomware**: Malware that encrypts a victim's files, with the attacker demanding payment to restore access.
4. **Zero-Day Exploits**: Attacks targeting software vulnerabilities unknown to the vendor or without a patch.
5. **Insider Threats**: Malicious threats from people within the organization, such as employees or contractors.

Best Practices for Mitigation

- **Regular Software Updates and Patching**: Keep all systems and software updated to protect against known vulnerabilities.
- **Firewalls and Intrusion Prevention Systems**: Implement and maintain robust firewall policies and intrusion detection/prevention systems.
- **Security Training and Awareness**: Regularly train employees about common attack methods and how to recognize them.
- **Regular Security Audits and Assessments**: Conduct thorough and regular audits of network security to identify and address vulnerabilities.

Understanding the various types of network attacks is vital in creating a robust network security posture. Equally important is implementing comprehensive mitigation strategies to protect against these threats, ensuring the confidentiality, integrity, and availability of network resources and data.

Section 4: Security Policies and Training

Development of Security Policies

Creating effective security policies is a critical step in safeguarding an organization's information technology assets. These policies provide a framework for setting expectations, defining procedures, and guiding the behavior of individuals within the organization. Key components often include incident response policies and acceptable use policies.

Steps to Create Security Policies

1. **Assess Risks and Needs**:
   - Conduct a thorough risk assessment to identify potential security threats and vulnerabilities.
   - Understand the organization's operational needs, regulatory requirements, and compliance obligations.
2. **Define Objectives**:

- Establish clear objectives for what the policies need to achieve, including protecting assets, ensuring data privacy, and complying with legal requirements.

3. **Draft Policies**:
   - Develop policy documents that address identified risks and align with the organization's objectives.
   - Key policies might include data protection, network access, password management, and remote access policies.

4. **Incident Response Policy**:
   - Develop procedures for detecting, reporting, and responding to security incidents.
   - Include roles and responsibilities, response steps, and communication plans.

5. **Acceptable Use Policy (AUP)**:
   - Create guidelines for the proper use of IT resources and the internet, clearly defining what is and is not permitted.
   - Address issues like software downloads, use of email, and access to social media.

6. **Review and Approval**:
   - Have the draft policies reviewed by key stakeholders, including IT staff, management, legal counsel, and HR.
   - Revise the policies based on feedback and obtain formal approval from top management.

7. **Implementation and Communication**:
   - Implement the policies across the organization.
   - Communicate the policies to all employees, ensuring they understand their roles and responsibilities.

8. **Training and Awareness Programs**:
   - Conduct regular training sessions to educate employees about security risks and the importance of compliance with policies.
   - Include scenario-based training to help employees understand how to apply policies in real-world situations.

9. **Regular Updates and Reviews**:
   - Periodically review and update the policies to adapt to new threats, technological changes, and business growth.
   - Ensure policies remain relevant and effective over time.

Developing comprehensive security policies is a foundational step in establishing a strong security posture. These policies not only guide how security is managed but also play a crucial role in creating a security-aware culture within the organization. Regular training and reviews are essential to keep these policies effective and relevant.

Training Programs: Employee Security Awareness

Employee security awareness training is an essential aspect of an organization's overall security strategy. Effective training programs are designed to educate employees about security threats, the importance of adhering to security policies, and best practices for maintaining a secure working environment.

Best Practices for Security Training Programs

1. **Regular and Continuous Training**: Security training should not be a one-time event. Schedule regular training sessions to keep security top of mind and update employees on new threats and policies.
2. **Engaging Content**: Use engaging and varied training materials, such as videos, interactive sessions, and real-world examples, to make the training more effective and memorable.
3. **Relevant to Roles**: Tailor training content to be relevant to different roles within the organization. Different departments may face different security risks and require specific guidance.
4. **Simulations and Testing**: Incorporate simulations, like phishing tests, to provide practical experience and reinforce the training content.
5. **Feedback and Improvement**: Encourage feedback from employees and continuously improve the training program based on this input and evolving security landscapes.
6. **Incentivize Participation**: Consider incentives or gamification to encourage active participation and completion of security training programs.
7. **Management Support and Involvement**: Ensure management leads by example and actively supports and participates in security training initiatives.

Outcomes of Effective Training

- **Enhanced Security Posture**: Well-trained employees are an organization's first line of defense against cyber threats.
- **Reduced Incidents**: Increased awareness leads to fewer security incidents and breaches.
- **Compliance**: Helps in maintaining compliance with various regulatory standards and requirements.

Employee security training is crucial in creating a security-aware culture, where every member understands their role in safeguarding the organization's assets and data. As we transition from understanding the intricacies of network security and the importance of comprehensive training, the next chapter will guide us through the world of **Network Troubleshooting and Tools**. This chapter will delve into the practical aspects of identifying, diagnosing, and resolving network issues, and the essential tools and techniques that facilitate effective network maintenance and problem-solving.

Chapter 5: Network Troubleshooting and Tools

Section 1: Troubleshooting Methodology

Step-by-Step Approach to Troubleshooting

Troubleshooting network issues effectively requires a systematic, methodical approach. This ensures that problems are not only resolved efficiently but also that the same issues can be prevented in the future. CompTIA's methodology for network troubleshooting provides a structured process that can be applied to various network problems.

CompTIA's Troubleshooting Methodology

1. **Identify the Problem**:
   - **Information Gathering**: Collect as much information as possible from the user experiencing the issue and from the network systems involved.
   - **Identify Symptoms**: Ask targeted questions to understand the symptoms and peculiarities of the issue.
   - **Determine if Anything has Changed**: Check for recent changes in the network that could have triggered the issue.
2. **Establish a Theory of Probable Cause (Question the Obvious)**:
   - Formulate hypotheses about what might be causing the problem based on the information gathered.
   - Consider the most common causes first.
3. **Test the Theory to Determine Cause**:
   - Once a theory is established, test it to see if it resolves the issue.
   - This may involve reproducing the problem, checking and testing network configurations, or swapping out hardware components.
4. **Establish a Plan of Action to Resolve the Problem and Implement the Solution**:
   - Develop a plan to resolve the issue based on the test results.
   - Implement the solution, ensuring it aligns with organizational policies and procedures.
5. **Verify Full System Functionality and, if Applicable, Implement Preventive Measures**:
   - After implementing a fix, verify that the system is functioning as expected.
   - Implement preventive measures to avoid recurrence of the same issue.
6. **Document Findings, Actions, and Outcomes**:
   - Document the problem, the process used to identify and resolve it, and the outcome.

- This documentation can help in resolving future issues and can be a valuable resource for training or reference.

Best Practices in Troubleshooting

- **Maintain Communication**: Keep relevant stakeholders informed throughout the troubleshooting process.
- **Stay Organized**: Keep track of your steps and findings. This can be crucial if the problem escalates or requires input from others.
- **Be Methodical**: Avoid jumping to conclusions or skipping steps in the process.
- **Knowledge and Resource Utilization**: Utilize available resources, such as knowledge bases, vendor support, and experienced colleagues.

A systematic, step-by-step approach to troubleshooting, as outlined by CompTIA, ensures that network issues are resolved effectively and efficiently. This methodology not only addresses the immediate problems but also contributes to the overall stability and reliability of the network infrastructure.

Section 2: Troubleshooting Tools

Hardware Tools for Network Troubleshooting

In network troubleshooting, hardware tools are essential for diagnosing and resolving physical and hardware-related issues. Tools such as cable testers, Time-Domain Reflectometers (TDRs), and multimeters are fundamental in a network technician's toolkit.

Cable Testers

1. **Purpose**: Cable testers are used to check the integrity of network cables (such as Ethernet cables) for faults like breaks, shorts, or wiring issues.
2. **Functionality**: They can test for continuity, verify wiring configuration (straight-through, crossover, etc.), and determine the length of a cable.
3. **Use Cases**: Essential for ensuring that cables are functioning correctly, particularly after installation or when network issues are suspected to be cable-related.

Time-Domain Reflectometers (TDRs)

1. **Purpose**: TDRs are advanced tools used to diagnose the condition of copper and fiber-optic cables.
2. **Functionality**: They work by sending a signal down the cable and measuring the reflections that return, which helps to identify the location and nature of cable faults.
3. **Use Cases**: Particularly useful in locating breaks, bends, or crimps in cables, especially over long distances where visual inspection is not feasible.

Multimeters

1. **Purpose**: Multimeters are versatile tools used for measuring electrical properties like voltage, current, and resistance.
2. **Functionality**: Can be used in both analog and digital formats, and some advanced models include capabilities like capacitance measurement and temperature readings.
3. **Use Cases**: In network troubleshooting, they are used to check power supplies, verify the presence and levels of voltage in network devices, and diagnose electrical issues with hardware.

Best Practices in Using Hardware Tools

- **Regular Calibration and Maintenance**: Ensure that these tools are regularly calibrated and maintained for accurate readings.
- **Proper Training**: Users should be properly trained in the operation and interpretation of results from these tools to avoid misdiagnosis.
- **Safety Precautions**: Follow all safety guidelines, especially when using tools like multimeters that interact with electrical components.

Hardware tools play a crucial role in the hands-on aspect of network troubleshooting. They provide direct and often immediate insights into the physical and electrical aspects of network components, making them indispensable in diagnosing and resolving network hardware issues.

Software Tools for Network Troubleshooting

Alongside hardware tools, software tools are equally important in diagnosing and resolving network issues. These include packet sniffers, network scanners, and monitoring software, each serving specific functions in the troubleshooting process.

Packet Sniffers

1. **Functionality**: Packet sniffers (or analyzers) capture and analyze network traffic. They can decode and display packet contents, helping in identifying network problems like traffic bottlenecks, unoptimized protocols, and unauthorized activity.
2. **Use Cases**: Useful for in-depth network analysis, security investigations, and optimizing network performance.
3. **Examples**: Wireshark is a widely used, free packet sniffer that supports a variety of network protocols.

Network Scanners

1. **Functionality**: Network scanners detect devices on a network and gather information about them, such as open ports, operating systems, and running services.

2. **Use Cases**: Essential for network mapping, security audits, and detecting unauthorized devices or vulnerabilities.
3. **Examples**: Tools like Nmap provide powerful network scanning capabilities and are frequently used for security assessments and troubleshooting.

Monitoring Software

1. **Functionality**: Network monitoring software continuously tracks network performance metrics like bandwidth utilization, packet loss, latency, and error rates.
2. **Use Cases**: Vital for maintaining network health, detecting performance degradation, and proactive troubleshooting.
3. **Examples**: Solutions like SolarWinds Network Performance Monitor and Nagios offer comprehensive monitoring features and alerting systems.

Best Practices in Using Software Tools

- **Regular Updates and Configuration**: Keep software tools updated for accuracy and security. Regularly review configurations to ensure they meet current network conditions and requirements.
- **Integration**: Integrate various software tools for a comprehensive view of network health and performance. This can provide more detailed insights and efficient troubleshooting.
- **Training and Familiarity**: Ensure network technicians are well-trained and familiar with these tools, including how to interpret their outputs effectively.

Software tools provide detailed insights into network operations, from the macro-level network performance to the micro-level packet analysis. They are crucial for both proactive network management and reactive troubleshooting, offering the necessary visibility to maintain and optimize network performance and security.

Section 3: Diagnostic Tools

Protocol Analyzers

Protocol analyzers, like Wireshark and similar tools, are essential in diagnosing a wide range of network issues. These software tools capture and analyze network traffic, allowing network administrators and technicians to inspect data packets in detail.

Use Cases for Protocol Analyzers

1. **Network Performance Analysis**:
   - Identify bottlenecks and performance degradation by analyzing traffic flow and packet loss.

- Monitor bandwidth usage and determine if the network infrastructure needs scaling or optimization.
2. **Troubleshooting Network Issues**:
   - Diagnose common problems like slow network speeds, intermittent connectivity, and application failures.
   - Identify and resolve misconfigurations in network protocols and devices.
3. **Security Analysis**:
   - Detect suspicious activities, such as unusual data patterns or traffic from unknown sources, which could indicate security threats like malware, spyware, or unauthorized access attempts.
   - Investigate and confirm security incidents, such as data breaches or Distributed Denial of Service (DDoS) attacks.
4. **Protocol and Application Testing**:
   - Verify that network applications and services are properly utilizing network protocols.
   - Test new network deployments and updates to ensure they operate as intended without disrupting existing services.
5. **Educational and Training Purposes**:
   - Use as a training tool to educate network professionals about network protocols, traffic patterns, and troubleshooting techniques.
   - Demonstrate real-world network scenarios and data flows.

Best Practices When Using Protocol Analyzers

- **Legal and Ethical Considerations**: Ensure that the use of protocol analyzers complies with legal requirements and ethical guidelines, particularly concerning privacy and data protection.
- **Targeted Analysis**: To avoid being overwhelmed by data, filter the traffic based on specific criteria relevant to the issue being investigated.
- **Continuous Learning**: Stay updated with network protocols and new features of the protocol analyzer tools, as networks and applications evolve continuously.

Protocol analyzers like Wireshark are powerful tools for network diagnostics, offering deep insights into network operations and the traffic that traverses it. They are indispensable in both proactive network management and in reactive troubleshooting scenarios, helping to ensure that networks remain secure, efficient, and reliable.

Network Scanners

Network scanners are software tools used to scan networks for various purposes, including assessing network health and identifying vulnerabilities. These tools play a crucial role in proactive network maintenance and security.

Vulnerability Scanners

1. **Functionality**: Vulnerability scanners probe networks, systems, and applications to identify weaknesses and vulnerabilities, such as unpatched software, open ports, and misconfigurations.
2. **Use Cases**:
   - Regular security assessments to identify and address potential vulnerabilities before they can be exploited by attackers.
   - Compliance audits to ensure that the network meets regulatory and industry security standards.
3. **Examples**: Tools like Nessus and OpenVAS are widely used for vulnerability scanning.

Network Health Scanners

1. **Functionality**: These scanners assess the overall health and performance of a network. They can identify issues like overloaded servers, failing network devices, or inefficient traffic patterns.
2. **Use Cases**:
   - Monitoring network performance to detect potential issues that could lead to downtime or degraded service.
   - Capacity planning by identifying areas of the network that require upgrades or optimization.
3. **Examples**: Software such as PRTG Network Monitor and SolarWinds Network Performance Monitor.

Best Practices When Using Network Scanners

- **Regular Scanning**: Conduct scans regularly to ensure continuous awareness of the network's state and vulnerabilities.
- **Analysis and Action**: It's not enough to simply identify issues; the key is in analyzing the results and taking appropriate actions to mitigate identified risks.
- **Customization and Configuration**: Tailor the scanning settings and parameters to suit the specific environment and requirements of the network.
- **Stay Updated**: Keep the scanner software updated with the latest features and vulnerability databases.

Network scanners, both for vulnerability assessment and network health, are essential tools in a network administrator's arsenal. They provide insights into the current state of the network, reveal potential security risks, and help in maintaining optimal network performance and security.

Throughput Testers

Throughput testers are tools designed to measure the performance of a network. These tools are instrumental in assessing how much data can be transferred over the network in a given time frame, which is essential for identifying potential network bottlenecks and for capacity planning.

Functionality of Throughput Testers

1. **Data Transfer Measurement**: They measure the rate at which data is successfully transferred over the network, typically reported in bits per second (bps), megabits per second (Mbps), or gigabits per second (Gbps).
2. **End-to-End Testing**: Often conduct tests between two endpoints in the network to assess the throughput of the entire network path.
3. **Simulated Traffic**: Generate network traffic to simulate various conditions and measure how the network performs under different types of loads.

Use Cases

1. **Network Performance Optimization**: Identify areas where the network may be underperforming and requires optimization or upgrade.
2. **Verifying SLAs (Service Level Agreements)**: Ensure that network providers are meeting their promised performance levels.
3. **Troubleshooting**: Help in diagnosing issues related to slow network speeds and in verifying the impact of any changes made to improve performance.

Popular Throughput Testing Tools

- **iPerf**: A widely used network testing tool that can create TCP and UDP data streams and measure the throughput of a network.
- **NetFlow/SFlow Analyzers**: For analyzing traffic patterns and volumes to provide insights into the throughput of the network over time.

Best Practices

- **Testing in Different Conditions**: Run throughput tests under various conditions, including different times of the day and using different data types, to get a comprehensive view of network performance.
- **Regular Testing**: Conduct regular throughput tests to continually monitor network performance and identify trends or emerging issues.
- **Balancing Network Load**: Use the insights gained from throughput tests to balance the network load and optimize the allocation of resources.

Throughput testers are key tools in measuring and understanding the actual performance of a network. They provide critical data that guides decisions in network optimization, troubleshooting, and capacity planning. As we wrap up our exploration of network troubleshooting tools and techniques, the next chapter will present a practical approach to applying this knowledge. We will delve into a **Practice Test** designed to solidify understanding and gauge readiness for real-world network challenges and certifications, providing hands-on scenarios and problem-solving exercises.

Chapter 6: Practice Test

Test

Q1: Which of the following is a primary function of the Network Layer in the OSI model?
a) Frame transmission
b) Path determination and logical addressing
c) Data encryption and decryption
d) Providing end-to-end data transport services and error recovery

Q2: Which protocol is used for securely browsing a website?
a) HTTP
b) FTP
c) HTTPS
d) SNMP

Q3: When setting up a small office network, which of the following is the best device to use for connecting multiple computers while providing network segmentation and traffic management?
a) Network hub
b) Network bridge
c) Network switch
d) Network repeater

Q4: In a wireless network, what does the term "SSID" stand for?
a) System Signal Identification
b) Secure System Internet Data
c) Service Set Identifier
d) Signal Strength Indicator Device

Q5: Which of the following is a public IP address?
a) 192.168.1.10
b) 10.0.0.1
c) 172.16.0.1
d) 131.107.10.29

Q6: Which of the following is a characteristic of UDP (User Datagram Protocol)?
a) Connection-oriented communication

b) Reliable data transfer with acknowledgments

c) Faster transmission with a lack of error checking

d) Sequence number tracking for data reconstruction

Q7: What is the primary purpose of using a VLAN (Virtual Local Area Network)?

a) To extend the range of a physical LAN

b) To increase the bandwidth of the network

c) To segment a network and reduce broadcast domains

d) To encrypt data traffic on a network

Q8: Which type of cable is most resistant to electromagnetic interference?

a) Unshielded Twisted Pair (UTP)

b) Shielded Twisted Pair (STP)

c) Coaxial cable

d) Fiber optic cable

Q9: What is the primary function of DNS (Domain Name System) in networking?

a) Assigning IP addresses to hostnames

b) Encrypting data packets for secure transmission

c) Translating domain names into IP addresses

d) Routing data packets between different networks

Q10: In a network, what is the purpose of a subnet mask?

a) To secure the network by masking IP addresses

b) To divide an IP address into network and host portions

c) To identify the protocol being used in the network

d) To detect errors in data transmission

Q11: What is the primary benefit of using SNMP (Simple Network Management Protocol) in a network?

a) Encrypting network traffic

b) Managing network configurations and devices

c) Providing wireless security

d) Segmenting the network

Q12: Which wireless networking standard operates at both 2.4GHz and 5GHz frequencies?

a) 802.11a

b) 802.11b

c) 802.11g

d) 802.11n

Q13: What type of firewall uses defined rules to make decisions about allowing or blocking traffic based on source and destination IP addresses, protocols, and ports?

a) Stateful firewall

b) Packet-filtering firewall

c) Proxy firewall
d) Next-generation firewall

Q14: In a network topology, which device is used to interconnect networks and route traffic between them?
a) Switch
b) Router
c) Hub
d) Modem

Q15: What is the primary purpose of a VPN (Virtual Private Network)?
a) To increase internet speed
b) To provide a secure connection over a public network
c) To increase the range of a network
d) To reduce network traffic

Q16: Which protocol is used to automatically assign IP addresses to devices on a network?
a) DNS
b) DHCP
c) SMTP
d) FTP

Q17: What technology is used to create multiple isolated networks on a single physical switch?
a) VPN
b) VLAN
c) NAT
d) MPLS

Q18: Which of the following is a characteristic of fiber optic cable?
a) It is susceptible to electromagnetic interference.
b) It has a higher risk of electrical fires compared to copper cables.
c) It transmits data in the form of light signals.
d) It is ideal for short-distance communication only.

Q19: What type of attack involves intercepting and altering communication between two parties without their knowledge?
a) DDoS attack
b) Phishing
c) Man-in-the-middle attack
d) Ransomware attack

Q20: In network security, what is the primary purpose of a WAF (Web Application Firewall)?
a) To monitor outbound traffic from an organization to the internet
b) To protect against internal threats within a corporate network

c) To filter and monitor HTTP/HTTPS traffic to and from a web application

d) To provide end-to-end encryption for data in transit

Q21: What does the term "latency" refer to in a network?

a) The physical length of the network cables

b) The bandwidth capacity of the network

c) The time it takes for a signal to travel from source to destination

d) The amount of data loss during transmission

Q22: Which network topology is most resilient to single points of failure?

a) Star

b) Bus

c) Ring

d) Mesh

Q23: In cybersecurity, what does "SIEM" stand for?

a) Signal Intelligence and Email Management

b) Security Information and Event Management

c) Simple Internet Encryption Method

d) Systematic Intrusion Evaluation Mechanism

Q24: What is the main purpose of using a network protocol analyzer?

a) To enhance the speed of network traffic

b) To manage network device configurations

c) To monitor and analyze network traffic

d) To encrypt data communication

Q25: Which of the following is an advantage of using IPv6 over IPv4?

a) Smaller header size for efficiency

b) Larger address space

c) Built-in encryption and authentication

d) Compatibility with all existing IPv4 networks

Q26: Which layer of the OSI model is responsible for ensuring error-free delivery of data?

a) Layer 2: Data Link

b) Layer 3: Network

c) Layer 4: Transport

d) Layer 7: Application

Q27: What technology is typically used to secure data transmission over a public Wi-Fi network?

a) WEP

b) WPA2

c) SNMP

d) MPLS

Q28: In a data center, what is the main purpose of using a KVM switch?
a) To increase the number of available ports
b) To manage and control multiple servers from a single console
c) To enhance the speed of the network
d) To provide backup power supply

Q29: Which protocol is commonly used for remote management of network devices?
a) RDP
b) SSH
c) FTP
d) HTTP

Q30: What is a primary difference between a hub and a switch?
a) A hub can filter data, whereas a switch cannot.
b) A switch operates at Layer 3 of the OSI model, while a hub operates at Layer 1.
c) A switch sends data to specific ports, whereas a hub broadcasts to all ports.
d) A hub is faster than a switch because it does not examine data packets.

Q31: Which type of DNS record is used to translate a domain name into an IPv6 address?
a) A record
b) AAAA record
c) MX record
d) CNAME record

Q32: What does NAT (Network Address Translation) primarily facilitate in a network?
a) Converting private IP addresses to public IP addresses
b) Encrypting network traffic
c) Assigning IP addresses to network devices
d) Filtering incoming internet traffic

Q33: In network security, what is the primary function of an IDS (Intrusion Detection System)?
a) To block malicious traffic
b) To encrypt data communications
c) To detect and alert about potential security threats
d) To analyze and optimize network traffic

Q34: Which wireless encryption standard is currently considered the most secure for Wi-Fi networks?
a) WEP
b) WPA
c) WPA2
d) WPA3

Q35: What is the primary purpose of a network patch panel in a structured cabling system?
a) To provide extra security for network connections

b) To connect network devices to each other

c) To manage and organize network cables

d) To amplify the signal strength across the network

Q36: Which protocol is commonly used to securely manage network devices via command-line interface?

a) Telnet

b) SSH

c) FTP

d) SNMP

Q37: What is the primary function of a firewall in a network?

a) To provide a DHCP service

b) To serve as a DNS server

c) To manage network traffic and block unauthorized access

d) To enhance the network's data transmission speed

Q38: In a wireless network, what does MIMO stand for and what is its benefit?

a) Multiple Input, Multiple Output; enhances signal strength and range

b) Modulation In, Modulation Out; improves data modulation efficiency

c) Management In, Management Out; streamlines network management tasks

d) Multiple Internet, Multiple Operations; allows simultaneous internet connections

Q39: Which IPv6 feature eliminates the need for NAT (Network Address Translation)?

a) Stateless address autoconfiguration

b) Anycast addressing

c) The vast address space

d) Integrated IPSec support

Q40: What is the main purpose of implementing QoS (Quality of Service) in a network?

a) To prioritize certain types of network traffic

b) To encrypt sensitive data traffic

c) To assign static IP addresses to devices

d) To detect and prevent network intrusions

Q41: Which type of address is used by IPv6 for local link communications only?

a) Multicast

b) Anycast

c) Global unicast

d) Link-local

Q42: In network security, what is 'social engineering'?

a) Manipulating people into revealing confidential information

b) Using advanced software to encrypt network data

c) Modifying network protocols for enhanced security
d) Building a social network to improve security awareness

Q43: Which protocol is responsible for automatic IP address allocation in a DHCP setup?
a) DNS
b) ARP
c) DHCP
d) ICMP

Q44: What is the primary use of a TDR (Time-Domain Reflectometer)?
a) To measure the length of a network cable and locate faults
b) To test the speed of a network connection
c) To analyze network traffic for security threats
d) To determine the data transfer rate of a fiber optic cable

Q45: Which OSI model layer is responsible for establishing, managing, and terminating sessions between applications?
a) Transport Layer
b) Session Layer
c) Network Layer
d) Presentation Layer

Q46: What is the primary purpose of a VLAN (Virtual Local Area Network)?
a) To connect multiple networks over the internet
b) To provide a secure connection for remote users
c) To segment a network into separate broadcast domains
d) To increase the speed of the network

Q47: Which of the following is a characteristic of a stateful firewall?
a) It filters traffic based solely on source and destination IP addresses.
b) It inspects the state of active connections and makes decisions based on the context.
c) It operates at the application layer of the OSI model.
d) It acts as an intermediary between the user and the web server.

Q48: In network troubleshooting, what is a 'ping' command used to test?
a) The strength of a Wi-Fi signal
b) The availability and reachability of a host on a network
c) The bandwidth capacity of a network connection
d) The security of a network connection

Q49: What does the 'tracert' (or 'traceroute') command help to identify?
a) Password strength
b) The path data takes from source to destination
c) The amount of traffic on a network
d) The encryption level of data

Q50: Which protocol is used for network automation and configuration management?
a) SNMP
b) SSH
c) Telnet
d) NETCONF

Q51: Which IEEE standard is known for defining Gigabit Ethernet over copper wiring?
a) 802.11ac
b) 802.3ab
c) 802.3z
d) 802.11n

Q52: What is the primary security benefit of segmenting a network with VLANs?
a) It encrypts data moving between VLANs.
b) It prevents denial-of-service attacks.
c) It limits the spread of viruses and worms.
d) It increases the speed of the network's firewall.

Q53: In a wireless network, what is the function of WPS (Wi-Fi Protected Setup)?
a) It automatically configures a secure wireless network connection between devices.
b) It allocates static IP addresses to wireless devices.
c) It increases the range of the wireless signal.
d) It encrypts the data transmitted over the Wi-Fi network.

Q54: What type of DNS record is commonly used to associate a subdomain with another domain name?
a) A record
b) MX record
c) CNAME record
d) PTR record

Q55: Which term describes a software application that runs on a network device and interacts with the operating system to gather information for monitoring and management?
a) SNMP agent
b) Syslog server
c) DHCP relay
d) Proxy server

Q56: Which protocol is used to encrypt and secure data transmitted over a network at the data link layer?
a) HTTPS
b) SSL
c) WPA2
d) SSH

Q57: What is the purpose of a demilitarized zone (DMZ) in network security?
a) To isolate internal network servers from the external internet
b) To provide a buffer zone between the internet and the internal network
c) To encrypt data leaving the network
d) To serve as the primary storage area for sensitive data

Q58: What type of attack involves flooding a targeted system with excessive network traffic, typically from multiple sources?
a) Man-in-the-middle attack
b) Phishing attack
c) Distributed Denial of Service (DDoS) attack
d) SQL Injection attack

Q59: In networking, what does the term "failover" refer to?
a) The process of upgrading network equipment
b) The automatic switching to a redundant or standby system upon failure
c) The loss of data during transmission
d) The degradation of network performance over time

Q60: What is the main purpose of using subnetting in a network?
a) To increase the internet speed
b) To encrypt data communication
c) To create smaller, more manageable network segments
d) To eliminate the need for routers

Q61: What technology is commonly used to monitor and analyze the performance of a network in real-time?
a) Network Attached Storage (NAS)
b) Virtual Private Network (VPN)
c) Network Management System (NMS)
d) Content Delivery Network (CDN)

Q62: Which of the following is a function of a proxy server in a network?
a) Allocating IP addresses to devices on the network
b) Filtering and forwarding client requests to other servers
c) Encrypting internal network communications
d) Providing additional storage for network devices

Q63: In IPv4 addressing, what is the purpose of a Classless Inter-Domain Routing (CIDR) notation?
a) To provide encryption for IP addresses
b) To designate private IP address ranges
c) To create a hierarchy of IP addresses
d) To allow for more efficient allocation of IP addresses

Q64: What type of DNS record is used to direct a domain to a mail server?
a) A record
b) AAAA record
c) MX record
d) SRV record

Q65: What is the primary purpose of STP (Spanning Tree Protocol) in network switches?
a) To encrypt data passing through the switch
b) To prevent loops in a network with redundant paths
c) To assign IP addresses to devices connected to the switch
d) To prioritize certain types of network traffic

Q66: Which technology is used to prioritize voice and video traffic in a network?
a) VPN
b) VLAN
c) QoS
d) MPLS

Q67: What is the main advantage of using an IPv6 address over IPv4?
a) Faster routing speeds
b) Smaller address space for easier management
c) Larger address space
d) Inherent encryption of data

Q68: Which of the following is a standard for wireless communication in the 5 GHz frequency band?
a) 802.11b
b) 802.11g
c) 802.11ac
d) 802.3

Q69: What is the primary function of a UTM (Unified Threat Management) appliance?
a) To enhance the speed and performance of network traffic
b) To provide a combination of security features such as firewall, antivirus, and intrusion prevention
c) To allocate IP addresses within a network
d) To balance network load across multiple servers

Q70: In network troubleshooting, what is the primary use of the nslookup command?
a) To display the routing path packets take to a network host
b) To identify the MAC address of a network device
c) To query DNS servers for information about domain name mappings
d) To monitor real-time network traffic

Q71: Which protocol is used for secure file transfer over a network?
a) FTP
b) HTTP
c) SNMP
d) SFTP

Q72: What type of network device is used to connect multiple devices on a LAN and make decisions based on MAC addresses?
a) Router
b) Switch
c) Modem
d) Hub

Q73: Which wireless standard operates in the 2.4GHz band and provides speeds up to 54 Mbps?
a) 802.11a
b) 802.11b
c) 802.11g
d) 802.11n

Q74: In a network, what is the function of a PoE (Power over Ethernet) switch?
a) To provide data and power over the same Ethernet cable to connected devices
b) To increase the speed of the Ethernet connection
c) To encrypt data passing through the Ethernet cable
d) To connect wireless devices to a wired network

Q75: What does APIPA (Automatic Private IP Addressing) do in a Windows-based network?
a) It encrypts IP addresses for secure communication.
b) It assigns a unique IP address from a DHCP server.
c) It automatically assigns a private IP address when a DHCP server is not available.
d) It converts private IP addresses to public IP addresses.

Answers and Explanations

Q1: b) Path determination and logical addressing

Explanation: The primary function of the Network Layer (Layer 3) in the OSI model is path determination and logical addressing. This layer is responsible for routing and forwarding packets, including determining the best path through the network using logical addressing (like IP addresses).

Q2: c) HTTPS

Explanation: HTTPS (Hypertext Transfer Protocol Secure) is used for securely browsing a website. It encrypts the data exchanged between a web browser and a website, ensuring secure transactions and protecting against eavesdropping.

Q3: c) Network switch

Explanation: A network switch is ideal for connecting multiple computers in a small office network. Unlike a hub, a switch provides network segmentation and can manage traffic efficiently by sending data only to its intended destination, thereby reducing network congestion.

Q4: c) Service Set Identifier

Explanation: SSID stands for Service Set Identifier. It's the name given to a wireless network. When you connect to a Wi-Fi network, you select it by its SSID. This identifier enables the distinction of one wireless network from another.

Q5: d) 131.107.10.29

Explanation: 131.107.10.29 is a public IP address. The other options (192.168.x.x, 10.x.x.x, and 172.16.x.x to 172.31.x.x) are private IP address ranges, typically used within a private network and not routable on the internet.

Q6: c) Faster transmission with a lack of error checking

Explanation: UDP (User Datagram Protocol) is known for faster transmission as it is a connectionless protocol and does not perform error checking and correction, unlike TCP. This makes it suitable for applications where speed is crucial and occasional data loss is acceptable, such as streaming media.

Q7: c) To segment a network and reduce broadcast domains

Explanation: The primary purpose of using a VLAN (Virtual Local Area Network) is to segment a larger network into smaller, isolated broadcast domains. This segmentation improves network performance and security by reducing the number of devices in each broadcast domain and containing broadcast traffic within the VLAN.

Q8: d) Fiber optic cable

Explanation: Fiber optic cables are most resistant to electromagnetic interference. Unlike copper cables (UTP, STP, and coaxial), which use electrical signals that can be affected by electromagnetic interference, fiber optic cables use light to transmit data, making them immune to such interference.

Q9: c) Translating domain names into IP addresses

Explanation: The primary function of the Domain Name System (DNS) is to translate human-readable domain names (like www.example.com) into numerical IP addresses that are used to locate and identify devices and resources on a network. This translation is crucial for navigating the internet easily.

Q10: b) To divide an IP address into network and host portions

Explanation: A subnet mask is used in IP networking to divide the IP address into two parts: the network portion and the host portion. This allows for the identification of the network a given IP address belongs to and the specific device (or host) on that network.

Q11: b) Managing network configurations and devices

Explanation: SNMP (Simple Network Management Protocol) is primarily used for managing network configurations and devices. It allows network administrators to remotely monitor, modify, and manage network devices like routers, switches, and servers.

Q12: d) 802.11n

Explanation: The 802.11n wireless standard operates at both 2.4GHz and 5GHz frequencies. This dual-band capability allows for better network performance and reduces interference, compared to standards that operate on a single frequency.

Q13: b) Packet-filtering firewall

Explanation: A packet-filtering firewall makes decisions about allowing or blocking traffic based solely on source and destination IP addresses, protocols, and port numbers. It checks the header of packets and filters traffic based on the set rules without considering the state of the connection.

Q14: b) Router

Explanation: A router is used to interconnect different networks and route traffic between them. It makes decisions based on IP addresses to determine the best path for data packets to travel from one network to another.

Q15: b) To provide a secure connection over a public network

Explanation: The primary purpose of a VPN (Virtual Private Network) is to create a secure and encrypted connection over a public network, such as the internet. This secure tunnel allows for the safe transmission of sensitive data and is commonly used for remote access to a private network, enhancing security and privacy.

Q16: b) DHCP

Explanation: DHCP (Dynamic Host Configuration Protocol) is used to automatically assign IP addresses to devices on a network. It simplifies the management of IP addresses and reduces the risk of IP address conflicts.

Q17: b) VLAN

Explanation: VLAN (Virtual Local Area Network) technology is used to create multiple isolated networks within a single physical switch. This allows for segmenting networks without requiring additional hardware, improving network management and security.

Q18: c) It transmits data in the form of light signals.

Explanation: Fiber optic cables transmit data in the form of light signals, offering higher bandwidth and greater resistance to electromagnetic interference compared to copper cables. They are suitable for both long and short-distance communications.

Q19: c) Man-in-the-middle attack

Explanation: A man-in-the-middle attack involves an attacker intercepting and potentially altering the communication between two parties without their knowledge. This type of attack can occur in various forms, including session hijacking and eavesdropping.

Q20: c) To filter and monitor HTTP/HTTPS traffic to and from a web application

Explanation: A Web Application Firewall (WAF) is specifically designed to filter and monitor HTTP/HTTPS traffic to and from web applications. It helps protect web applications by filtering and monitoring HTTP requests and by blocking malicious traffic.

Q21: c) The time it takes for a signal to travel from source to destination

Explanation: Latency in a network refers to the delay from the time a signal is sent from its source to when it is received at the destination. It's a measure of the time delay experienced in a system, which can affect network performance, especially in real-time applications.

Q22: d) Mesh

Explanation: A mesh topology is most resilient to single points of failure because each node is connected to multiple other nodes. If one connection fails, data can typically still be transmitted through alternative paths, making this topology highly fault-tolerant.

Q23: b) Security Information and Event Management

Explanation: SIEM stands for Security Information and Event Management. It's a cybersecurity solution that provides real-time analysis of security alerts generated by applications and network hardware. It helps organizations to quickly detect, analyze, and respond to potential security threats.

Q24: c) To monitor and analyze network traffic

Explanation: The main purpose of using a network protocol analyzer is to monitor and analyze network traffic. These tools capture network packets and help in diagnosing network problems, analyzing network performance, and detecting security breaches.

Q25: b) Larger address space

Explanation: One of the main advantages of IPv6 over IPv4 is its larger address space. IPv6 uses 128-bit addresses, significantly expanding the number of available IP addresses compared to the 32-bit addressing used in IPv4, addressing the issue of IP address exhaustion.

Q26: c) Layer 4: Transport

Explanation: The Transport layer (Layer 4) of the OSI model is responsible for ensuring error-free delivery of data. It provides services such as segmentation, acknowledgement, and error correction which are essential for reliable data transmission.

Q27: b) WPA2

Explanation: WPA2 (Wi-Fi Protected Access 2) is the technology typically used to secure data transmission over a public Wi-Fi network. It provides enhanced security measures compared to its predecessor, WEP (Wired Equivalent Privacy), making it the preferred choice for Wi-Fi security.

Q28: b) To manage and control multiple servers from a single console

Explanation: A KVM (Keyboard, Video, Mouse) switch is used in data centers to manage and control multiple servers from a single console. It allows network administrators to switch between different servers using the same keyboard, monitor, and mouse, thereby simplifying management and saving space.

Q29: b) SSH

Explanation: SSH (Secure Shell) is a protocol commonly used for the secure remote management of network devices. It provides a secure channel over an unsecured network, enabling network administrators to securely log in to servers, switch configurations, and manage devices remotely.

Q30: c) A switch sends data to specific ports, whereas a hub broadcasts to all ports.

Explanation: The primary difference between a hub and a switch is how they handle data packets. A switch sends data only to the specific port to which the destination device is connected, whereas a hub broadcasts the data to all of its ports regardless of the destination, leading to potential network inefficiencies and security concerns.

Q31: b) AAAA record

Explanation: An AAAA record in DNS (Domain Name System) is used to translate a domain name into an IPv6 address. While A records are used for IPv4 addresses, AAAA records are specifically for mapping domain names to IPv6 addresses.

Q32: a) Converting private IP addresses to public IP addresses

Explanation: NAT (Network Address Translation) is used in networks to convert private IP addresses to public IP addresses. This process allows multiple devices on a local network to access the internet using a single public IP address, conserving public IP addresses and adding a level of privacy and security.

Q33: c) To detect and alert about potential security threats

Explanation: The primary function of an IDS (Intrusion Detection System) is to monitor network traffic and detect potential security threats. Unlike an Intrusion Prevention System (IPS), an IDS does not take action to block the threats but instead alerts network administrators about suspicious activities for further investigation.

Q34: d) WPA3

Explanation: WPA3 (Wi-Fi Protected Access 3) is currently the most secure wireless encryption standard for Wi-Fi networks. It provides more robust security than its predecessors, WEP, WPA, and WPA2, by offering enhanced cryptographic strength and improved protection against brute-force attacks.

Q35: c) To manage and organize network cables

Explanation: The primary purpose of a network patch panel in a structured cabling system is to manage and organize network cables. Patch panels consolidate all the network cables in a central location, simplifying cable management and making it easier to reconfigure network connections as needed.

Q36: b) SSH

Explanation: SSH (Secure Shell) is commonly used to securely access and manage network devices via a command-line interface. It provides a secure channel over an unsecured network, encrypting the data exchanged between the client and the server, which makes it ideal for remote administration.

Q37: c) To manage network traffic and block unauthorized access

Explanation: The primary function of a firewall in a network is to manage network traffic and block unauthorized access. Firewalls monitor incoming and outgoing network traffic based on security rules and act as a barrier between trusted internal networks and untrusted external networks.

Q38: a) Multiple Input, Multiple Output; enhances signal strength and range

Explanation: MIMO stands for Multiple Input, Multiple Output. It's a technology used in wireless communications where multiple antennas are used at both the source (transmitter) and the destination (receiver). The main benefits of MIMO are increased data throughput and range for wireless systems, improving the performance of wireless networks.

Q39: c) The vast address space

Explanation: The vast address space of IPv6 eliminates the need for NAT (Network Address Translation). Unlike IPv4, which has a limited number of public IP addresses and often requires NAT to conserve addresses, IPv6 has a significantly larger address space, making it possible to assign unique public IP addresses to a vast number of devices.

Q40: a) To prioritize certain types of network traffic

Explanation: The main purpose of implementing QoS (Quality of Service) in a network is to prioritize certain types of network traffic. This ensures that critical network traffic, such as VoIP or streaming video, receives higher priority and maintains performance standards, especially in congested network environments.

Q41: d) Link-local

Explanation: In IPv6, link-local addresses are used for local link communications only. These addresses are automatically configured on all IPv6-enabled devices and are not routable beyond the local network segment.

Q42: a) Manipulating people into revealing confidential information

Explanation: Social engineering in network security refers to the psychological manipulation of people into revealing confidential information or performing actions that may compromise security. It often involves tricking individuals into breaking standard security procedures.

Q43: c) DHCP

Explanation: DHCP (Dynamic Host Configuration Protocol) is responsible for automatic IP address allocation in a network. It dynamically assigns IP addresses to devices on the network, simplifying the management of IP addresses and reducing configuration errors.

Q44: a) To measure the length of a network cable and locate faults

Explanation: A TDR (Time-Domain Reflectometer) is used to measure the length of a network cable and locate faults such as breaks or imperfections. It sends a signal along the cable and measures the reflections that return, which indicate the location of faults.

Q45: b) Session Layer

Explanation: The Session Layer, Layer 5 of the OSI model, is responsible for establishing, managing, and terminating sessions between applications. This layer sets up, coordinates, and terminates conversations, exchanges, and dialogues between the applications at each end.

Q46: c) To segment a network into separate broadcast domains

Explanation: The primary purpose of a VLAN (Virtual Local Area Network) is to segment a larger physical network into separate broadcast domains. This segmentation helps in reducing broadcast traffic, improving network management, and enhancing security by isolating network traffic.

Q47: b) It inspects the state of active connections and makes decisions based on the context.

Explanation: A stateful firewall inspects the state of active connections and makes decisions based on the context of the traffic, not just on predetermined static rules. It keeps track of the state of network connections (such as TCP streams) and can make more informed decisions about which network packets to allow through.

Q48: b) The availability and reachability of a host on a network

Explanation: The 'ping' command is used to test the availability and reachability of a host on a network. It sends ICMP echo request messages to the target host and listens for echo reply messages. The responses help determine whether the target host is reachable and responding.

Q49: b) The path data takes from source to destination

Explanation: The 'tracert' (in Windows) or 'traceroute' (in Unix/Linux) command is used to identify the path data takes from the source to the destination. It maps out each hop along the route and can help diagnose where potential issues are occurring in the network path.

Q50: d) NETCONF

Explanation: NETCONF (Network Configuration Protocol) is used for network automation and configuration management. It provides mechanisms to install, manipulate, and delete the configuration of network devices through a network-wide, standard interface.

Q51: b) 802.3ab

Explanation: The IEEE 802.3ab standard, also known as 1000BASE-T, defines Gigabit Ethernet transmission over copper wiring, specifically unshielded twisted pair (UTP) cables. It supports a maximum length of 100 meters and is widely used in local area networks.

Q52: c) It limits the spread of viruses and worms.

Explanation: Segmenting a network with VLANs (Virtual Local Area Networks) helps limit the spread of viruses and worms within a network. By dividing the network into smaller, isolated segments, VLANs can contain security threats to a single segment, preventing them from propagating across the entire network.

Q53: a) It automatically configures a secure wireless network connection between devices.

Explanation: WPS (Wi-Fi Protected Setup) is designed to simplify the process of connecting devices to a wireless network while maintaining security. It allows users to easily set up a secure wireless network connection, often by pressing a button on the router and the device or entering a PIN.

Q54: c) CNAME record

Explanation: A CNAME (Canonical Name) record in DNS (Domain Name System) is used to associate a subdomain with another domain name (the "canonical" domain name). It allows multiple subdomains to be mapped to a single domain, simplifying domain management.

Q55: a) SNMP agent

Explanation: An SNMP (Simple Network Management Protocol) agent is a software application that runs on a network device. It collects data about the device's operation and communicates this information to an SNMP manager, used for network monitoring and management.

Q56: c) WPA2

Explanation: WPA2 (Wi-Fi Protected Access 2) is a security protocol used to encrypt and secure data transmitted over a wireless network at the data link layer. It provides strong data protection by using advanced encryption standards, thereby securing wireless communication from eavesdropping and attacks.

Q57: b) To provide a buffer zone between the internet and the internal network

Explanation: A Demilitarized Zone (DMZ) in network security is used to provide a buffer zone between the internet and an organization's internal network. It's a segregated network that contains public-facing servers and services, protecting the internal network from direct exposure to the internet while allowing external access to specific services.

Q58: c) Distributed Denial of Service (DDoS) attack

Explanation: A Distributed Denial of Service (DDoS) attack involves overwhelming a targeted system, such as a website or network, with excessive traffic, typically originating from multiple sources. This flood of traffic can render the system unusable, denying service to legitimate users.

Q59: b) The automatic switching to a redundant or standby system upon failure

Explanation: "Failover" refers to the automatic switching process to a redundant or standby system when the primary system fails. This ensures continuous operation and availability, especially in critical systems, by having a backup system take over seamlessly when the main system encounters an issue.

Q60: c) To create smaller, more manageable network segments

Explanation: Subnetting is the practice of dividing a larger network into smaller, more manageable segments or subnets. This helps in improving network performance and security by reducing broadcast traffic, simplifying management, and allowing for more efficient use of IP addresses.

Q61: c) Network Management System (NMS)

Explanation: A Network Management System (NMS) is commonly used to monitor and analyze the performance of a network in real-time. It helps in managing, monitoring, and optimizing network resources efficiently, providing insights into network performance, traffic patterns, and potential issues.

Q62: b) Filtering and forwarding client requests to other servers

Explanation: A proxy server in a network primarily functions to filter and forward client requests to other servers. It acts as an intermediary between end users and the servers they are accessing, providing functions like web request filtering, caching of web content, and controlled access to websites.

Q63: d) To allow for more efficient allocation of IP addresses

Explanation: Classless Inter-Domain Routing (CIDR) notation in IPv4 is used for more efficient allocation of IP addresses. It allows for flexible subnetting by specifying an IP address and a subnet mask, which can vary in length to allocate IP addresses more precisely and reduce waste.

Q64: c) MX record

Explanation: An MX (Mail Exchange) record in DNS is used to direct a domain to a mail server. This record specifies the mail server responsible for accepting email messages on behalf of a domain, directing email to the correct server.

Q65: b) To prevent loops in a network with redundant paths

Explanation: The primary purpose of the Spanning Tree Protocol (STP) in network switches is to prevent loops in a network that has redundant paths. STP ensures there is only one active path between two network devices, which prevents broadcast storms and network failures due to multiple paths.

Q66: c) QoS

Explanation: QoS (Quality of Service) is a technology used to prioritize certain types of network traffic, such as voice and video. It ensures that critical applications, like VoIP and video conferencing, receive the necessary bandwidth and low latency to function properly, even when the network is congested.

Q67: c) Larger address space

Explanation: The main advantage of using an IPv6 address over IPv4 is its larger address space. IPv6 uses 128-bit addressing, which significantly increases the number of available IP addresses compared to the 32-bit addressing of IPv4. This expansion addresses the issue of IPv4 address exhaustion and supports a larger number of devices on the internet.

Q68: c) 802.11ac

Explanation: 802.11ac is a wireless communication standard that operates in the 5 GHz frequency band. It offers higher data rates and less interference compared to standards operating in the 2.4 GHz band (like 802.11b and 802.11g), making it well-suited for bandwidth-intensive applications like streaming video and online gaming.

Q69: b) To provide a combination of security features such as firewall, antivirus, and intrusion prevention

Explanation: A UTM (Unified Threat Management) appliance provides a comprehensive security solution by combining multiple security features into a single device. This typically includes a firewall, antivirus, intrusion prevention, and sometimes additional services like spam filtering and VPN capabilities, offering an all-in-one approach to network security.

Q70: c) To query DNS servers for information about domain name mappings

Explanation: The nslookup command is primarily used to query DNS servers to obtain domain name mapping information. It helps in diagnosing DNS-related issues by enabling users to query the DNS to find out the IP address associated with a domain name or vice versa.

Q71: d) SFTP

Explanation: SFTP (Secure File Transfer Protocol) is used for secure file transfer over a network. It provides a secure method of transferring files by utilizing SSH (Secure Shell) to encrypt both commands and data. This prevents sensitive data from being transmitted in plain text over the network.

Q72: b) Switch

Explanation: A switch is a network device used to connect multiple devices on a Local Area Network (LAN). It makes decisions based on MAC addresses of the devices. Unlike a hub, which broadcasts data to all connected devices, a switch intelligently sends data only to the intended recipient, improving network efficiency and security.

Q73: c) 802.11g

Explanation: The 802.11g wireless standard operates in the 2.4GHz band and offers speeds up to 54 Mbps. It is backward compatible with 802.11b and was a significant improvement over the earlier standard in terms of data transmission speed.

Q74: a) To provide data and power over the same Ethernet cable to connected devices

Explanation: PoE (Power over Ethernet) switches have the capability to deliver power along with data over the same Ethernet cable. This feature is particularly useful for powering devices like IP cameras, VoIP phones, and wireless access points, where it would be inconvenient or impractical to have a separate power supply.

Q75: c) It automatically assigns a private IP address when a DHCP server is not available.

Explanation: APIPA (Automatic Private IP Addressing) is a feature in Windows-based networks that automatically assigns a private IP address in the range of 169.254.x.x to a computer when a DHCP server is not available to assign an IP address. This allows the computer to communicate with other devices on the same local network, though it cannot access the internet.

CONTACT THE AUTHOR

I always strive to make this guide as comprehensive and helpful as possible, but there's always room for improvement. If you have any questions, suggestions, or feedback, I would love to hear from you. Hearing your thoughts helps me understand what works, what doesn't, and what could be made better in future editions.
To make it easier for you to reach out, I have set up a dedicated email address:
epicinkpublishing@gmail.com

Feel free to email me for:

- Clarifications on any topics covered in this book
- Suggestions for additional topics or improvements
- Feedback on your experience with the book
- Any problem (You can't get the bonuses for example, please before releasing a negative review, contact me)

Your input is invaluable.

I read every email and will do my best to respond in a timely manner.

GET YOUR BONUSES

Dear reader,

First and foremost, thank you for purchasing my book! Your support means the world to me, and I hope you find the information within valuable and helpful in your journey.

As a token of my appreciation, I have included some exclusive bonuses that will greatly benefit you.

To access these bonuses, scan the QR Code with your phone:

Once again, thank you for your support, and I wish you the best of luck in your Exam. I believe these bonuses will provide you with the tools and knowledge to excel.

Made in the USA
Las Vegas, NV
19 December 2024

14962949R00188